I0803195

IMAGES
of America

LIGHTHOUSES OF THE VENTURA COAST

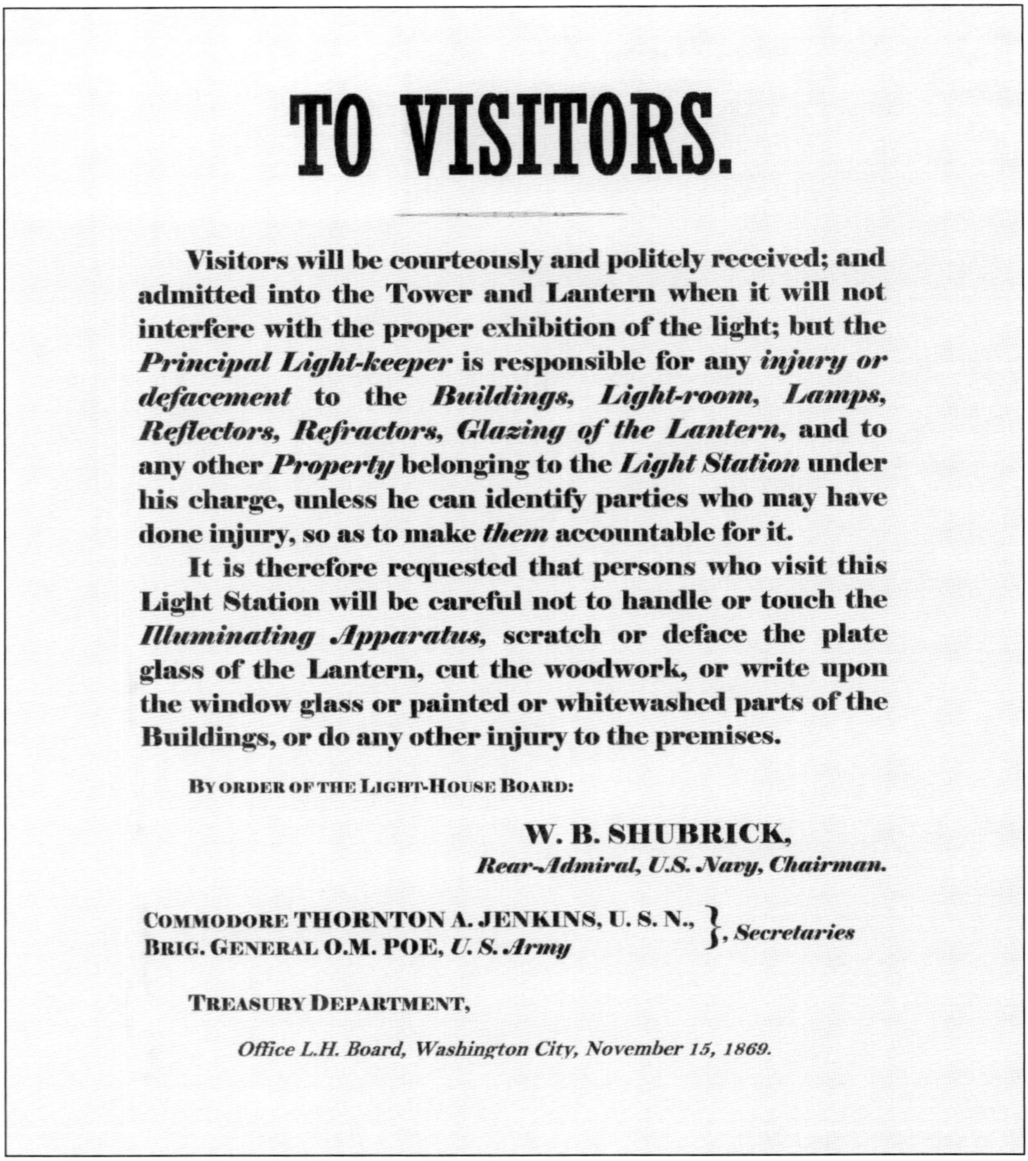

TO VISITORS.

Visitors will be courteously and politely received; and admitted into the Tower and Lantern when it will not interfere with the proper exhibition of the light; but the *Principal Light-keeper* is responsible for any *injury or defacement* to the *Buildings, Light-room, Lamps, Reflectors, Refractors, Glazing of the Lantern,* and to any other *Property* belonging to the *Light Station* under his charge, unless he can identify parties who may have done injury, so as to make *them* accountable for it.

It is therefore requested that persons who visit this Light Station will be careful not to handle or touch the *Illuminating Apparatus,* scratch or deface the plate glass of the Lantern, cut the woodwork, or write upon the window glass or painted or whitewashed parts of the Buildings, or do any other injury to the premises.

BY ORDER OF THE LIGHT-HOUSE BOARD:

W. B. SHUBRICK,
Rear-Admiral, U.S. Navy, Chairman.

COMMODORE THORNTON A. JENKINS, U. S. N.,
BRIG. GENERAL O.M. POE, *U. S. Army*
}, *Secretaries*

TREASURY DEPARTMENT,

Office L.H. Board, Washington City, November 15, 1869.

As visitors entered the Point Hueneme Lighthouse in the early 1900s they saw this notice, informing them of accountability if damage should occur on any part of the Light Station grounds. (Courtesy Laverne White-Dornberger.)

ON THE COVER: Aerial view of the Anacapa Lighthouse Station. (Courtesy U.S. Coast Guard.)

IMAGES of America

LIGHTHOUSES OF THE VENTURA COAST

Rose Castro-Bran

ARCADIA PUBLISHING

ISBN 978-0-7385-8186-6

Published by Arcadia Publishing
Charleston, South Carolina

Printed in the United States of America

Library of Congress Control Number: 2010932248

For all general information, please contact Arcadia Publishing:
Telephone 843-853-2070
Fax 843-853-0044
E-mail sales@arcadiapublishing.com
For customer service and orders:
Toll-Free 1-888-313-2665

Visit us on the Internet at www.arcadiapublishing.com

Nothing indicates the liberality, prosperity or intelligence of a nation more clearly than the facilities which it affords for the safe approach of the mariner to its shores.

—Report of the Lighthouse Board, 1868

This book is dedicated to the men and women of the U.S. Lighthouse Service and the U.S. Coast Guard for their devotion to duty.

CONTENTS

ACKNOWLEDGMENTS

This book was only made possible with the generosity and assistance of the following individuals and groups. I would like to thank Charles Johnson of the Ventura County Museum of History and Art; Gina Nichols, archivist for the U.S. Naval Base Ventura County; Dr. David Rosen, U.S. Coast Guard historian; Wayne Wheeler and Jeff and Richard Gales of the U.S. Lighthouse Society; Michael Redmon of the Santa Barbara Museum; the Santa Barbara Special Collections Department; the National Archives; Joyce Carlson, chairperson of the Murals of Santa Paula; Joanna Bard Newton; Georgia Pulos; Ann Thiermann; Michael K. Ward; and Jan Timbrook. Thanks to Anne Hansford and Joe McKenzie of the San Pedro Bay Historical Society and Abra Klinger of Samy's Camera.

Many thanks to Lisa Donley of the City of Port Hueneme Parks and Recreation, Kathleen Misewitch of the Port Hueneme Chamber of Commerce, and to Dorothy Ramirez and Helen Brant of the Hueneme Historical Society, not only for their time but for their interesting and hilarious stories. Thank you to Julie Tumamait, whose dedication in her efforts to preserve the traditions and legacies of the Chumash people is an inspiration. Special thanks to Laverne White-Dornberger and Margaret Kellogg-Anderson for keeping the legacies of their fathers alive for generations to come and for their amazing help.

A special thank you to Master Chief Petty Officer John Hurst, U.S. Coast Guard (Ret.), for his entrusting the Point Hueneme Lighthouse to a couple of Auxiliarists to create exhibits and opening it up for tours. Thank you to Eric Castro-Bran, my father-in-law, who has been keeper of Point Vicente Lighthouse for over 18 years, for his expertise, dedication, and love of lighthouses. A heartfelt thank you to the members of the U.S. Coast Guard Aids to Navigation Team Los Angeles–Long Beach for their hard work and dedication to duty. Thank you to my husband, Kim, who is my partner in everything I do. Thank you for your endless support and love, and for always being my light in the darkness.

INTRODUCTION

In 1848, when the United States acquired California at the end of the Mexican-American War, there was an expanse of well over 800 miles of barren coastline completely void of any lighthouses. The main challenge that remained for mariners was that the coastline was relatively unknown. However, that same year, Congress established an act authorizing construction of lighthouses for the West Coast and appointed the Coast Survey to study feasibility and provide recommendations. From 1852 through 1858, the Lighthouse Board established 16 lighthouses, with the first ones on the West Coast. The Cape Cod–design style was incorporated into all of these lighthouses. Only later would California's Spanish influence factor into design.

In 1853, when the *Winfield Scott* wrecked on Anacapa Island, the Coast Survey recommended a permanent lighthouse facility on the island. The U.S. Coast Survey visited the island in 1854 and concluded, "it is inconceivable for a lighthouse to be constructed on this mass of volcanic rock—perpendicular on every face, with an ascent inaccessible by any natural means."

The more feasible location was Hueneme (pronounced why-NEE-mee) on the southeast end of the Santa Barbara Channel. In 1874, an elaborate Victorian stick-style lighthouse was established at the point. It was the nearest point on the mainland and the fastest way to cross the Santa Barbara Channel to Anacapa Island, with only an 11-mile separation.

Shipping in the Santa Barbara Channel increased, and with the increase of traffic came more shipwrecks. In 1909, the Lighthouse Board stated, "Anacapa Island is one of the most difficult points on the Southern California coast to pass in foggy or otherwise thick weather and is regarded as the most important point for a light station on any of the Channel Islands." However, Congress did not want to pay the estimated $100,000 cost to erect a lighthouse and opted for an unmanned acetylene light placed at the east end of the island in 1911. The light did little to warn mariners, and tragedy struck again in 1921 when the *Liebre* ran aground directly below the light, necessitating a permanent lighthouse structure.

Construction of the Anacapa station finally began in the spring of 1930 and was carried out in two phases. The sheer remoteness of the island proved a daunting task for transporting supplies and construction materials; however, the greatest challenge of all was trying to build upon the harder-than-stone volcanic rock. In 1932, the light was finally completed.

The style was a complete departure from Hueneme's Victorian-style lighthouse. Anacapa light was built in the more typically known cylindrical style or column-shaped lighthouse design, with a twist. The lighthouse was created in Spanish Revival–style, which was influenced by the Spanish Colonial architecture of earlier centuries. It is an ideal location for a lighthouse and, according to the U.S. Coast Guard, "is a valuable aid for both trans-pacific and coast-wise vessel traffic."

From 1931 through the 1960s, a crew of about 15 to 25 personnel stationed at Anacapa maintained the light and fog signal. They also conducted hourly weather and radar monitoring reports, as well as manning the radio tower.

With increased traffic, the desire for a harbor at Hueneme was growing. The name "Hueneme," or "Wyneme," has origins dating back to the Chumash Indians. It means "resting place," or "halfway point." The would-be port was an ideal location because it would lie midway between where Point Mugu is today and the mouth of the Santa Clara River.

The idea of building a port at Hueneme was the vision of Thomas Bard in 1867. Bard had learned of a natural submarine valley more than 1,000 feet deep that came within 300 feet of the proposed channel. This canyon enabled the proposed channel to be free of silt and debris. Utilizing this submarine valley, Bard's 1,500-foot wharf was constructed in 1872 for smaller transports between the coast and ships offshore.

The son of Thomas Bard, Richard, would carry his father's dream even further. Richard Bard and area farmers applied for a loan to construct a commercial port but were rejected by Washington. Undeterred, these men applied for and were awarded a bond issue in the amount of $1.75 million to finance the project without having to rely on any funds from the federal government. According to the City of Oxnard, "It was proposed and accepted by the City of Oxnard that the harbor property it had previously annexed, be released to the Harbor District and that it should never be a part of any incorporated city."

On February 4, 1939, Richard Bard dug the first shovel of dirt during ground-breaking exercises. The construction of the port continued from 1939 into 1940 and marked the conclusion of constant work by the developers of the district, as well as the start of sound expansion for the future.

The fate of the 1874 Point Hueneme Lighthouse was hanging in the balance. The location of the lighthouse was too close to the harbor's edge, making it ineffective. The need for a new Hueneme Lighthouse was evident. In 1940, an art moderne–style lighthouse (a design very typical of the 1920s and 1930s) was constructed.

The Fresnel lens from 1897 was removed from the original structure and relocated to the new lighthouse. The lighthouse keeper at the time, Walter White, also transferred from one lighthouse to the other with ease, and he stayed at the new structure until his retirement.

The realization of the historical significance of the original Victorian lighthouse resulted in its move, with great care and planning. On February 16, 1940, it became the first lighthouse in history to be put on a barge and moved across a harbor. Unfortunately, only one bid resulted at an auction for the old structure. The cost of relocating the lighthouse by truck, plus additional expenses and 1941 wartime cutbacks, proved to be too much. The building was eventually razed.

One

The Ventura Coast
Discovery of New Land

For hundreds of years, the Channel Islands and the coast of the Ventura area in Southern California were populated by the Chumash people, who lived off the land. The fires they set for survival and warmth would have been some of the first navigational aids dotting the California coastline. The Chumash considered the Pacific Ocean their first home and referred to themselves as "the first people."

The Chumash numbered in the tens of thousands, and archaeological research demonstrates that they have a deep history in the Santa Barbara Channel and lived along the Southern California coast for millennia. Utilizing the vast resources of the islands, which they referred to as "Limuw," the Chumash subsisted on the abundant seafood encompassing the islands and on hunting, as well as mining chert (a type of quartz). They developed specialized crafts and traded among themselves and then with the explorers and those who came after them.

Portuguese navigator Juan Rodriguez Cabrillo is most noted for his exploration of the West Coast of North America as he sailed from Spain in search of new land. Cabrillo was the first European explorer to navigate the coast of present-day California. Cabrillo witnessed the then swamp grass–filled area and was the first to lay anchor and declare San Buenaventura for Spain in 1542.

In 1602, Sebastian Vizcaino led the final Spanish exploration to California and noted on his map the name of Santa Cruz Island as the "Isla de Gente Barbuda" (island of the bearded people). In 1769, explorer Don Gaspar de la Portola reached Santa Cruz Island accompanied by Fr. Juan Gonzalez Vizcaino and Fr. Francisco Palou and made contact with the native people.

Today Ventura continues to flourish thanks to its natural resources, rich soil, and bustling port. The Channel Islands, on the other hand, have benefited from their lack of development, as these fragile islands have been able to maintain their natural splendor and resources, thanks in part to an act of Congress.

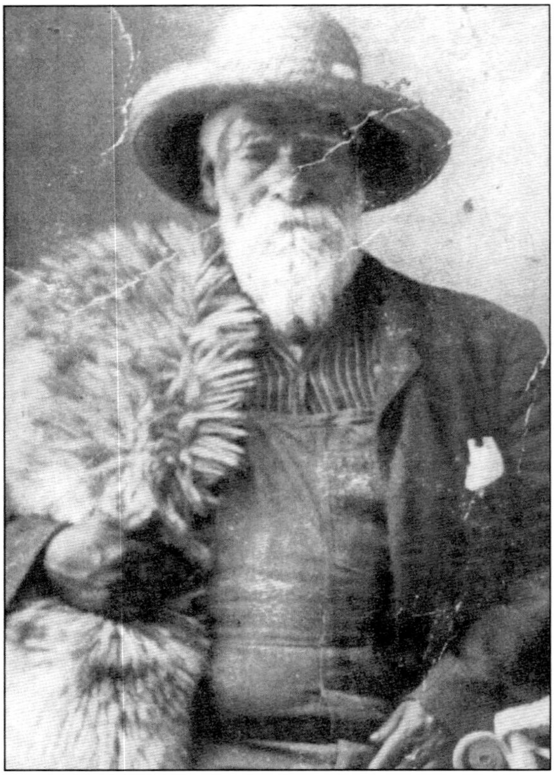

The Chumash Indians were once the largest cultural group in California. Much of their history would have been lost if it wasn't for Fernando Librado. Born in 1839, Librado, a full-blooded Chumash, assisted in relaying the stories and history of his people in 1912 to John P. Harrington. The book *Breath of the Sun* was the result of this endeavor. (Courtesy Santa Barbara History Museum.)

Librado is also credited with reconstructing a tomol, or canoe, and helping to save the history of this amazing craftsmanship and lost art. The tomol was key to the lifestyle of the Chumash, as they used it to travel up and down the Pacific coast and out to the Channel Islands of Santa Cruz, Santa Rosa, and Anacapa. (Courtesy Jan Timbrook.)

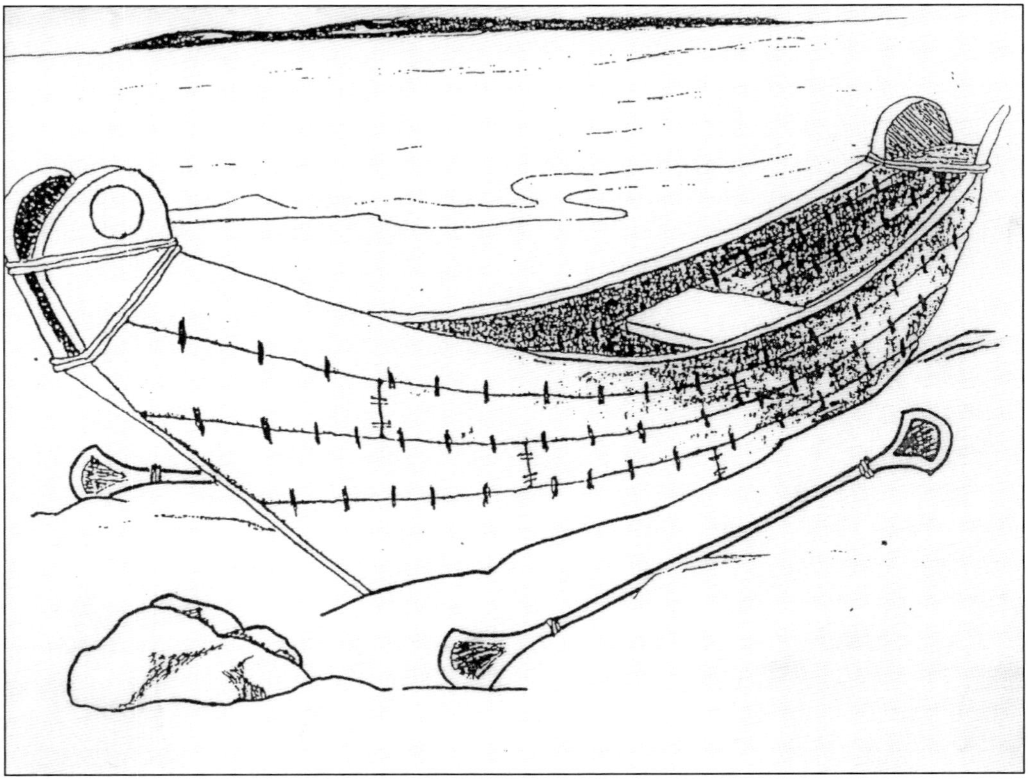

A Chumash man with painted face readies for a special event. The hairpins, nose piercing, and shell beads were indicative of the Chumash heritage. Face painting is an important tradition among Native Americans. Each tribe of Indians has its own unique way of face painting. More than just a beautifying practice, face painting is done on special occasions. The customs are rooted in displaying social acts of distinction and cultural heritage. (Courtesy Michael K. Ward.)

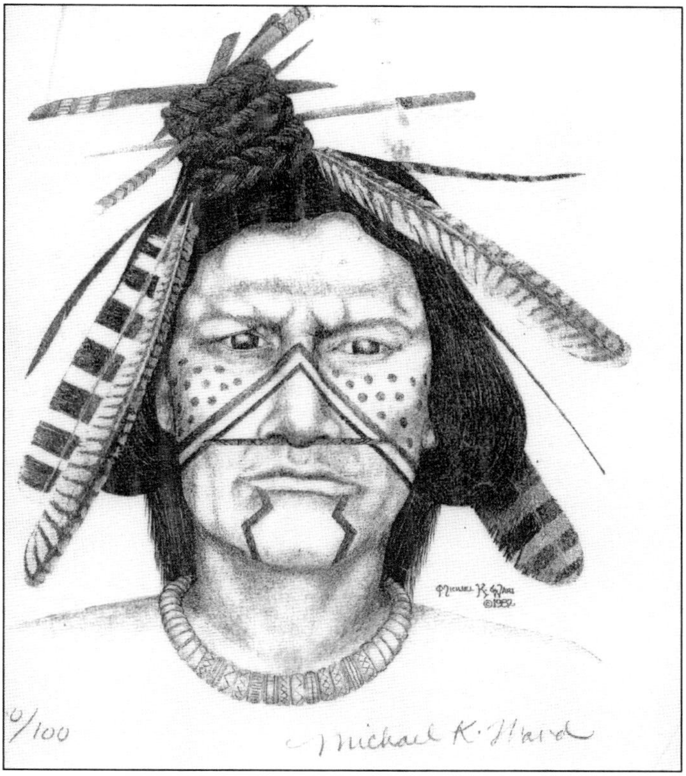

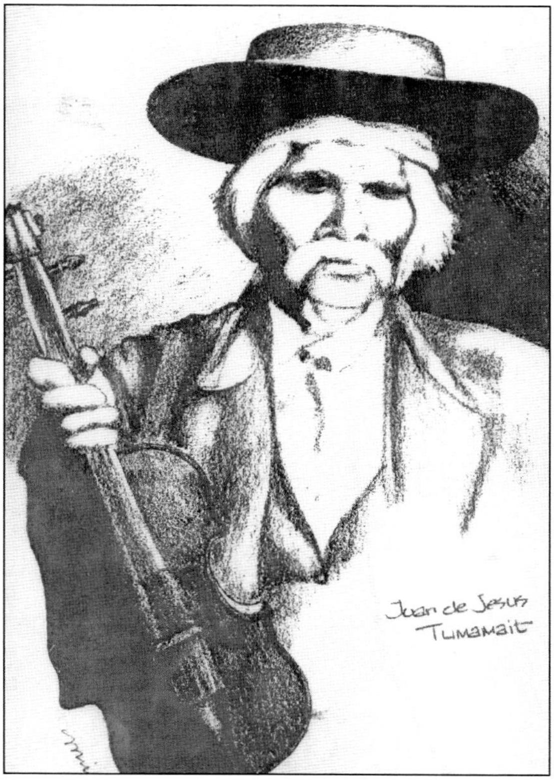

Juan De Jesus Tumamait was born August 29, 1811, in San Buenaventura, California, and died November 8, 1895, in Ventura, California. He was a leader among the Ventureno Chumash in post-mission times. (Courtesy Michael K. Ward.)

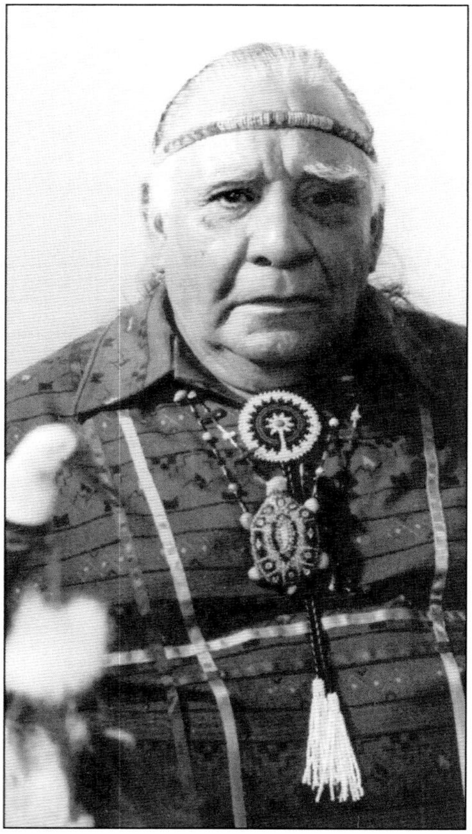

Vincent Tumamait (1919–1992), grandson of Juan de Jesus Tumamait, was the son of a full-blooded Chumash father and half-blooded Chumash mother. Both his parents came from Santa Cruz and Santa Rosa Island. He was an elder and chief of the Ojai Valley and was referred to as "Paha," or one who does invocations. An accomplished storyteller and singer, Vincent traveled around the country, sharing the knowledge of his people. (Courtesy Julie Tumamait.)

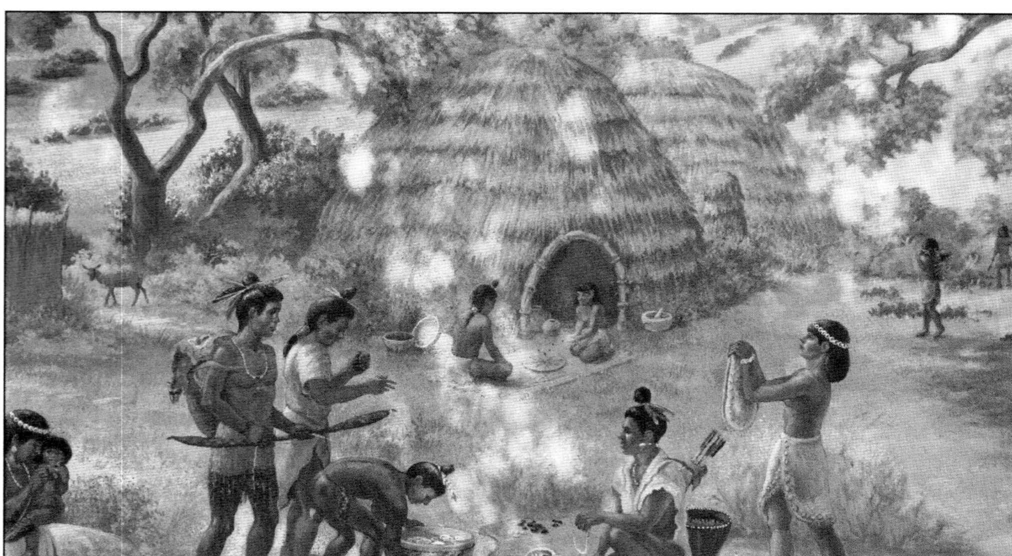

Early Chumash lived near the water's edge, placing their villages in close proximity to farming, fishing, and plant gathering. This mural depicts life in a Chumash village historically located along the Santa Paula Creek in Ventura County. The Chumash villages were distributed over approximately 7,000 square miles and numbered in the hundreds. (Courtesy Artist Ann Thiermann and Chairperson of Murals Joyce Carlson.)

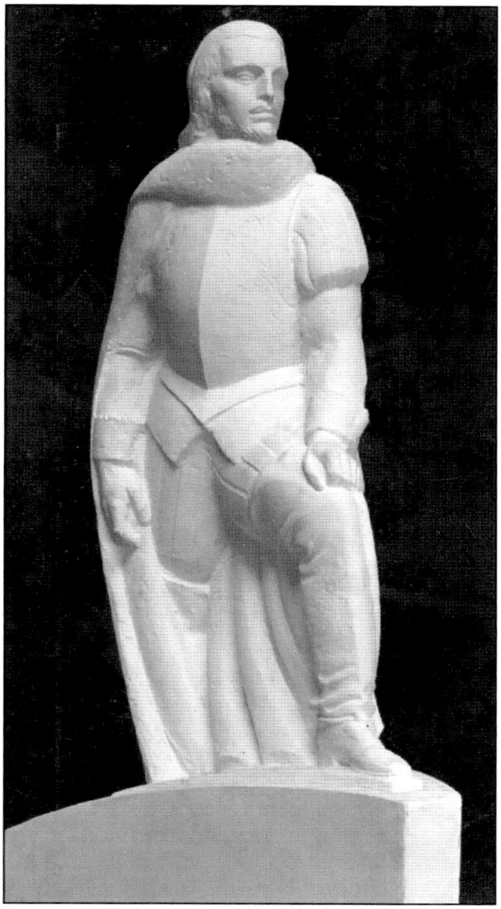

A San Pedro monument commemorates Juan Rodriguez Cabrillo's voyage of discovery. In 1542, Cabrillo led the first European expedition to explore what is now the West Coast of the United States. Making his way up the California coastline, Cabrillo made what is believed to be his last anchorage and final resting place on San Miguel Island, which is today one of the Channel Islands off the coast of Ventura County. (Courtesy San Pedro Bay Historical Society.)

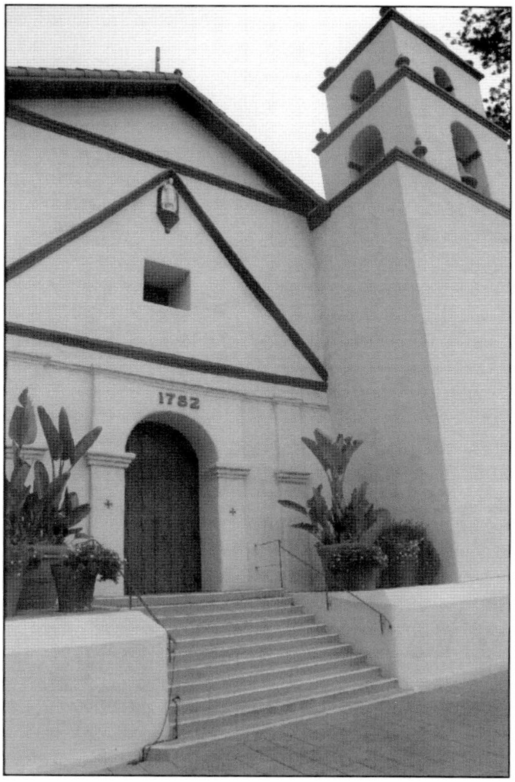

Mission San Buenaventura was founded on Easter Sunday, March 31, 1782. Named after a Franciscan theologian, Saint Bonaventure, it was the last of the missions founded by Father Serra. (Courtesy Kim Castro-Bran.)

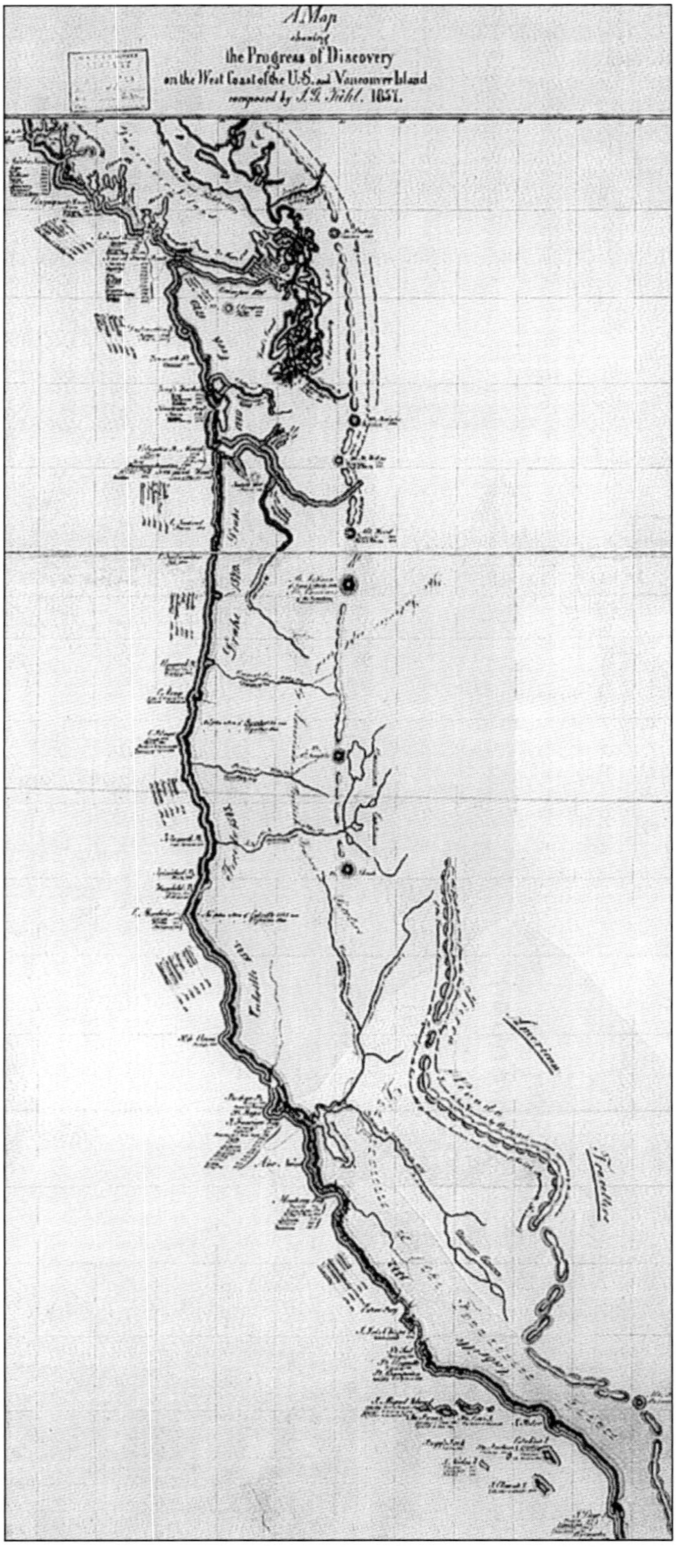

This map, by Johann Georg Kohl, shows the "Progress of Discovery of the West Coast of the U.S. and Vancouver Island" around 1857. (Courtesy National Archives.)

Two

Point Hueneme

The Original Lighthouse

With the decision to build a lighthouse at Point Hueneme, plans needed to be drawn up for the structure, which would house not only the light but its keepers as well.

The chief draftsman for the lighthouse board, architect Paul Pelz, was tasked with creating what would be the blueprint for six lighthouses: Mare Island, Hereford, East Brother, Point Fermin, Point Hueneme, and Point Adams. All of these were constructed from 1872 through 1875. Point Fermin and Point Hueneme were built at the same time and activated on December 15, 1874. Pelz is best known for assisting in designing the Library of Congress in Washington, D.C.

The style of these lighthouses is known as Swiss Carpenter Gothic, or more commonly, Victorian stick style. The Point Hueneme Lighthouse was built on a brick foundation, as was Point Fermin Lighthouse. The structure itself was constructed of oak. The house had 10 rooms, with four fireplaces and a three-story, 65-foot tower.

The head keeper and his family lived on the first floor, with the assistant keeper and his family on the second. The second floor consisted of a living room, kitchen and bedroom. The tower weight ran through both the living room and kitchen.

The light was changed from fixed red to occulting white on April 15, 1892. The apparatus used was a new type devised by Maj. D. P. Heap, engineer for the Third Lighthouses District, New York. A second Fresnel lens was introduced, which was manufactured in Paris in 1897 and installed at Hueneme in 1899. This lens continues to shine to this very day, having been removed from the original structure and installed in the newer lighthouse.

A total of 12 head and assistant keepers and their families resided at the original lighthouse from 1874 through 1940. Technology aided the keepers in operating the lighthouse as the building was electrified in 1925, and an electric motor was installed on the light in 1934.

The lighthouse continued to guide ships to safety until 1940, when it was replaced by the structure that stands to this day.

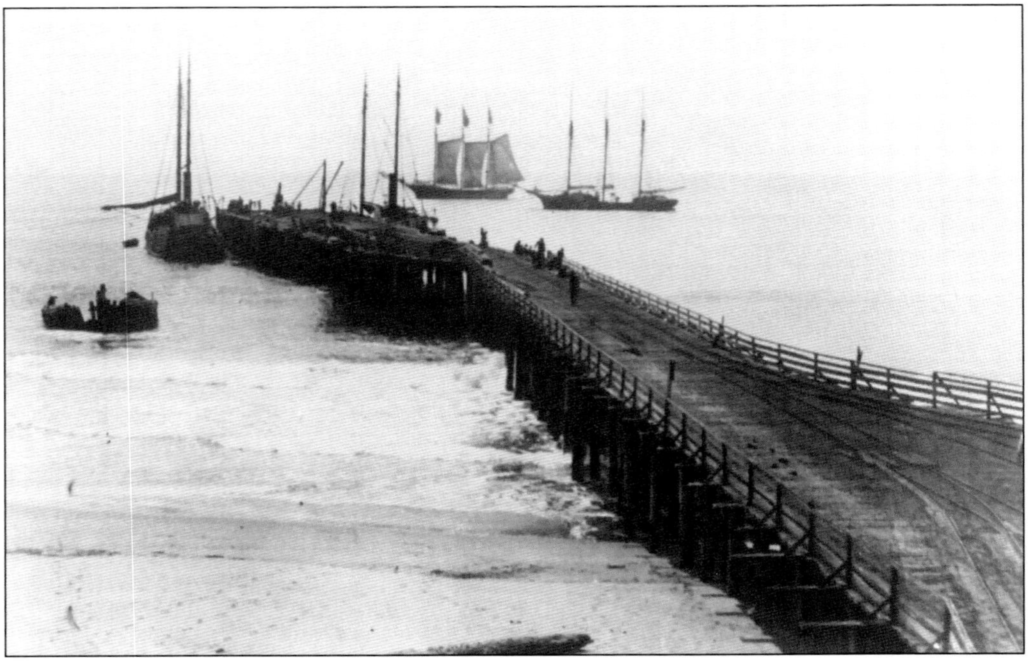

The wharf at Hueneme, constructed in 1872, was only made possible when a natural underground river, or submarine valley, was discovered during coastal exploration by Thomas Bard in 1867. The canyon was over 1,000 feet deep and came within 300 feet of the proposed channel. This sweeping river flow, which kept the canyon free of sand and debris, was the catalyst for the wharf and the future port. (Courtesy Port Hueneme Historical Society.)

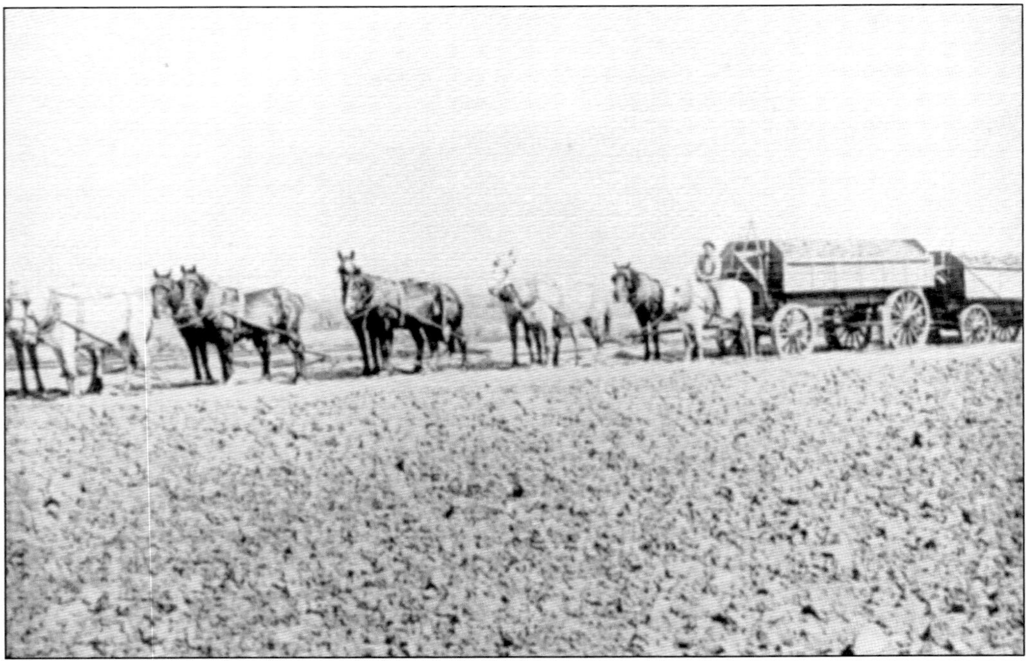

A 10-horse team heads from the Russell Ranch in the Conejo Valley toward the station at Simi around 1894. Before 1904, the ranches on the Conejo shipped their grain via the Hueneme Wharf. (Courtesy Port Hueneme Historical Society.)

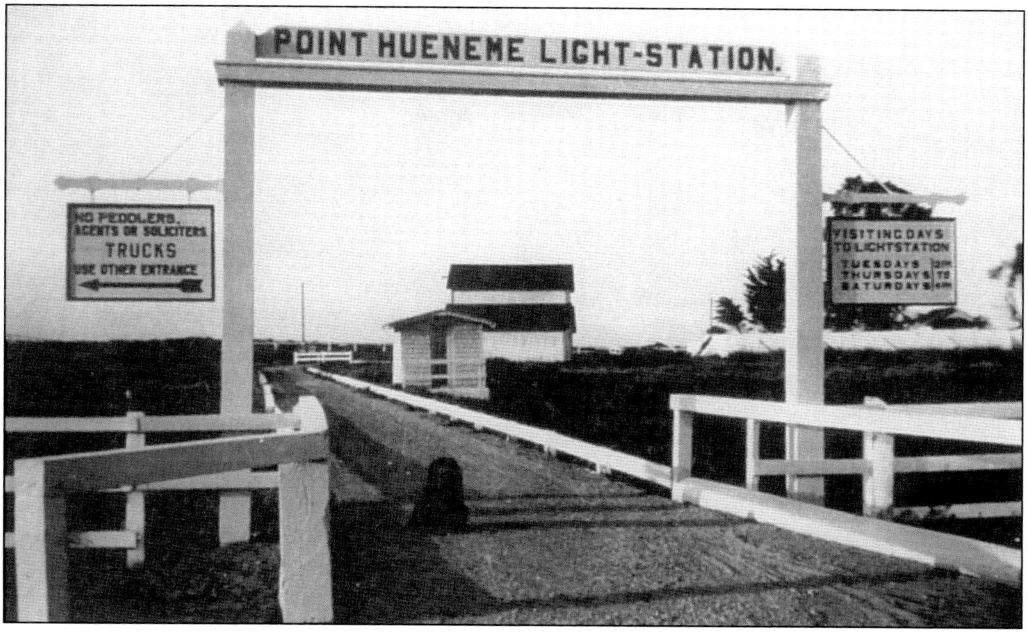

The main entrance to the Point Hueneme Light-Station (above) was followed by a long dirt road that led to the lighthouse prior to the construction of the harbor. The front view (below) is of the very ornate Point Hueneme Victorian stick–style lighthouse constructed in 1874. It was located on the north side of the east entrance to the Santa Barbara Channel. The lighthouse consisted of 10 rooms and was constructed primarily of oak. The assistant keeper's family lived on the second floor, which consisted of a living room, kitchen, and bedroom. (Both courtesy Laverne White-Dornberger.)

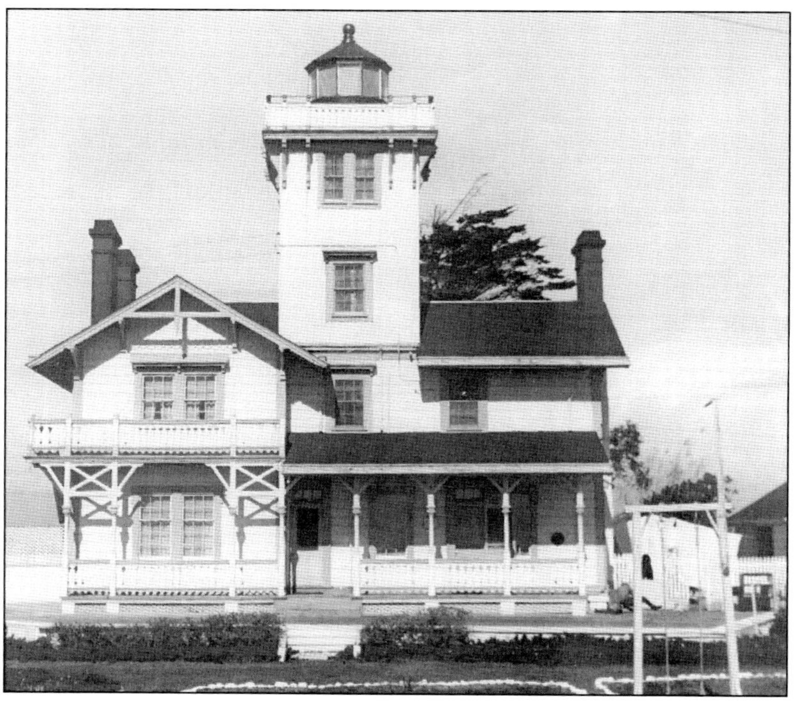

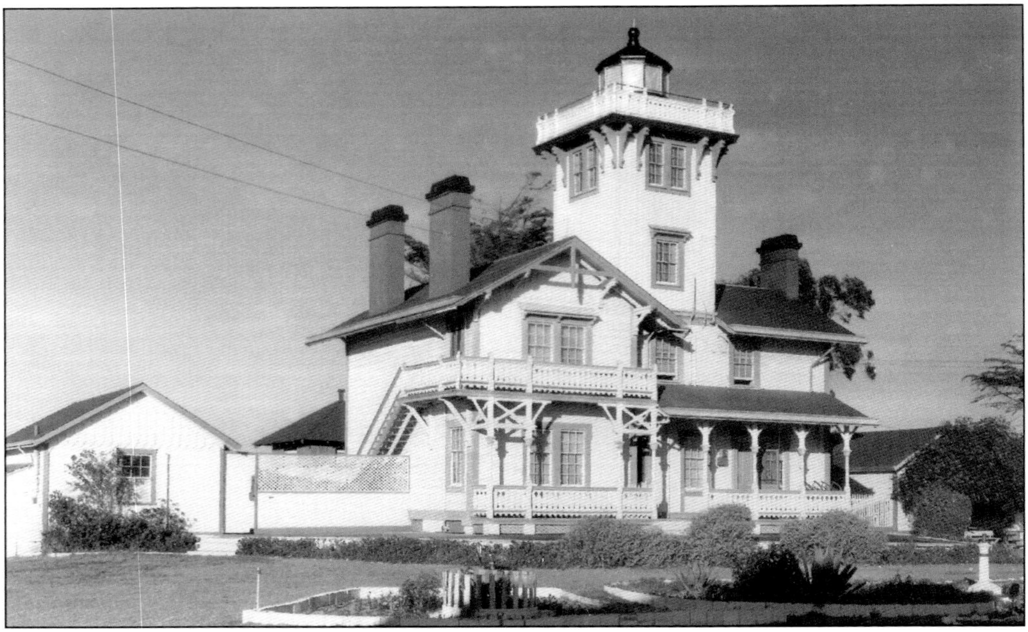

This side view (above) shows the lighthouse grounds. The sketch below shows the elaborate Victorian stick–style house noted for having a series of stick work, exposed trusses, and other details borrowed from medieval times. Many of these very ornate elements were purely decorative. The benefit of this style of lighthouse was that the keeper and the assistant keeper could live in the residence with their family and mind the light at the same time. (Above, courtesy Wayne Wheeler, U.S. Lighthouse Society; below, sketch by the author.)

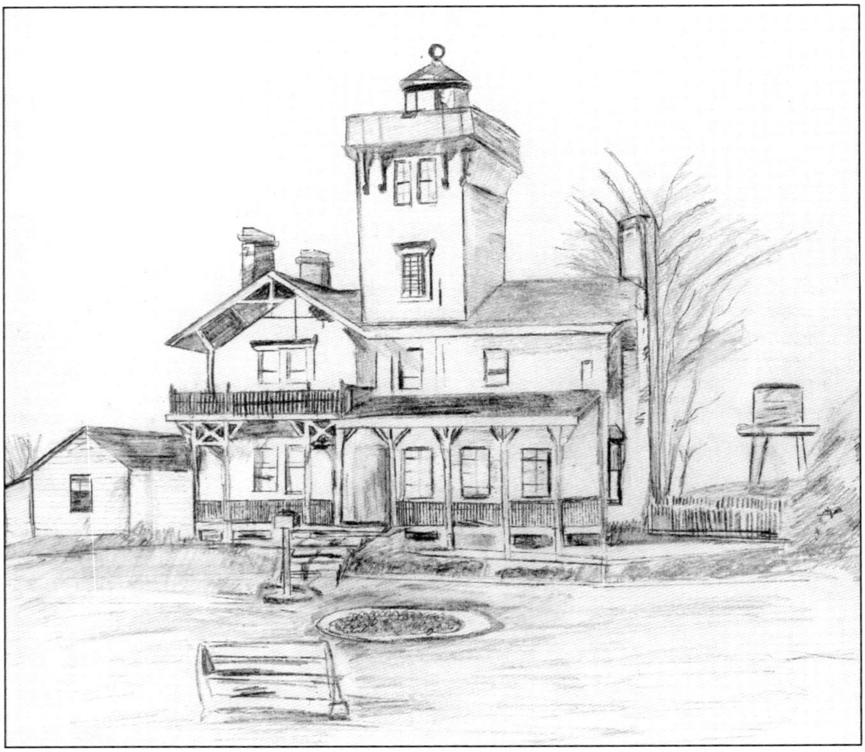

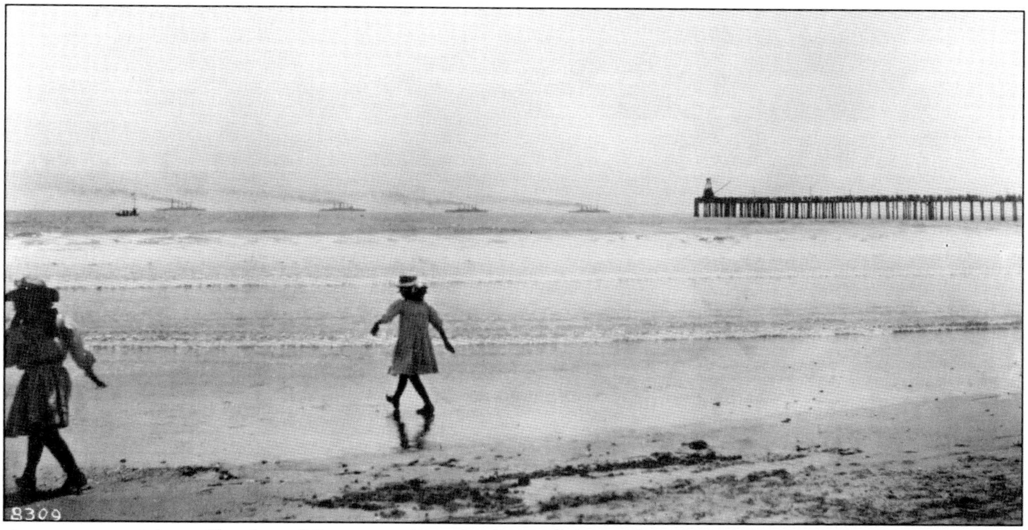

As a young girl strolls along Hueneme Beach, four of the 16 battleships that later became known as the Great White Fleet can be seen in the background as they make their way around the world. The 14-month voyage, which started on December 16, 1907, and ended on February 22, 1909, allowed Pres. Theodore Roosevelt to demonstrate America's mighty sea power to the world. (Courtesy Ventura County Museum of History and Art.)

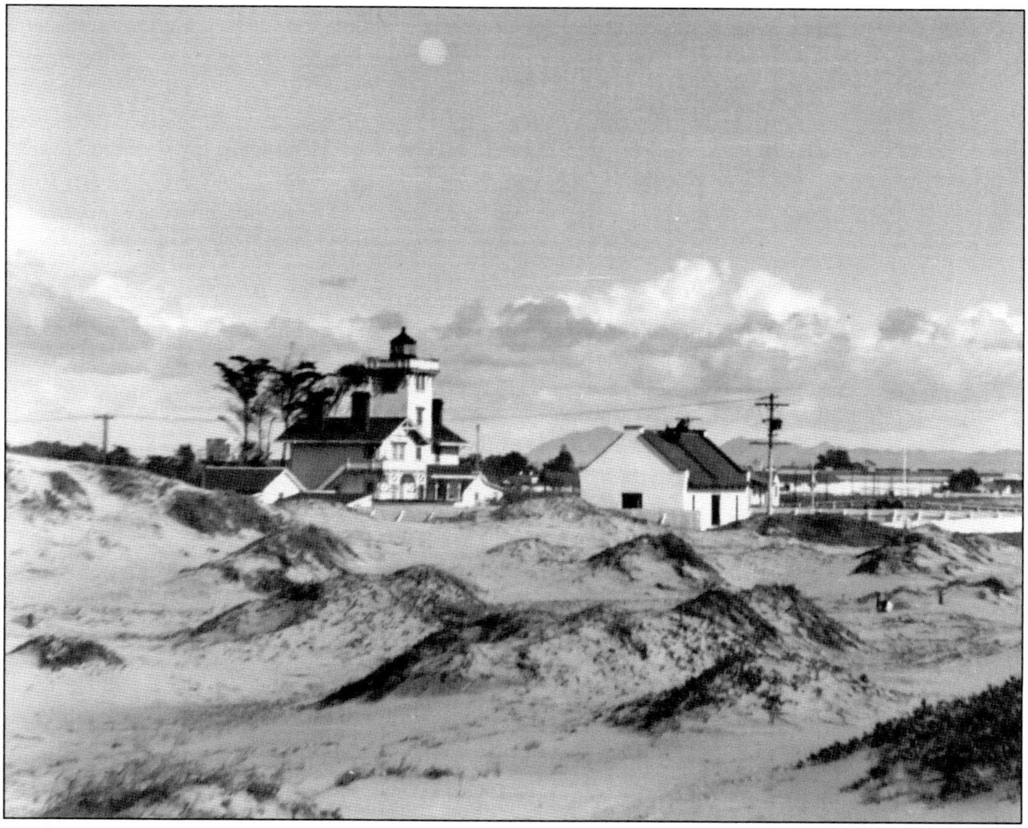

With the lighthouse in the background, dunes created by loose sands and the prominent winds of the area are seen in the foreground. (Courtesy Port Hueneme Historical Society.)

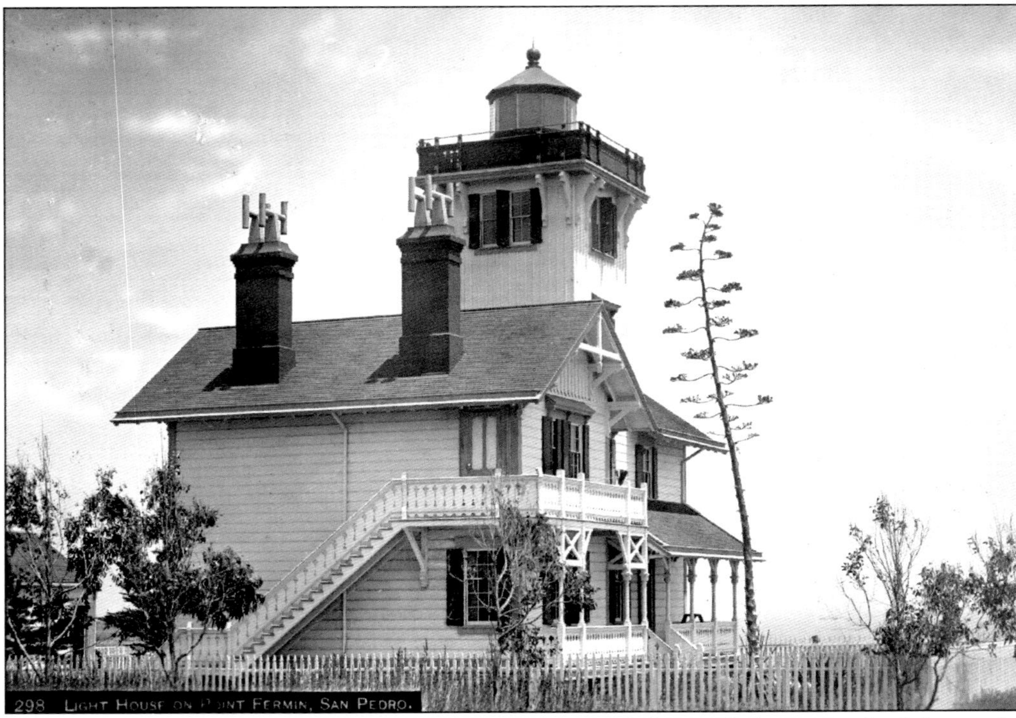

Point Fermin Lighthouse (above) and Point Hueneme Lighthouse (below) were both lit on the same day, December 15, 1874. Both lighthouses were constructed from the same plans, with only slight variations, by architect Paul J. Pelz. Pelz's design was used for six lighthouses, of which three are still standing (East Brothers in San Francisco Bay, Hereford Inlet in New Jersey, and Point Fermin in San Pedro). (Above, courtesy San Pedro Bay Historical Society; below, courtesy Ventura County Museum of History and Art.)

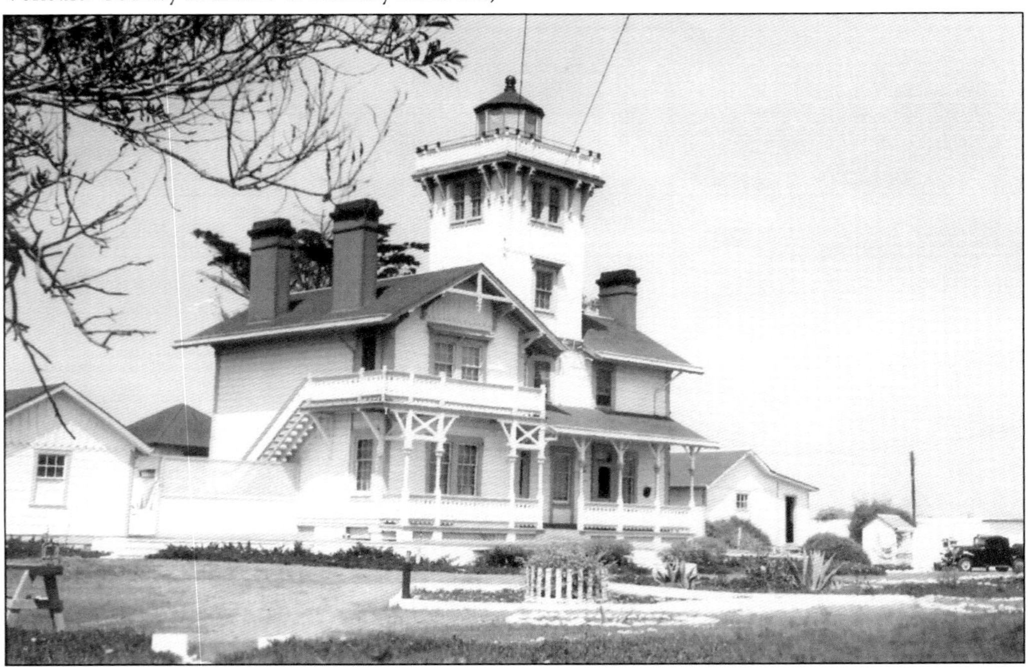

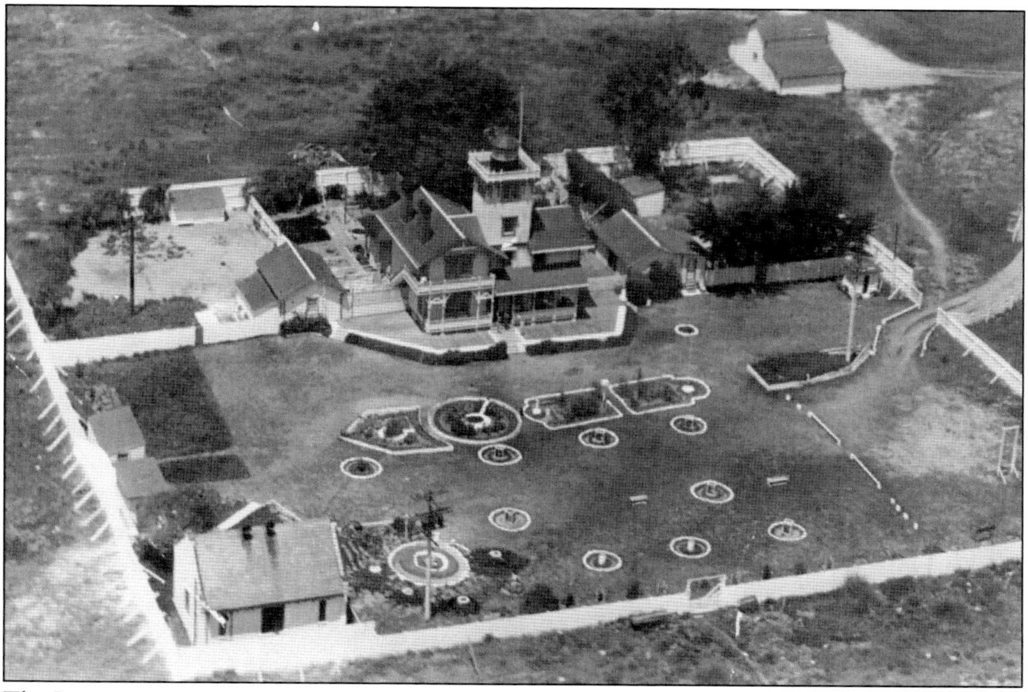

The Point Hueneme Lighthouse reservation is shown in an aerial photograph (above) and diagram (below), outlining each area of the lighthouse grounds. (Both courtesy Laverne White-Dornberger.)

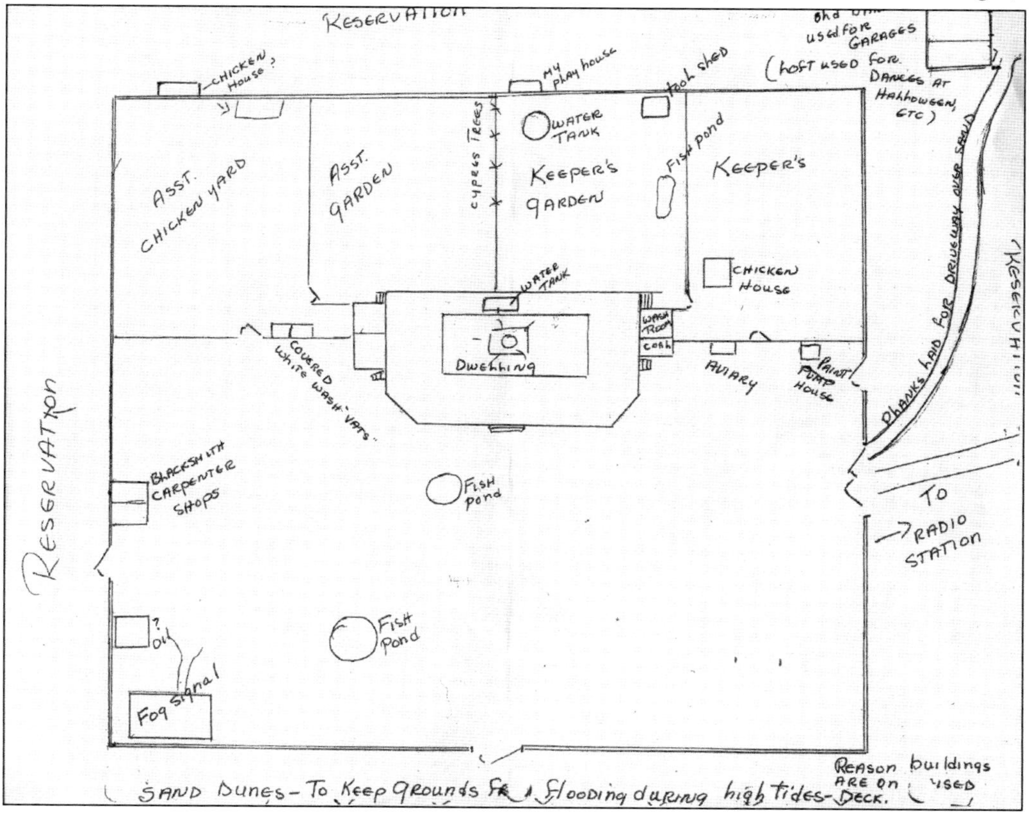

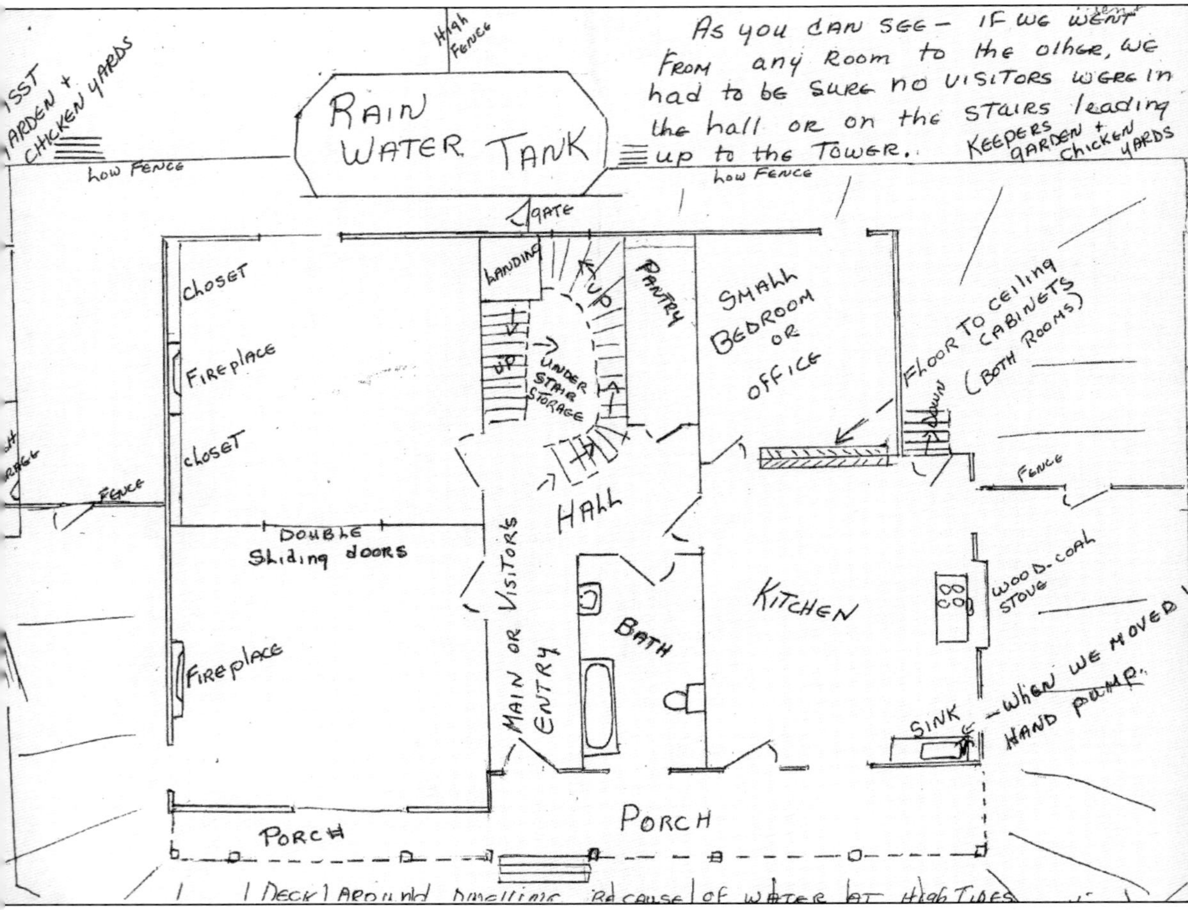

This diagram shows the layout of the first floor of the lighthouse. The lighthouse keeper and his family resided on the first floor. For the keeper and his family, 90 percent of the living and entertaining was done in the kitchen. The other rooms—living and bedroom—were dark, damp, and chilly by contrast. The only heat in those rooms came from fireplaces that were seldom lit. But as Laverne White, youngest daughter of Walter and Frankie White, recalls, "it was a carefree and enjoyable childhood and we did not lack much." As noted in the diagram, if the family went from one room to the other, they had to make sure no visitors were in the hall or on the stairs leading up to the tower. Also noted is the deck around the dwelling that helped to deflect flooding during high tide. (Courtesy Laverne White-Dornberger.)

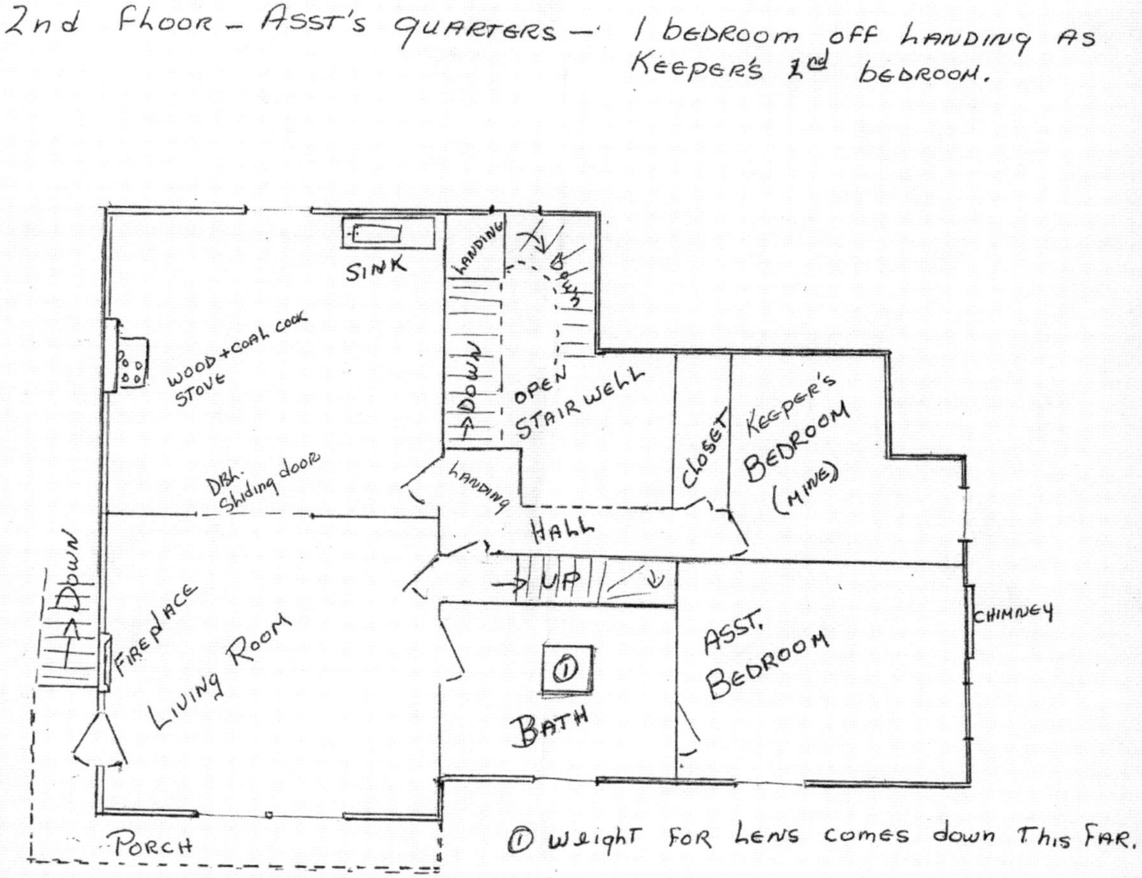

This diagram illustrates the layout of the second floor of the lighthouse. The assistant keeper and his family resided on the second floor except for one small room under the upper right roof, which was used by the keeper as a spare bedroom. There was a kitchen on the second floor for the family to have their own meals, as well as a living room and bedroom. The light would rotate on a pendulum or "clockworks" system from the base of the rotating lens attached to ropes, pulleys, and weights that would descend straight down the tower, through the assistant keeper's quarters, and into the first floor bathroom. This enabled the light to rotate and create a flash sequence and also made it obvious to the keeper and assistant when the light needed to be cranked again. (Courtesy Laverne White-Dornberger.)

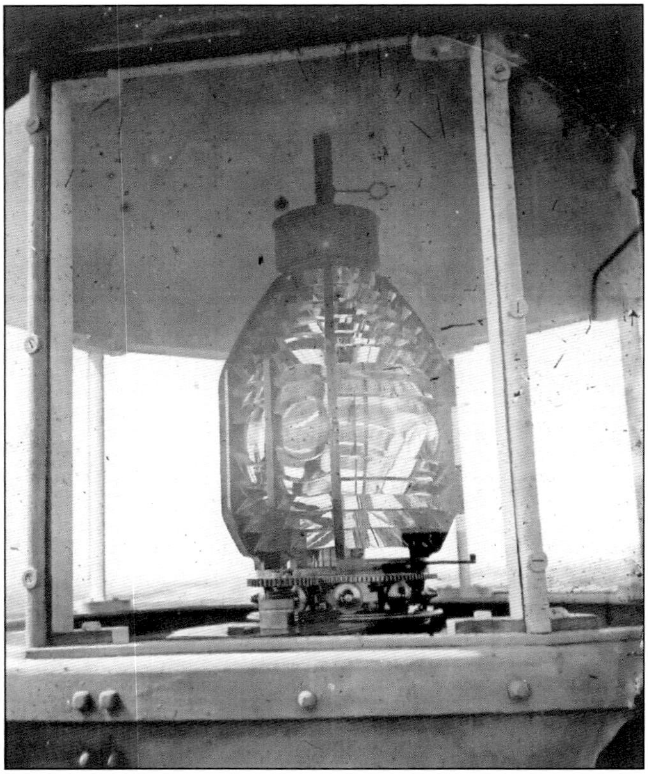

This is the only known photograph of Point Hueneme Lighthouse's first Fresnel (pronounced fru-NELL) lens, installed in December 1874. The characteristics of the light changed from fixed red to occulting white on April 15, 1892, and remained until 1899, when a second Fresnel lens was installed. (Courtesy Ventura County Museum of History and Art.)

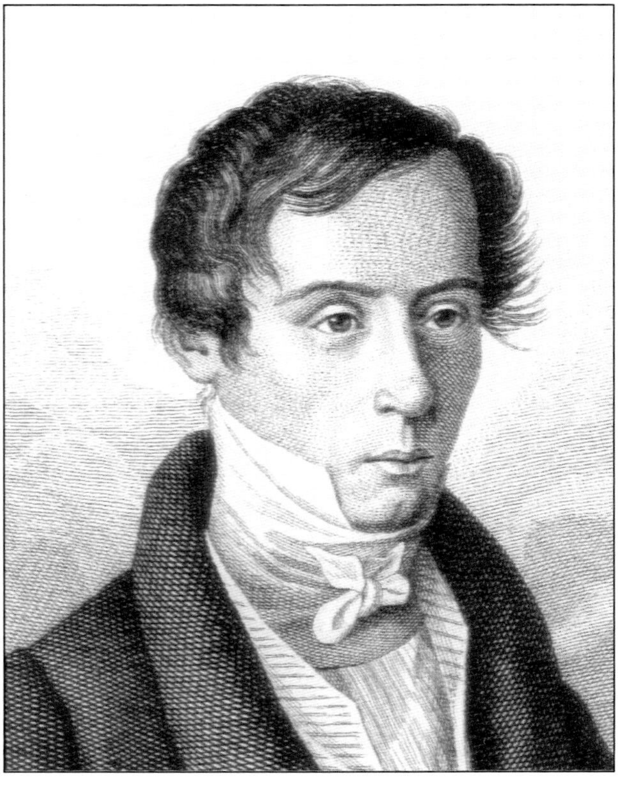

The light was named after its inventor, Augustine Fresnel, a French physicist and inventor who revolutionized navigation and saved countless lives. Using hand-carved glass prisms positioned at various angles to capture light rays, Fresnel was able to bend (refract) and project (reflect) light for miles upon miles out to sea. Car headlights, studio lighting, and cameras have all benefited from his invention. (Courtesy U.S. Lighthouse Society.)

Taken from the keeper's log, this is Walter White's transcription of the keepers' names and years served at the lighthouse, starting with the very first keeper, Samuel Ensign, in 1874, to White's own service in 1927. The circled date of 21 is the number of years Walter White served at Point Hueneme. The 44 is for his combined service. He predicted that Ward would be the next keeper, but Ward would continue on as assistant. (Courtesy Laverne White-Dornberger.)

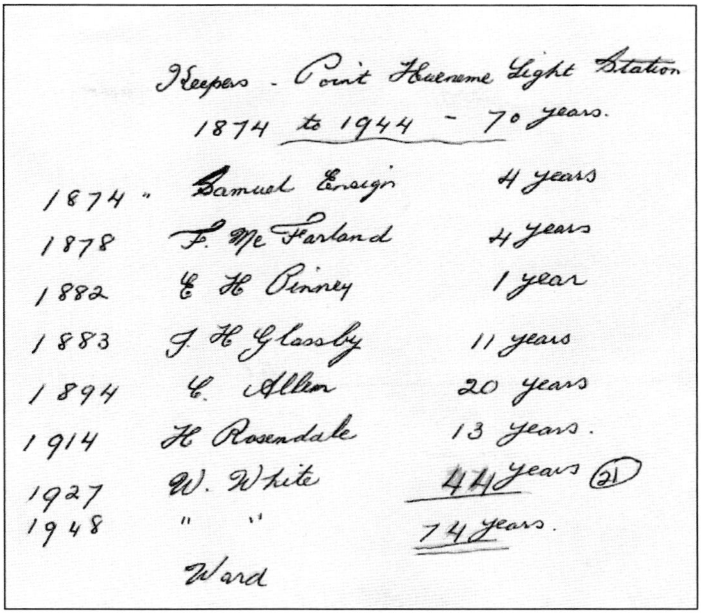

Keepers - Point Hueneme Light Station
1874 to 1944 - 70 years.

1874 "	Samuel Ensign	4 years
1878	F. McFarland	4 years
1882	E H Pinney	1 year
1883	J. H Glassby	11 years
1894	C. Allen	20 years
1914	H Rosendale	13 years.
1927	W. White	44 years (21)
1948	" "	74 years.
	Ward	

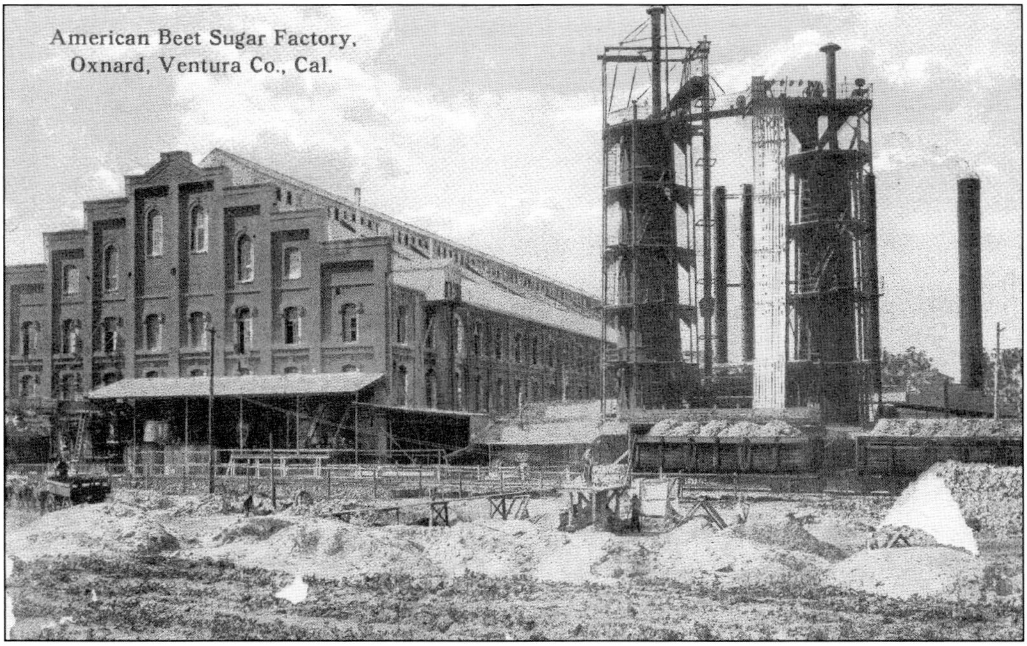

When the Dingley Tarriff Bill imposing a heavy duty on the import of sugar was passed in 1897, Henry, James, and Oxnard seized the opportunity to establish the American Beet Sugar Factory in Oxnard, Ventura County. As a result, they created 700 jobs and refined nearly 200 tons of beets by 1903. (Courtesy Laverne White-Dornberger.)

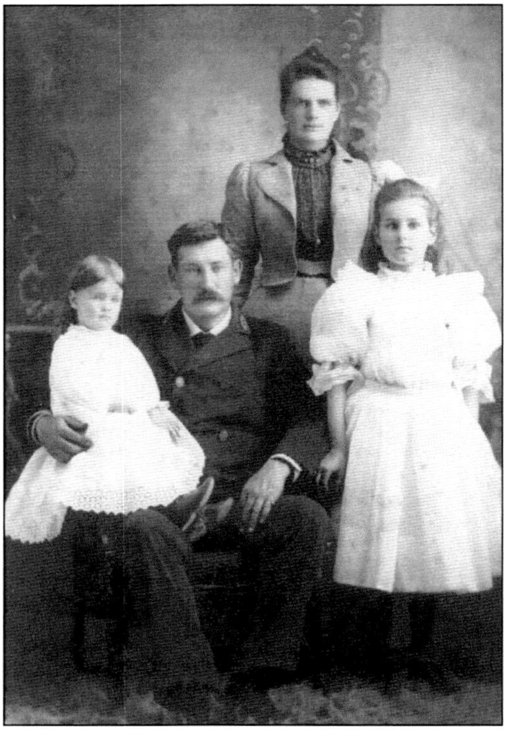

This family portrait depicts lighthouse keeper Charles Allen with his wife, Anna, and daughters May and Melba. Charles Allen was the fifth lighthouse keeper and served from 1894 until he resigned in 1914. This photograph was taken around 1920, after his 20 years of service. (Courtesy Ventura County Museum of History and Art.)

Anna Allen, wife of Charles Allen, is sitting sidesaddle on a horse with keeper Charles Allen standing in front. Daughters Melba and May are standing to the left. (Courtesy Ventura County Museum of History and Art.)

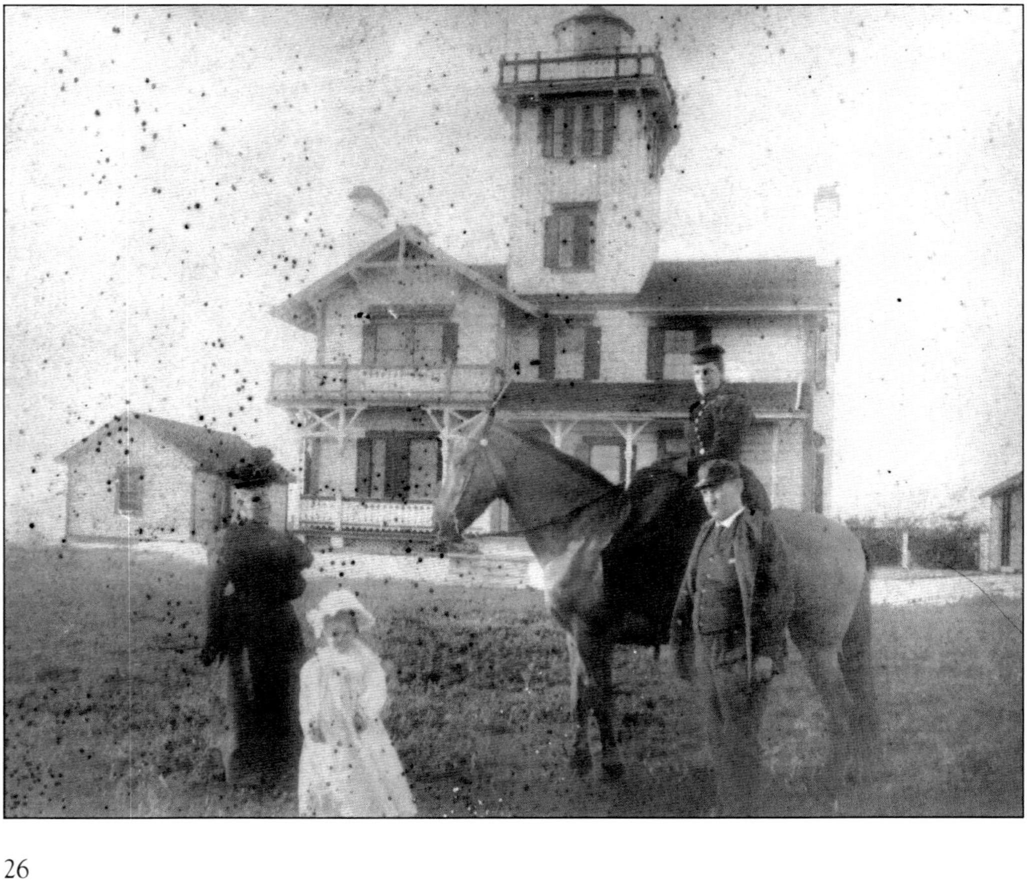

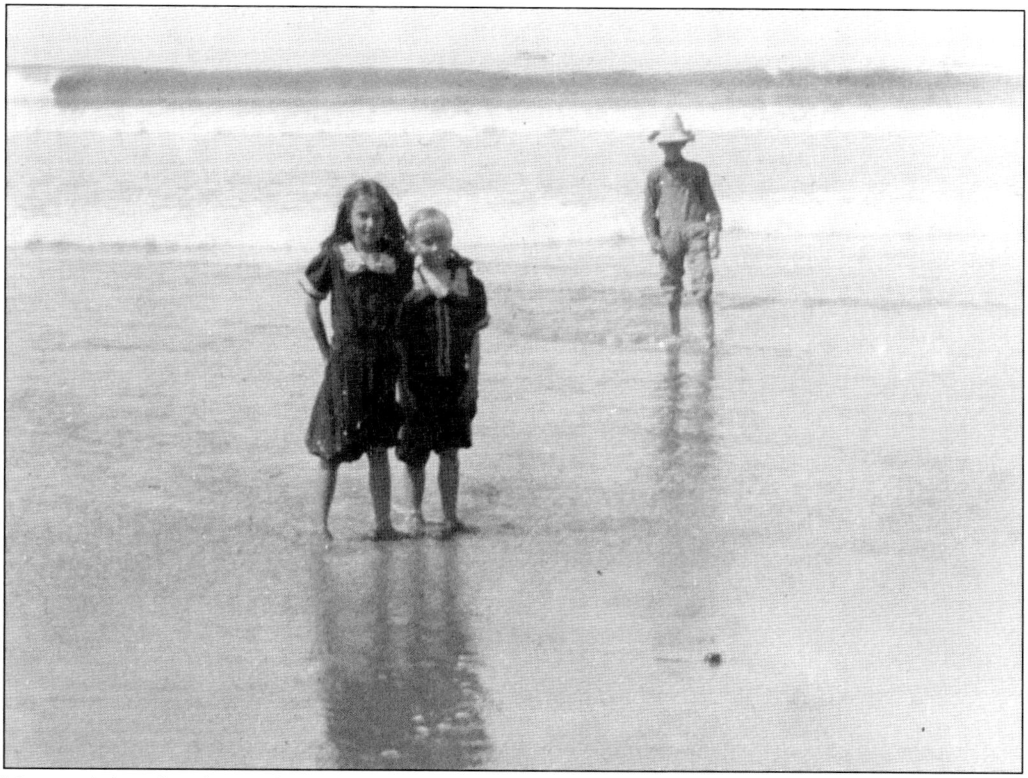

Ventura's beaches have always been a haven for sun worshipers and outdoor adventurers of all backgrounds. Seen in these two photographs taken around 1900 are a farmer with his two girls and residents wearing their Sunday best. (Both courtesy Port Hueneme Historical Society.)

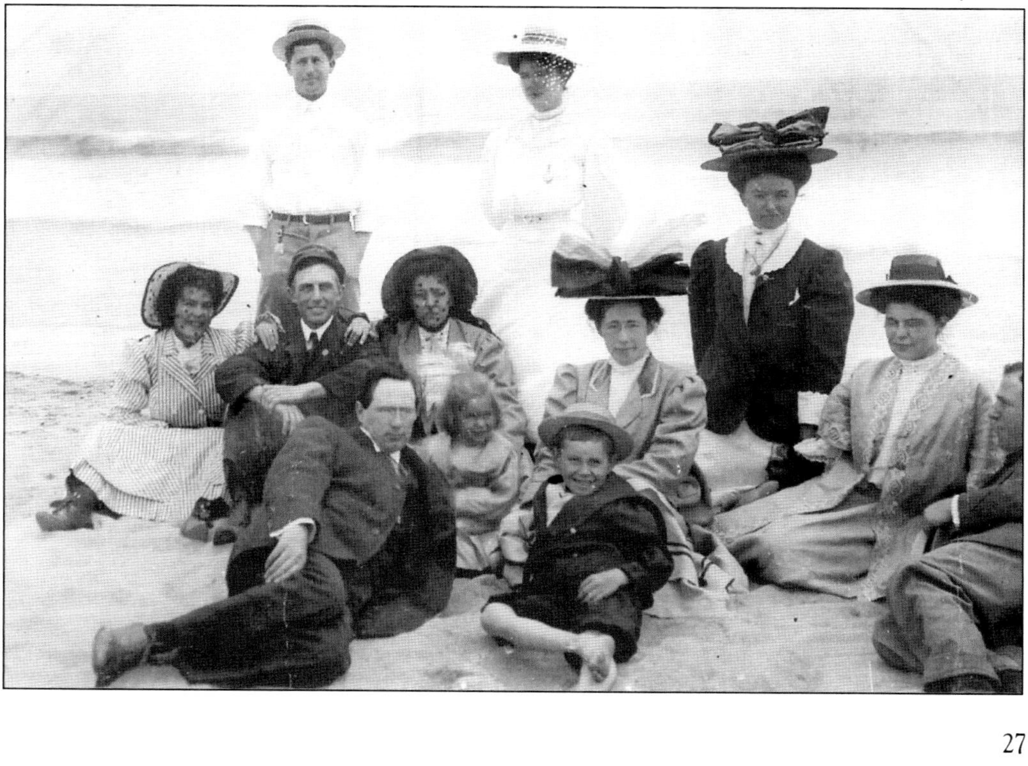

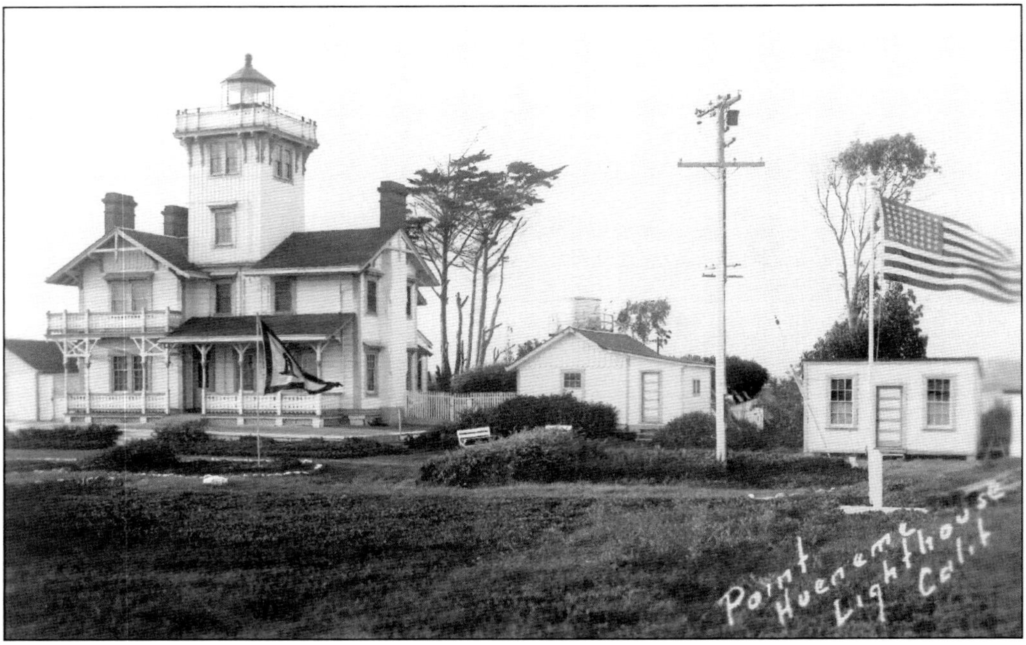

This vintage postcard shows the Point Hueneme Lighthouse, with the flagpole and flag on the right. (Courtesy Laverne White-Dornberger.)

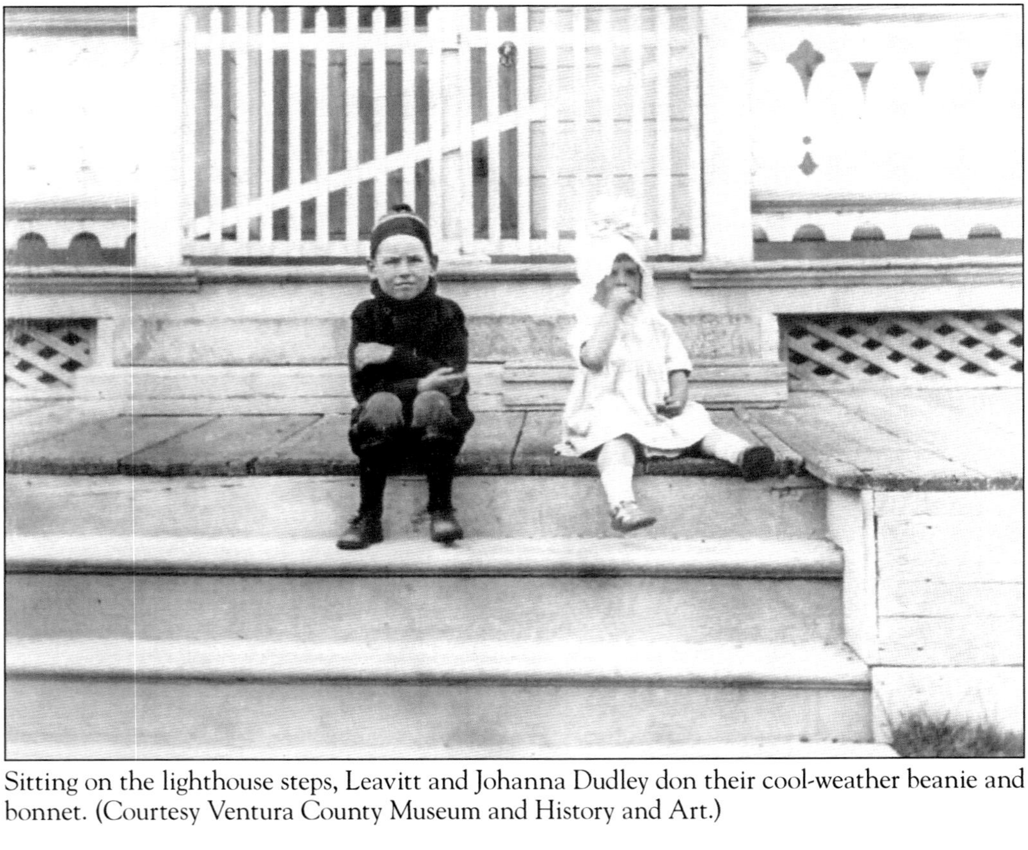

Sitting on the lighthouse steps, Leavitt and Johanna Dudley don their cool-weather beanie and bonnet. (Courtesy Ventura County Museum and History and Art.)

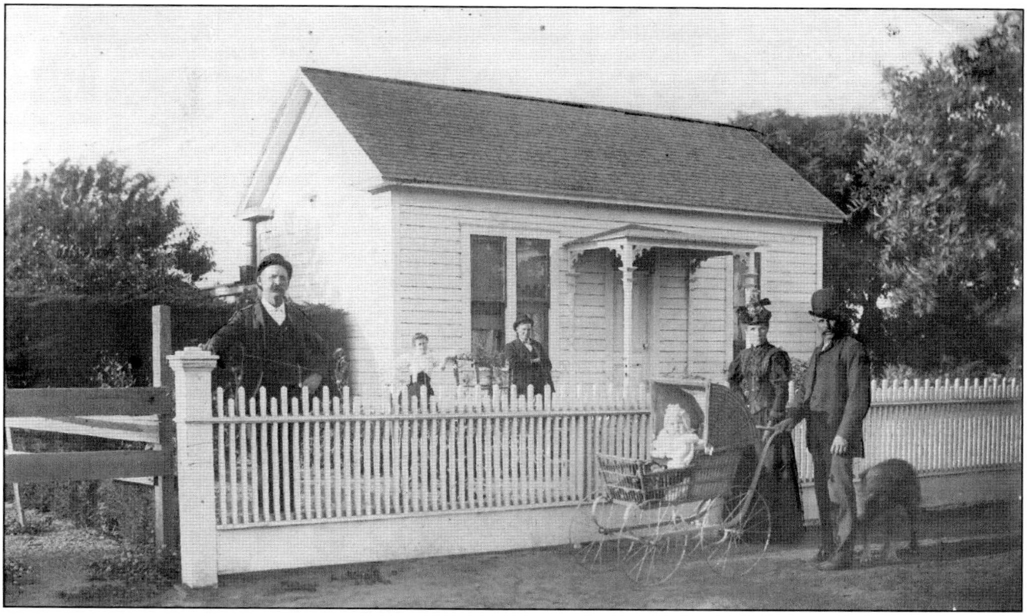

The Woodruff home (above) and the Pitt home (below) are pictured in the late 1800s. From the porch, the Woodruffs enjoyed the company of their neighbors as they passed by. (Courtesy Port Hueneme Historical Society.)

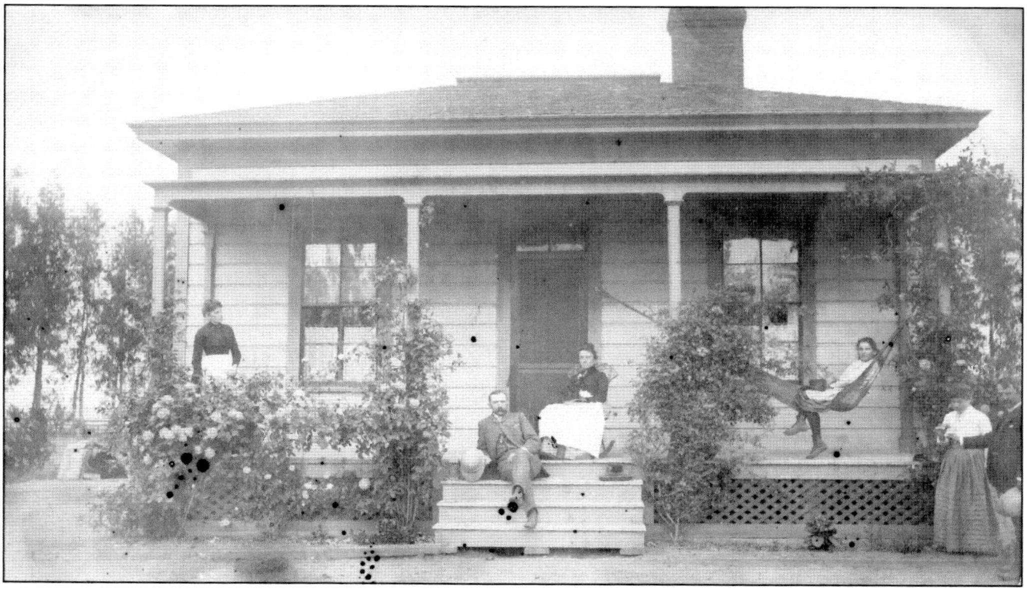

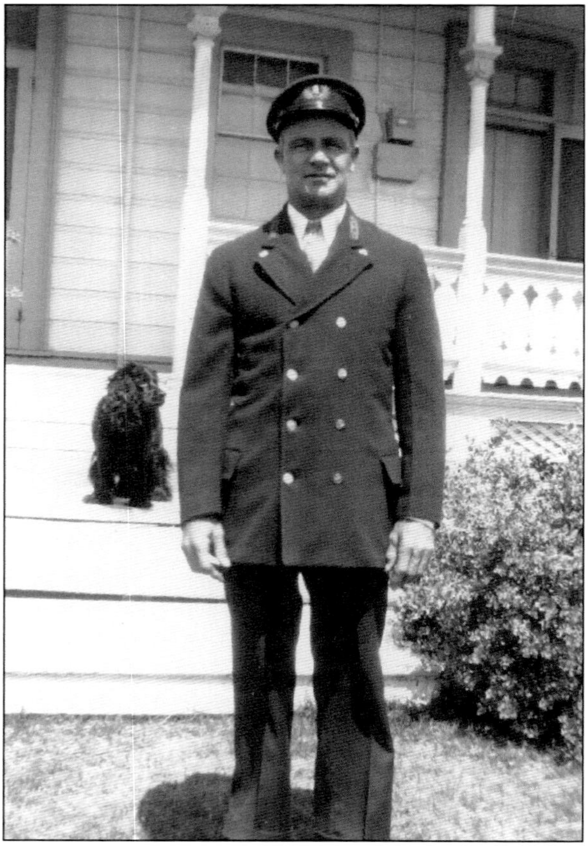

Walter White (left) stands in front of the lighthouse while the family's loyal cocker spaniel sits on the stairs, waiting for the kids to return home from school. Walter White's service at Point Hueneme Lighthouse began in 1927. In his 21 years of service as lighthouse keeper, White used kerosene and a wick to light the Fresnel lens, witnessed the advent of electricity in the house in 1925 and to the lens in 1934, and served in the current structure. He is the longest serving lighthouse keeper at Point Hueneme, with a total of 21 years. White and Lew Oppel (below right), who served as assistant keeper from 1933 to 1935, are seen chopping down the best-looking Christmas tree they could find. (Both courtesy Laverne White-Dornberger.)

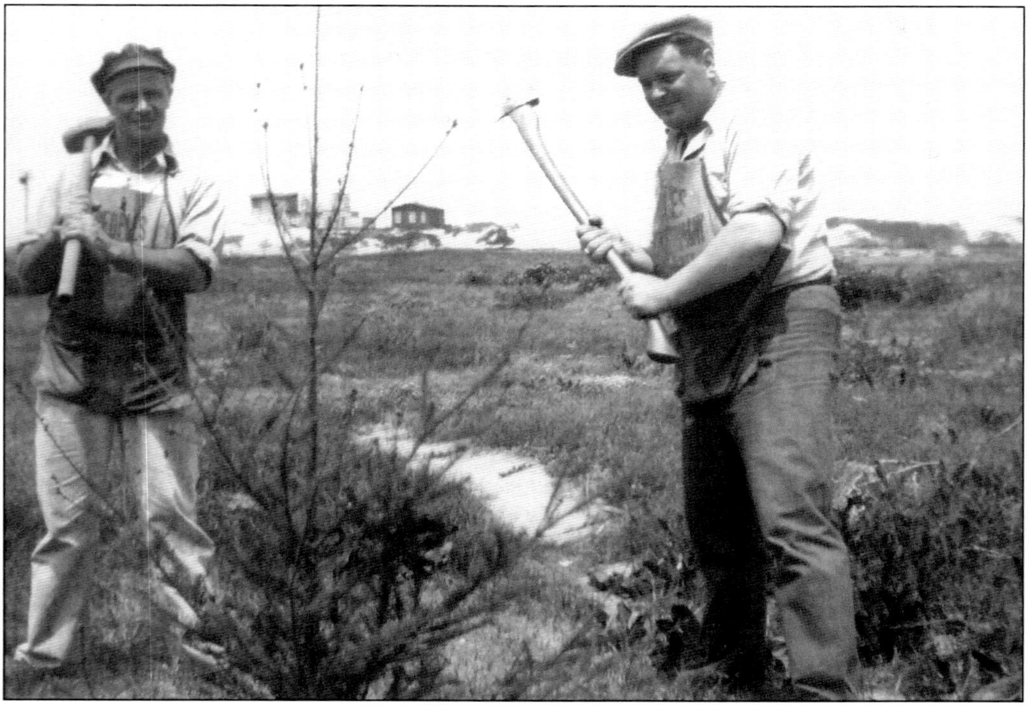

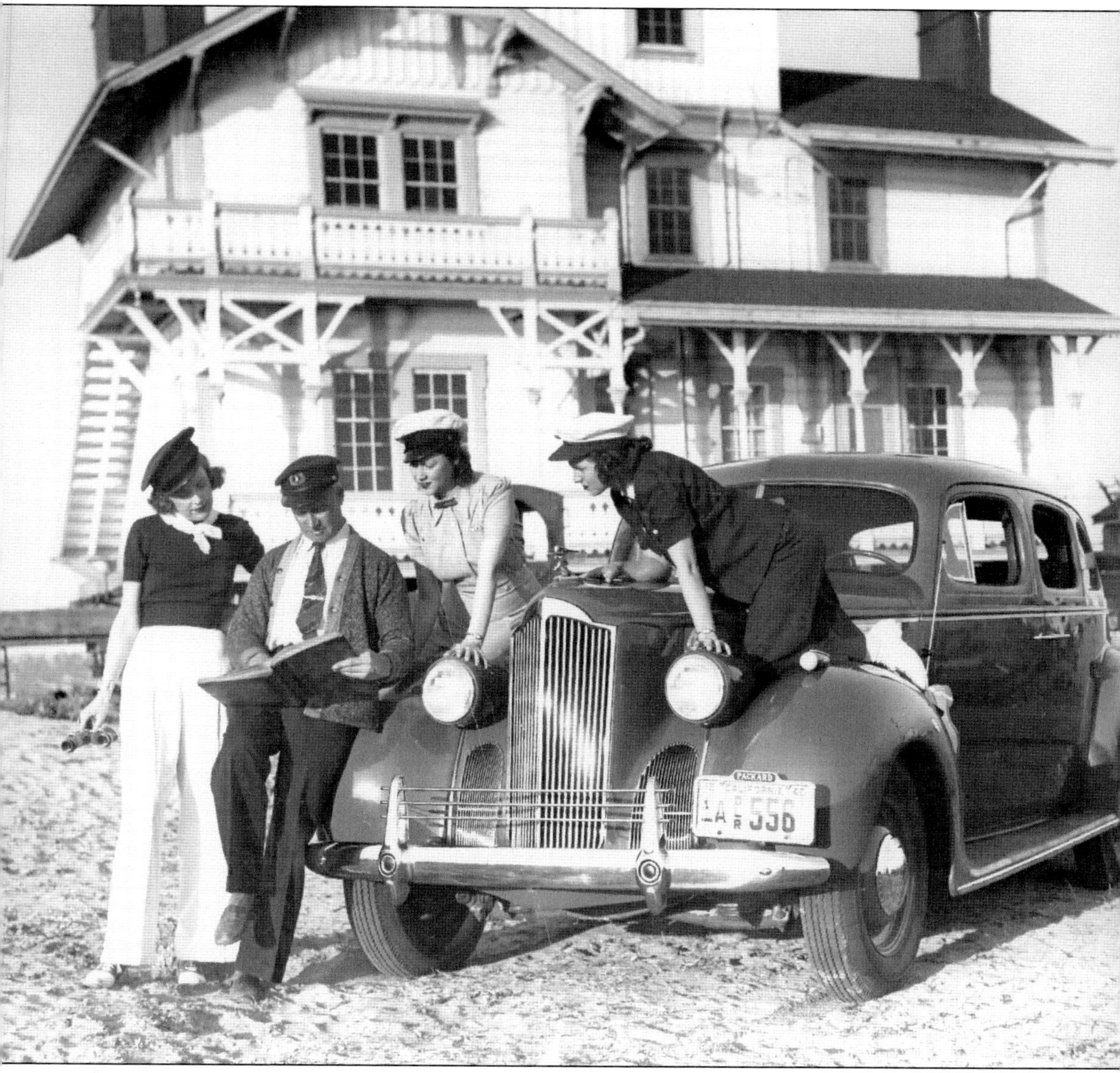

Huddled around lighthouse keeper Walter White are Lorraine Liddle on the left and Lavonne Sinkie and Jerry Chapman on the right. Walter, pictured here in the late 1930s, is reading from the logbook and recanting the history of the lighthouse. (Courtesy Laverne White-Dornberger.)

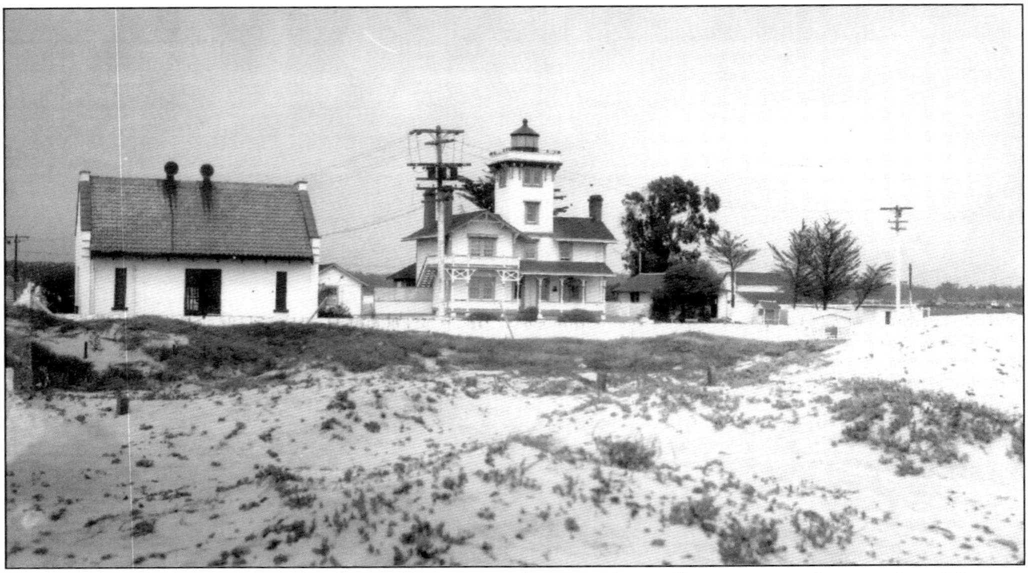

When the light was obscured due to heavy sea fog, which is often more widespread and longer lasting than land fog, an audible warning or fog signal is used to warn mariners of the approaching rocks and shoals. The foggiest months are July through October, and the foghorn is on almost constantly. Shown on the left is the fog signal building around the 1930s. The diaphone gave a 4-second blast every 41 seconds. If the diaphone was disabled, a siren was used in the interim until the diaphone was put back into operation. (Courtesy Wayne Wheeler, Lighthouse Society.)

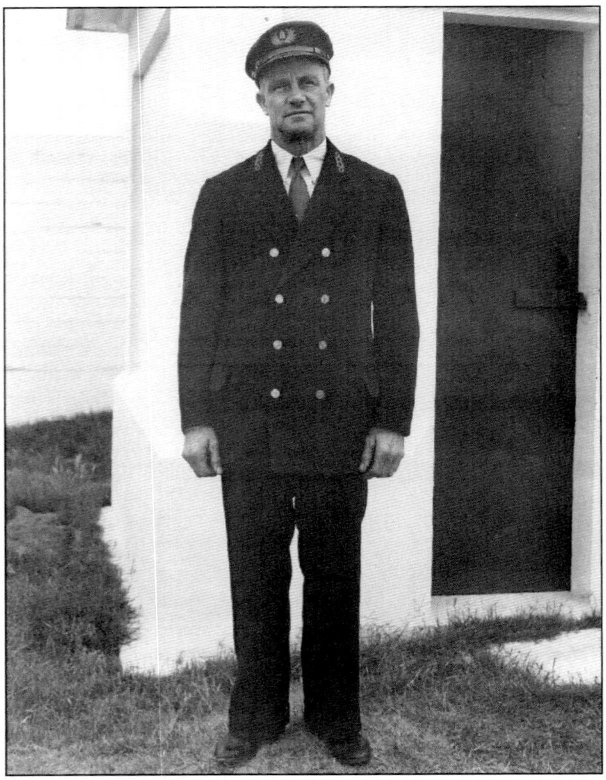

Keeper Walter White stands outside the fog signal building. Since the fog signal was in a separate building from the lighthouse, there were many times when the assistant had to tend to the operation of the fog signal with the keeper minding the lighthouse. (Courtesy Laverne White-Dornberger.)

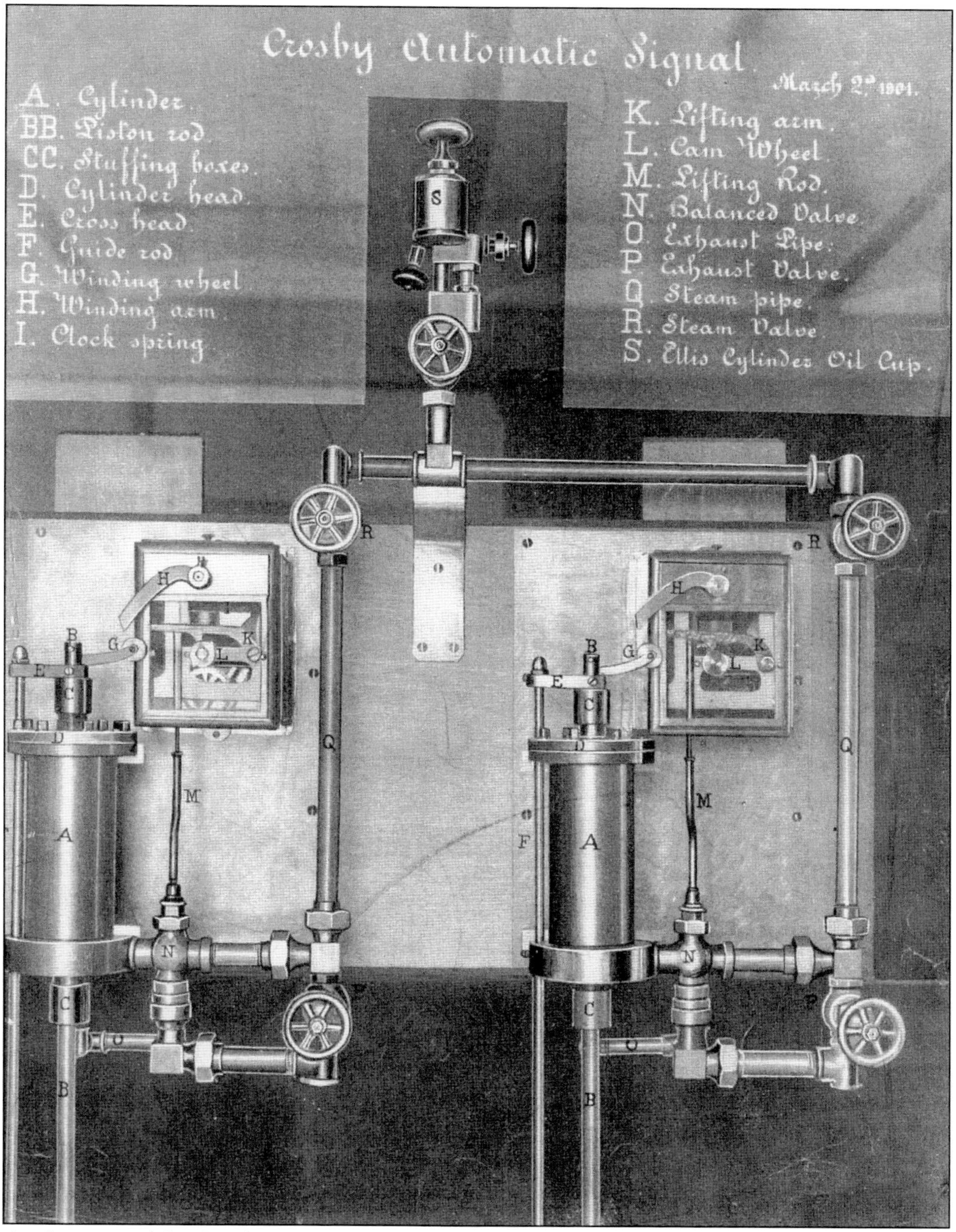

A schematic of the Crosby Automatic Signal from March 2, 1901, was on hand in the fog signal building for operating the fog signal. (Courtesy Laverne White-Dornberger.)

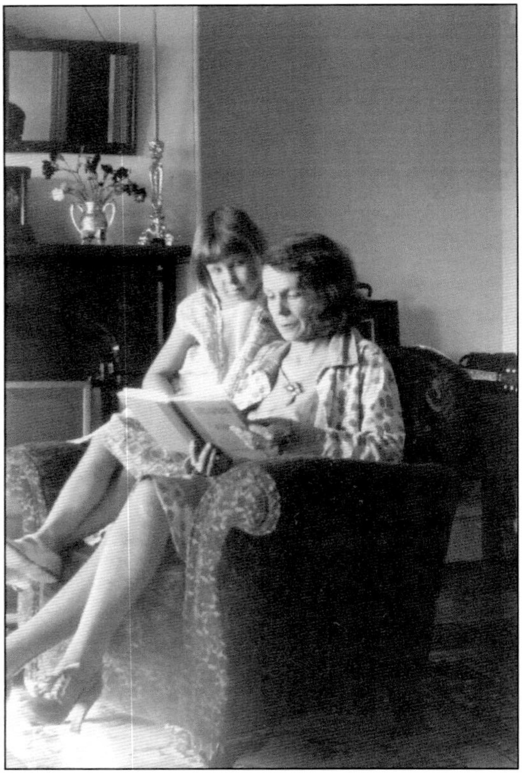

At left, Francis White, wife of keeper Walter White, and daughter Laverne, are shown in the first floor of the lighthouse, reading together in a cozy chair in the living room. Below, Laverne, an avid reader, is enjoying reading on her own. (Both courtesy Laverne White-Dornberger.)

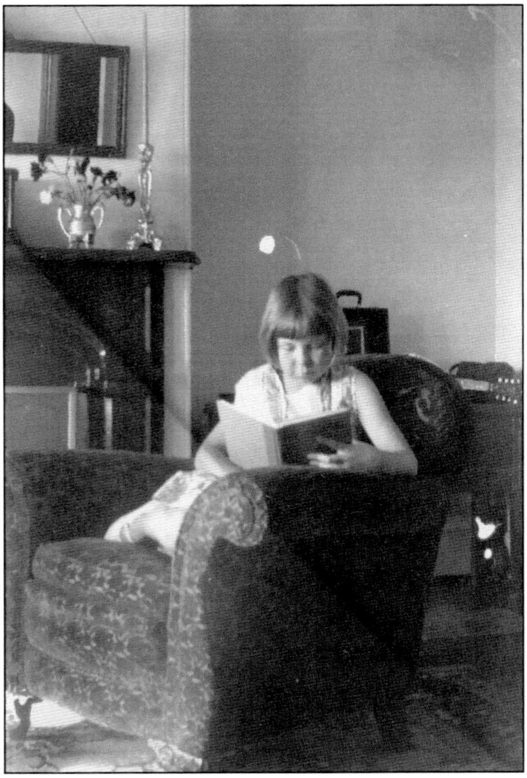

Walter White, pictured at right in the 1930s, holds the flagpole rope that he would raise and lower regularly. Today, the flagpole is on display inside the current Point Hueneme Lighthouse. Beatrice White (below), eldest daughter of Walter and Frankie White, is posed on the lawn of the lighthouse grounds. The garden in the background was due to the green thumb of Walter White, who enjoyed gardening and planting evergreens, roses, shrubs, herbs, and a vegetable garden. He also painstakingly whitewashed rocks to highlight the various areas of the lighthouse grounds, and also painted the perimeter fences that extend to the town of Hueneme and out to the ocean. The whitewash was made on the premises in a lime box, located near the coal house. (Courtesy Laverne White-Dornberger.)

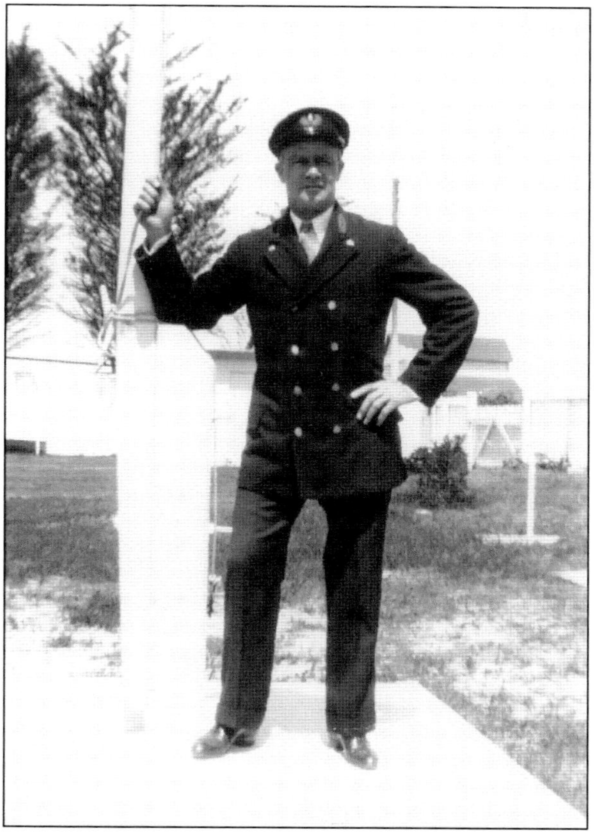

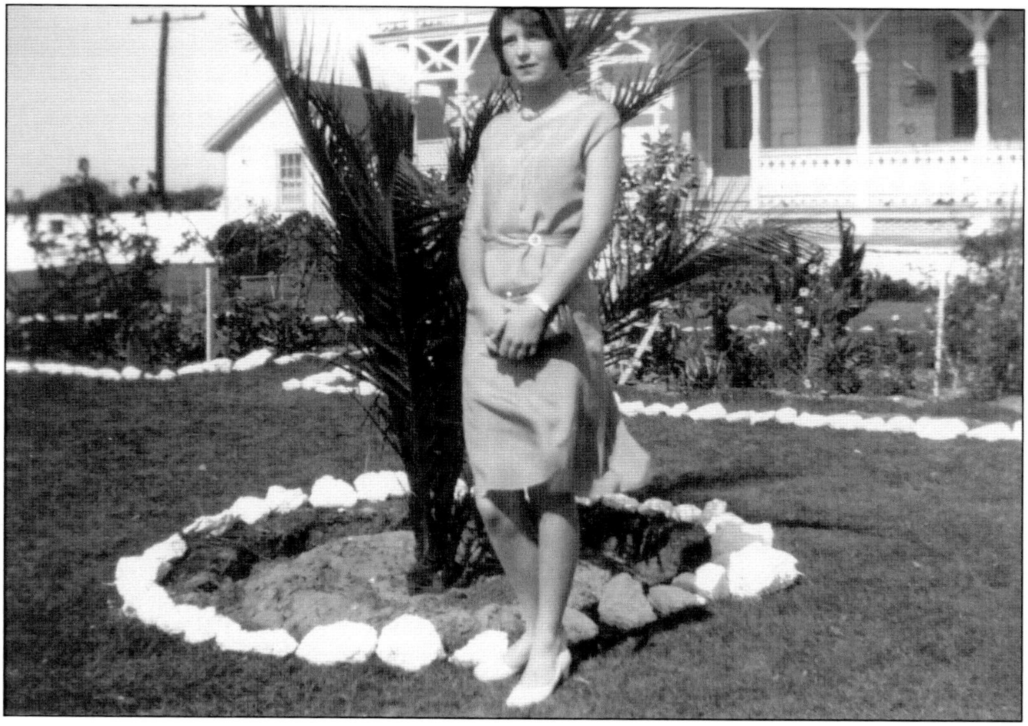

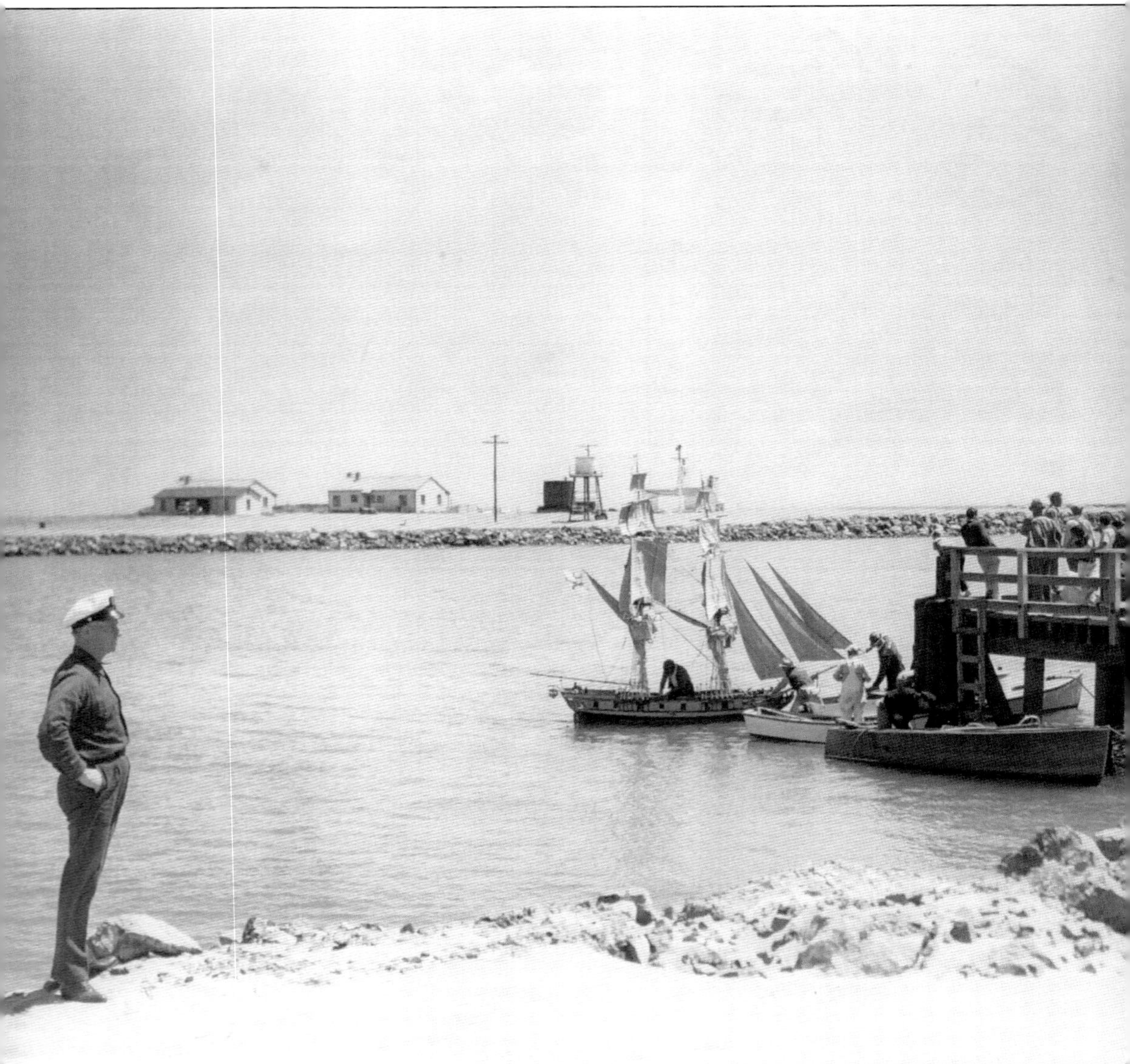

Walter White, wearing his lighthouse keeper hat around 1939, is watching the filming of the motion picture *Captain Caution*, starring Victor Mature and Louise Platt. Model ships, as seen here, were used to create the setting of the War of 1812 during filming. The temporary light pole in the background (middle of the photograph) was put in place for preparations of the proposed harbor and would be used until the new lighthouse was constructed and put into operation. (Courtesy Laverne White-Dornberger.)

Three

ANACAPA
THE LIGHT ACROSS THE WAY

The Channel Islands rose from the ocean millions of years ago, born of plate tectonics, volcanic activity, and fluctuating sea levels. The islands lie in a region between the mainland coast and the deep ocean beyond the continental shelf. They have been referred to as the Galapagos of the United States and the rain forest of the sea. It is their unique water currents, winds, and weather that have created an ecosystem that supports a rich diversity of life comprising over 2,000 species (145 of them can be found nowhere else on earth).

On December 2, 1853, the side-wheel steamer *Winfield Scott* collided with the middle islet (one of three) of Anacapa Island. Due to the notoriety of the wreck, Pres. Franklin Pierce signed an executive order the following year that preserved Anacapa solely for lighthouse purposes.

Anacapa—or as the Chumash called it, "Anyapakh," meaning ever changing or mirage—seemed to rise out of nowhere, leaving little warning for mariners. As a quick solution, the Lighthouse Board placed an unmanned acetylene lens lantern on a 50-foot skeletal tower, which only required servicing twice a year, and a whistling buoy anchored five-eighths of a mile off the east end of the island. On February 28, 1921, the steamship *Liebre* ran aground directly under the light.

In 1932, the current permanent light station was built. It is a 39-foot tower and fog signal on the highest point of the island. It is a traditional cylindrical-style lighthouse. In 1938, under the direction of Franklin D. Roosevelt, Santa Barbara and Anacapa Islands became Channel Island National Monument.

There are eight Channel Islands off the coast of Southern California spanning 160 miles. The four northern islands are San Miguel, Santa Rosa, Santa Cruz, and Anacapa. The four southern islands are San Nicholas, Santa Barbara, Santa Catalina, and San Clemente. The National Park Service owns and operates all of the northern islands and Santa Barbara on the southern side. To this day, the park service continues to preserve and protect the islands.

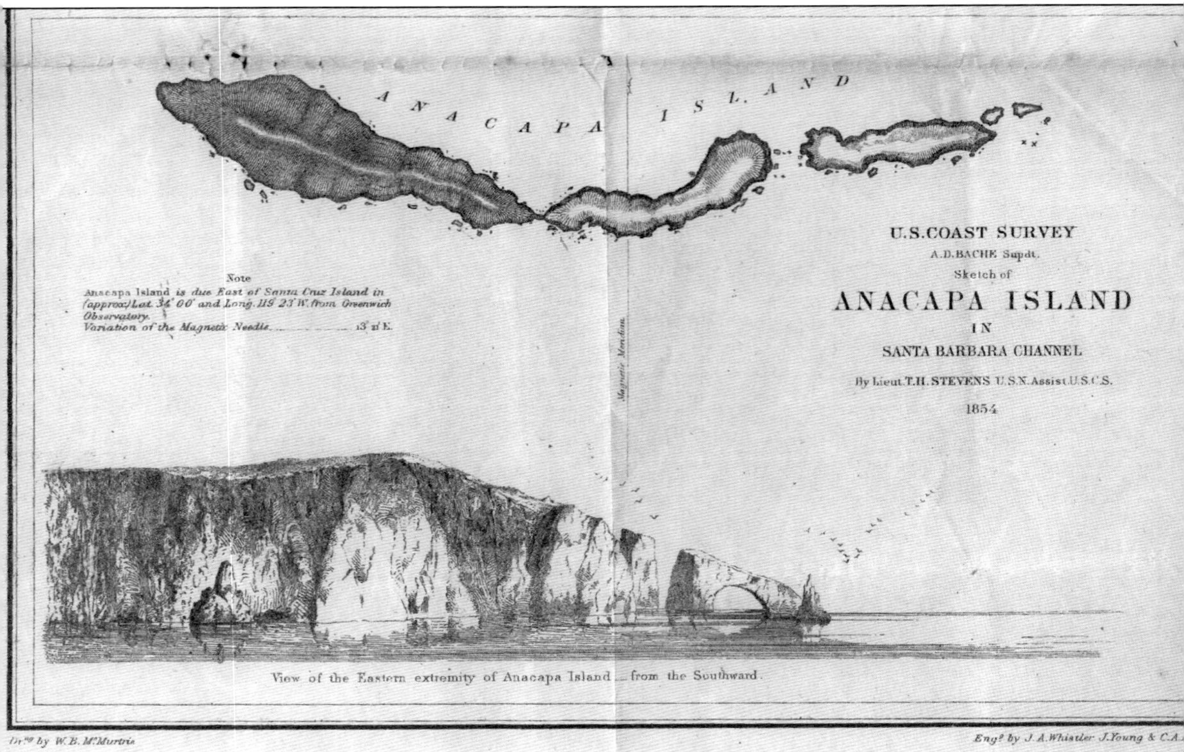

This engraved map of Anacapa Island was made by artist James Whistler, of *Whistler's Mother* fame, in 1854. A later revised version of the map had the seagulls removed because the U.S. Coast Survey did not approve of them. Whistler was fired from the U.S. Coast Survey after only one month. It was, however, this vision of Anacapa that would begin his professional career. (Courtesy University of California, Santa Barbara, Library, Special Collections Department.)

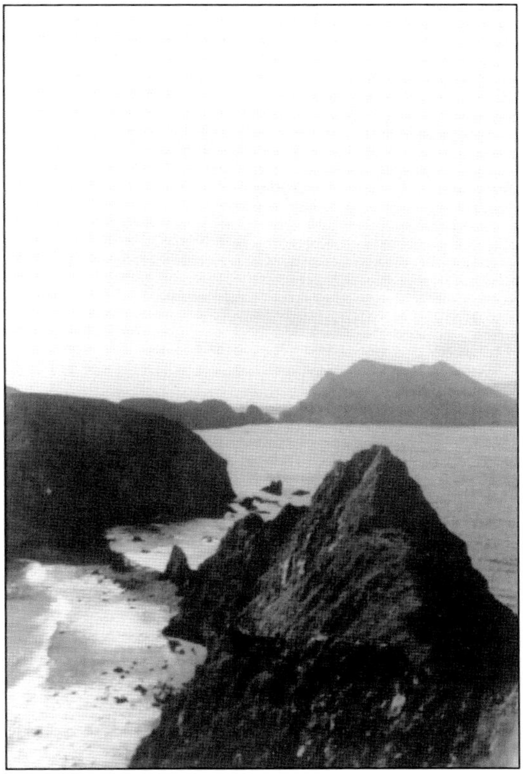

A 5-mile-long spine of rock emerges from the ocean and breaks into three islets known as Anacapa Island. The island is located on the southern side of the eastern end of the Channel Islands, forming the southern boundary to the Santa Barbara Channel approximately 12 miles from the mainland. Both Anacapa and San Nicolas Islands are located in Ventura County. On charts, the 737-acre island appears as East, Middle, and West Anacapa. The islands of San Miguel, Santa Rosa, Santa Cruz, and Anacapa were once joined as a single island called Santarosae. When the sea levels increased again, it created the four islands seen today. (Both courtesy Port Hueneme Historical Society.)

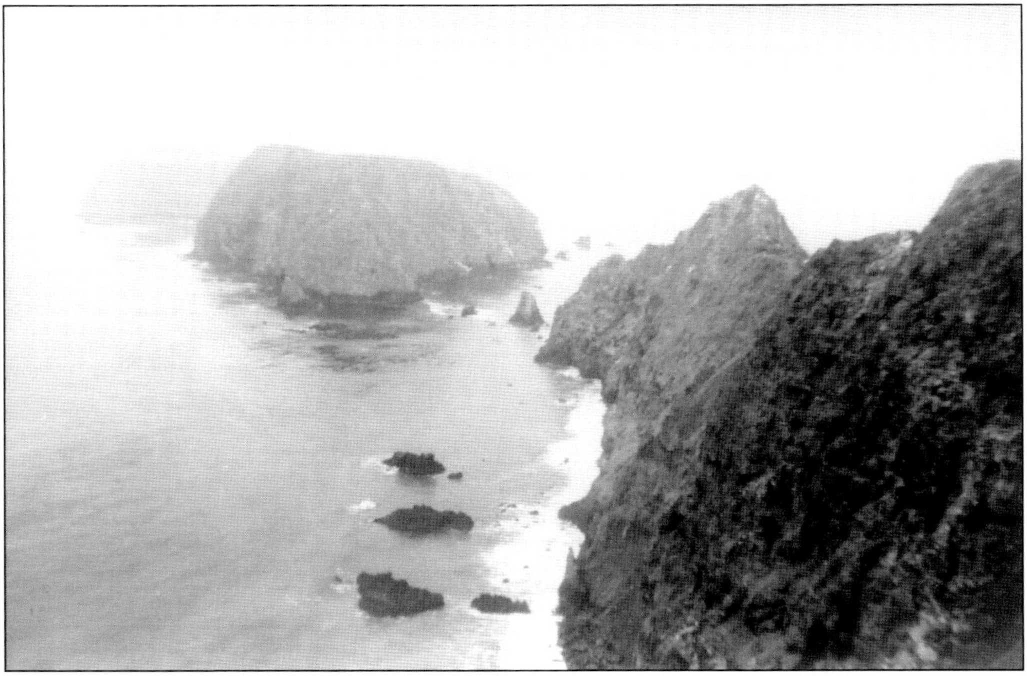

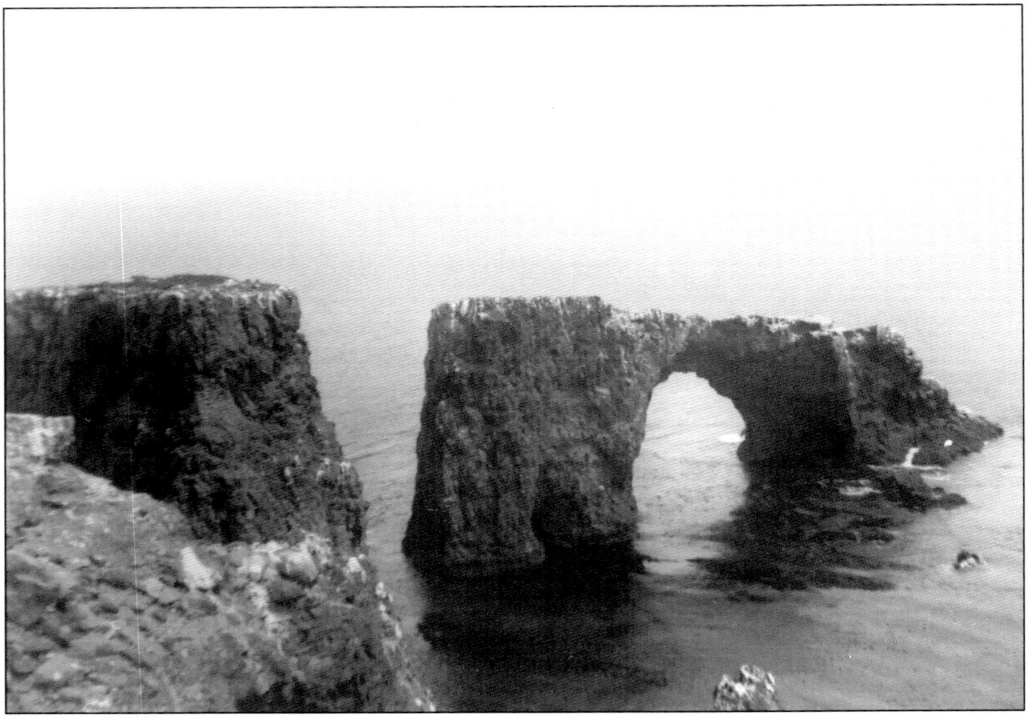

Arch Rock is a natural feature carved by the wind and the sea, rising 40 feet above the surface of the water. Visible from quite a distance away, it has become one of the most recognizable features of Anacapa Island, along with the lighthouse. Unfortunately, as the rock succumbs to the bombardment of the elements, at some point it will no longer be visible. (Both courtesy Port Hueneme Historical Society.)

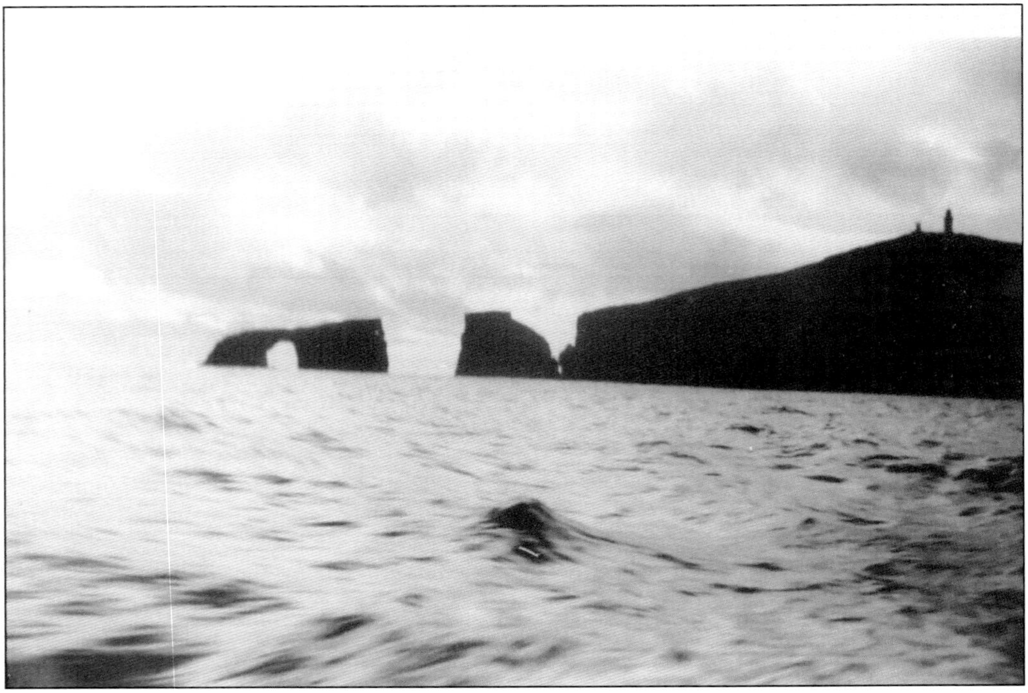

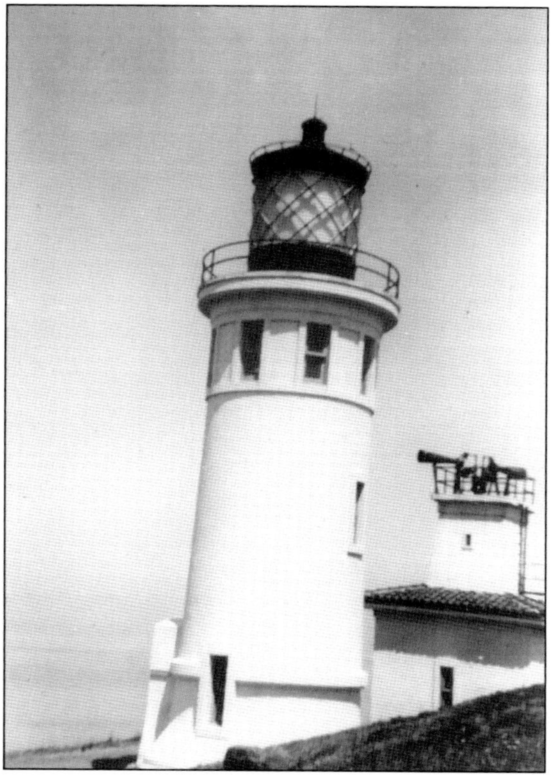

Marking the entrance to the Santa Barbara Channel, Anacapa Lighthouse is located on East Anacapa and was constructed in 1932. It is a cylindrical-shaped lighthouse constructed of brick and reinforced concrete. The stark white and black-trim paint emphasizes the Spanish Revival–style architecture highlighted in the iron cross-pattern work of the windows. Next to the lighthouse is the foghorn (diaphragm-type), which sounds a one- to two-second blast followed by two seconds of silence, then it sounds again for two seconds and completes the cycle with 14 seconds of silence. (Courtesy Port Hueneme Historical Society.)

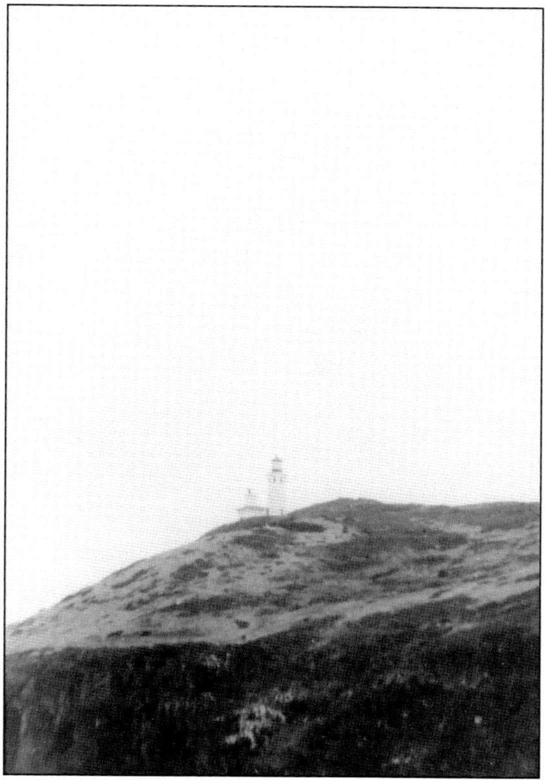

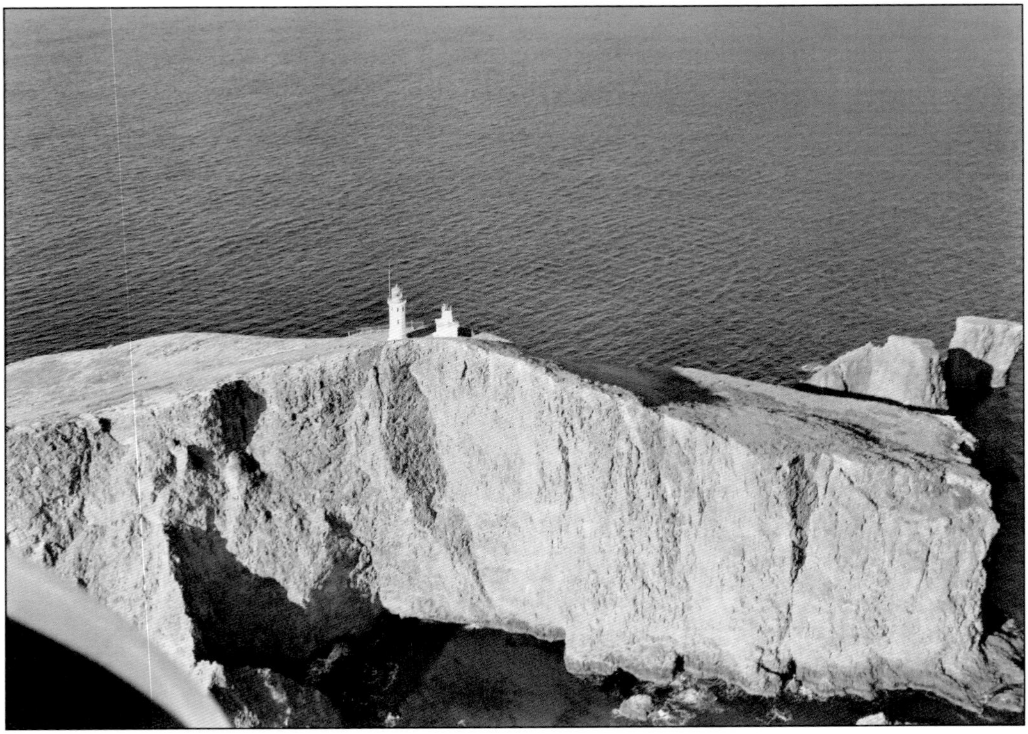

As seen in these aerial views from the 1940s, the lighthouse seems both barren and isolated. But because of its proximity to the mainland, those stationed on the island were only a 12-mile boat ride from replenishing supplies or going on liberty. (Both courtesy U.S. Coast Guard.)

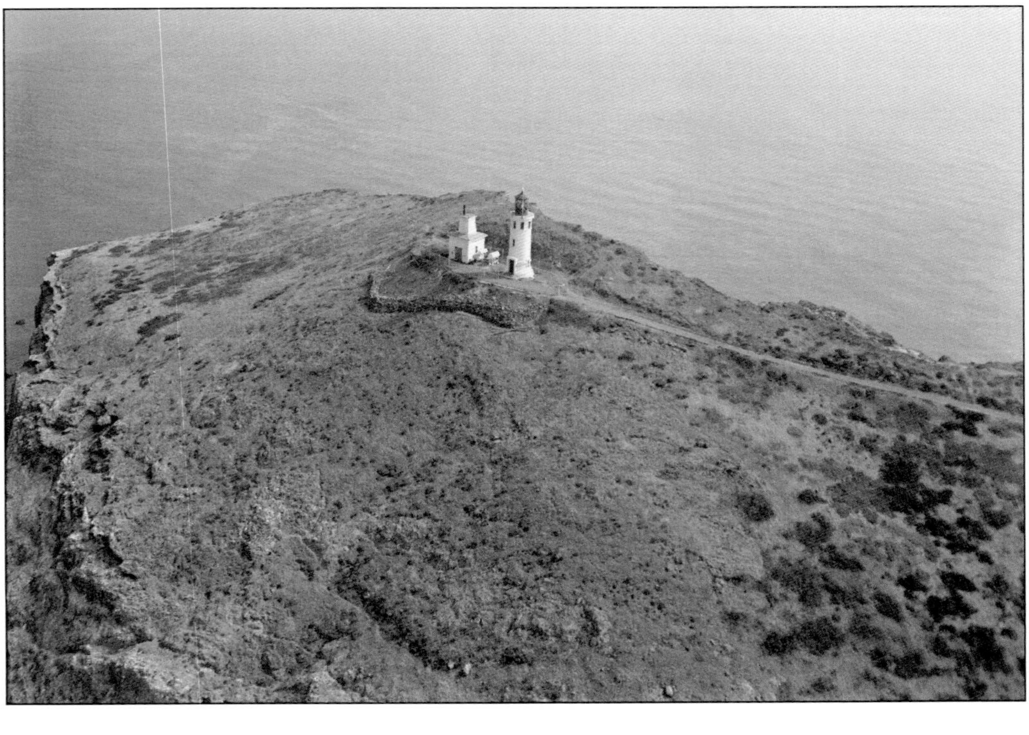

Construction of the Anacapa station began in the spring of 1930 and was carried out in two phases. Before construction could begin on the light, supplies and construction materials needed to be delivered; therefore, a landing dock and hoisting crane needed to be constructed. The hoisting crane, pictured here around 1950, continues to be the optimal way of delivering supplies to the island. (Courtesy U.S. Coast Guard.)

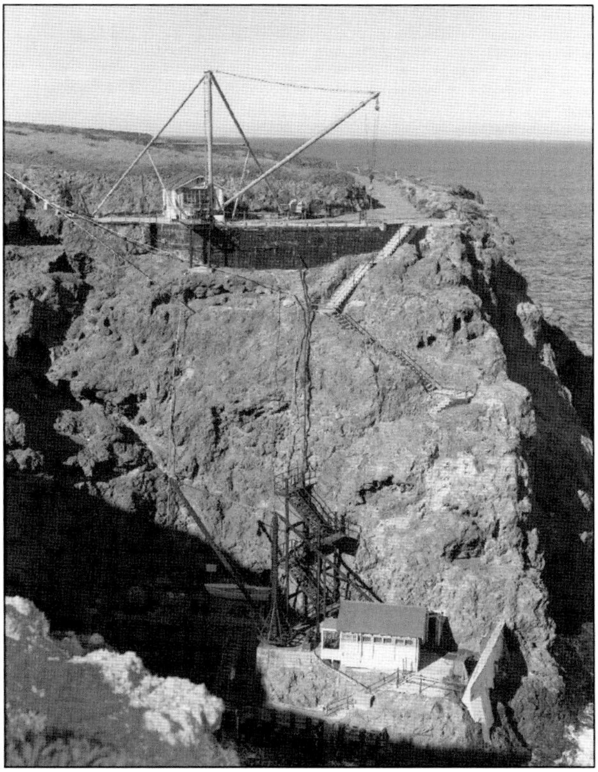

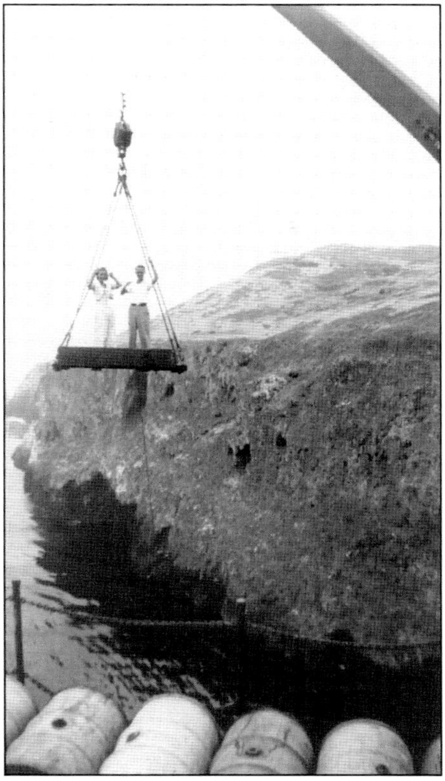

Taking in a beautiful day, Margaret Kellogg, daughter of keeper Leo Kellogg, and her future husband are being lifted past the 200-foot-high cliffs onto the island. The crane did have its risks. In the 1930s, a keeper plummeted to his death after falling off the platform. In 1934, a keeper's wife was seriously injured in a fall. (Courtesy Margaret Kellogg-Anderson.)

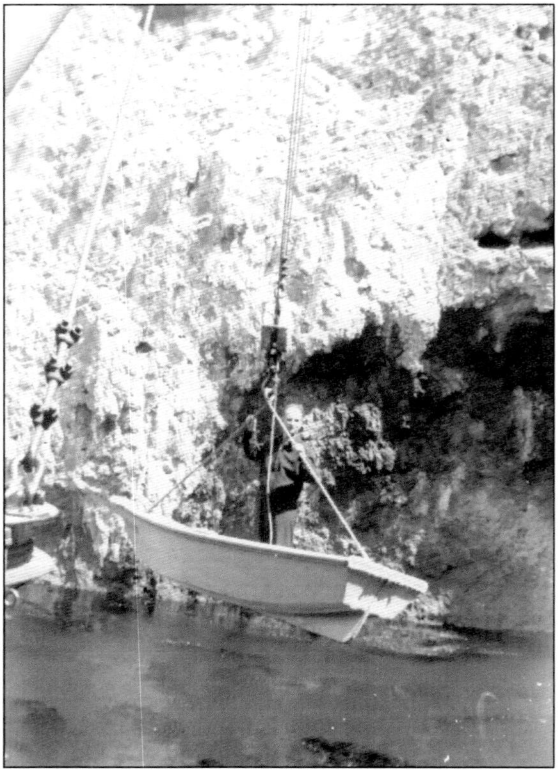

A dory, or small boat (left), is being hoisted out of the water and will be placed on a cradle. Supplies (below) are carefully packed and are being delivered to the top of the island. From there a truck will deliver the goods to the four homes. A routine trip to the grocery store was a daylong affair and, depending on the weather, could take even longer. (Both courtesy Margaret Kellogg-Anderson.)

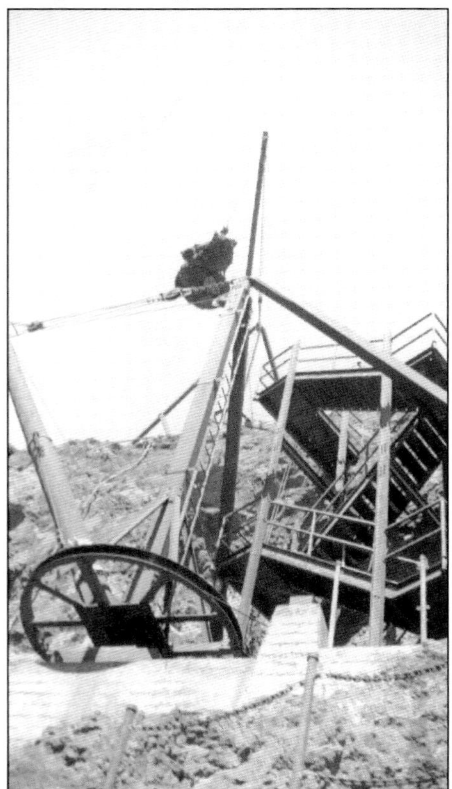

Joe May looks out over the horizon for approaching vessels. He served as keeper of Anacapa in the 1930s and was then transferred to Point Vicente Lighthouse in Palos Verdes, California, where this photograph was taken. (Courtesy Margaret Kellogg-Anderson.)

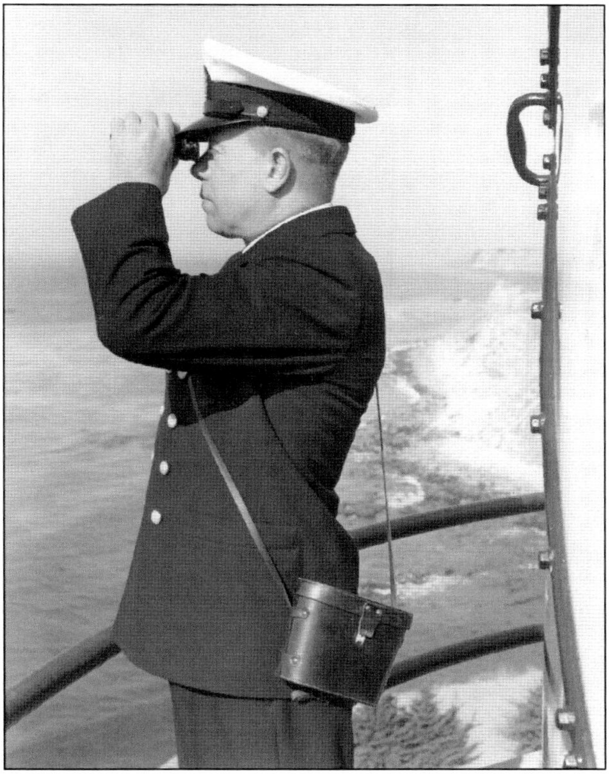

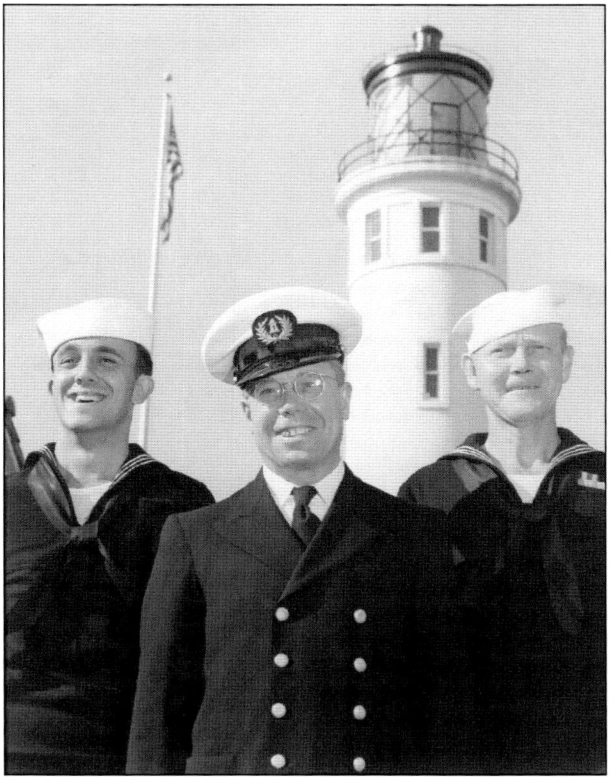

Joe May is standing in front of Point Vicente Lighthouse with two Coast Guard personnel at his side. To the left of May is George Livesey, and an unidentified serviceman is on the right. Anacapa light is a similar version of Point Vicente Lighthouse, and in photographs it is hard to tell them apart. The main difference is that Anacapa stands 40 feet tall compared to Point Vicente's 67 feet. (Courtesy Margaret Kellogg-Anderson.)

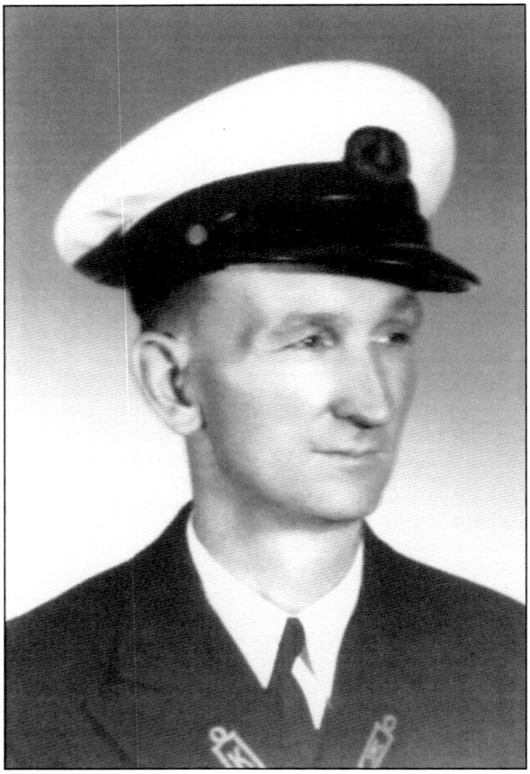

Assistant keeper Leo Kellogg wears his keeper's uniform. Kellogg began as assistant keeper at Anacapa in the mid-1930s. He was there until World War II, at which time he was transferred to Point Arguello, and then on to Point Hueneme as keeper. As the civilian officer in charge, he served as Point Hueneme's keeper from 1948 to 1952. (Courtesy Margaret Kellogg-Anderson.)

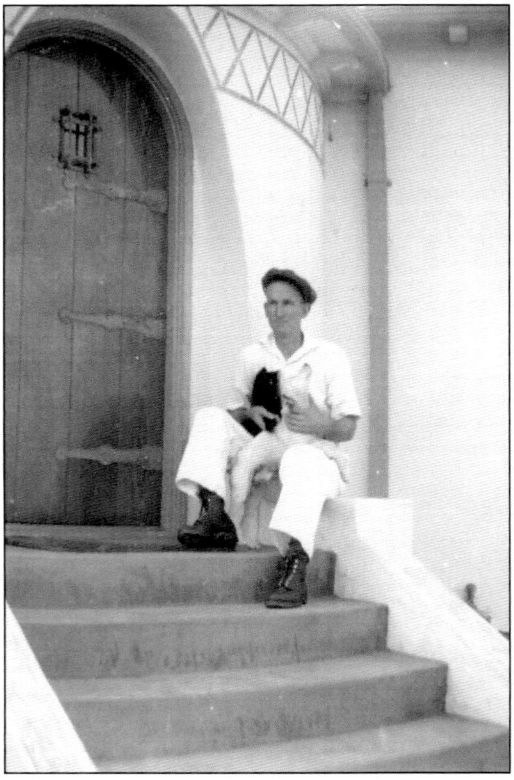

Leo Kellogg rests on the steps while holding Skippy the dog and a cat. Skippy was abandoned on the island by another family but quickly won over Leo Kellogg, and as daughter Margaret remembers, Skippy adopted them. (Courtesy Margaret Kellogg-Anderson.)

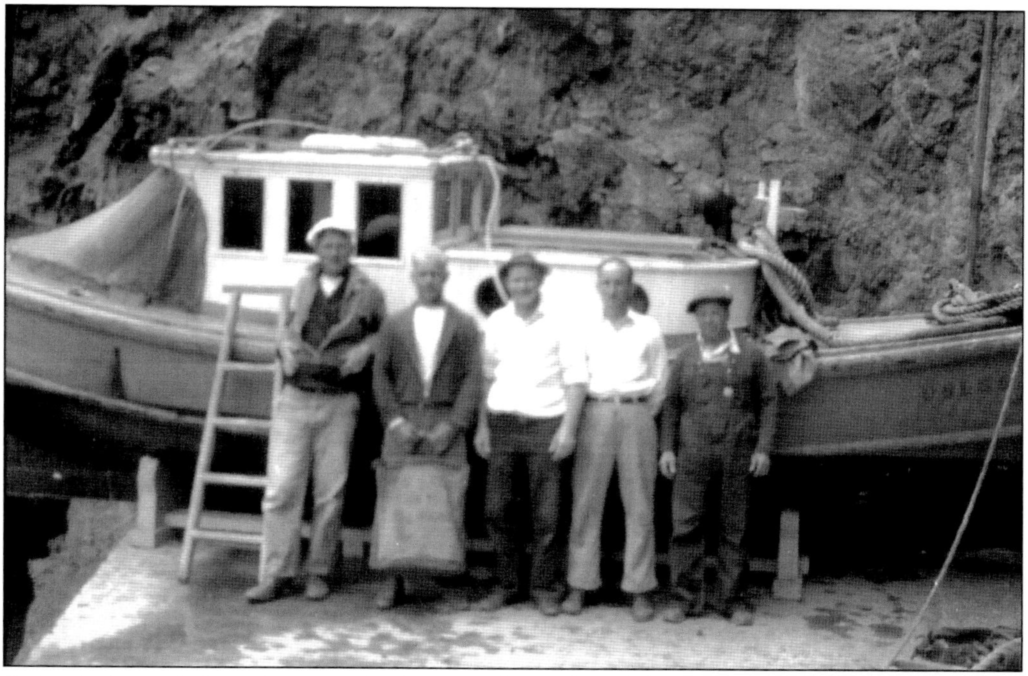

Posing in front of a boat that is resting in its cradle are, from left to right, Howard Fawcett, Livesoy's son, George Livesoy, Leo Kellogg, and Joe May. (Courtesy Margaret Kellogg-Anderson.)

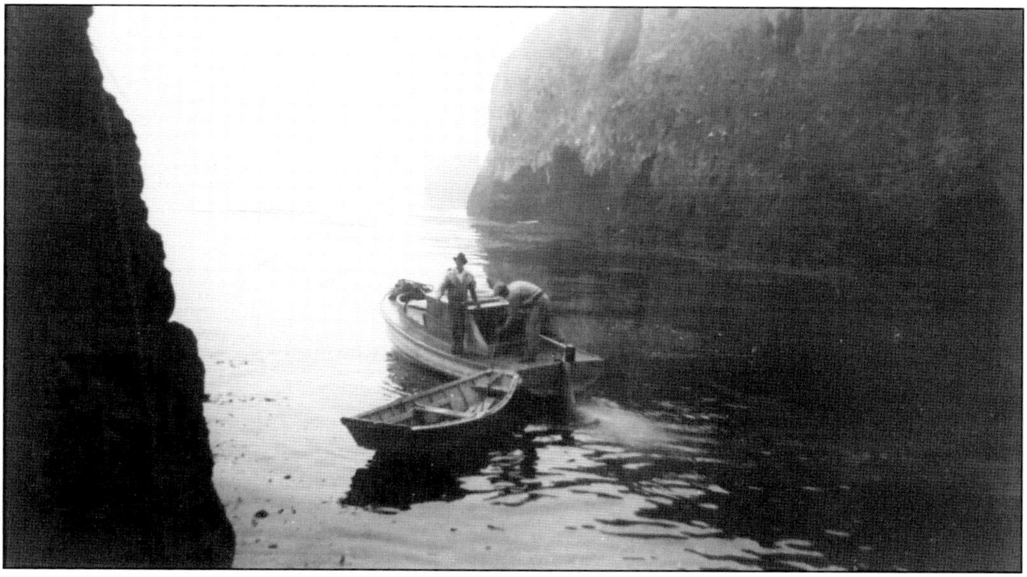

The only landing for a boat is a small cove, which is completely surrounded by 100-foot vertical cliffs, as seen here. A vessel must approach an improvised landing platform that has been cut out of the cliff face in order to discharge its load of goods. It is imperative to be constantly vigilant of the conditions of the sea to avoid the risk of slamming into the rocks. (Courtesy Margaret Kellogg-Anderson.)

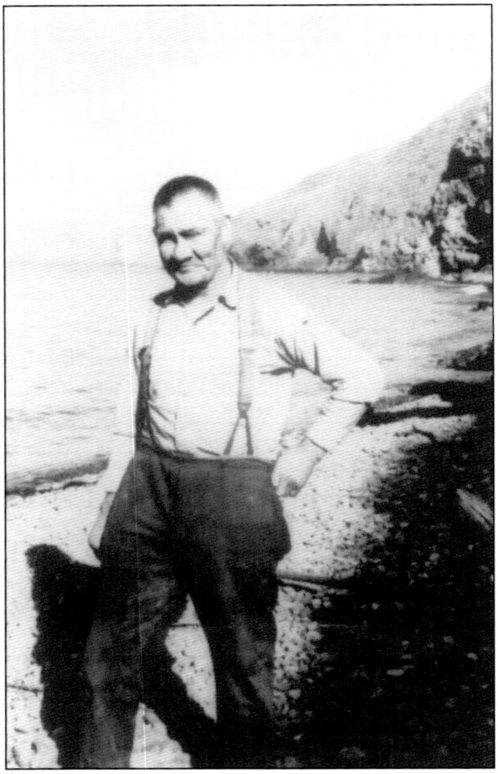

Charles "Charlie" Johnson is a famous hermit of Anacapa Island, second only to Raymond "Frenchy" LaDreau, who lived on the island for 28 years. Charlie was known as the unofficial mayor of the island and would help govern the lighthouse and the staff. He arrived in 1931 and passed away on the island about eight years later. Prior to his self-imposed exile, he was an avid fisherman, served as a steamship skipper on the Great Lakes, and was a veteran of the Spanish-American War. As the mayor, he always made it a point to greet any fishing parties and would row his skiff alongside them, spin a few yarns, and barter for a few bottles of beer. The Samoyed dog (below) belonged to seaman Ralph Lewis and ran free on the island. (Left, courtesy Margaret Kellogg-Anderson; below, courtesy U.S. Coast Guard.)

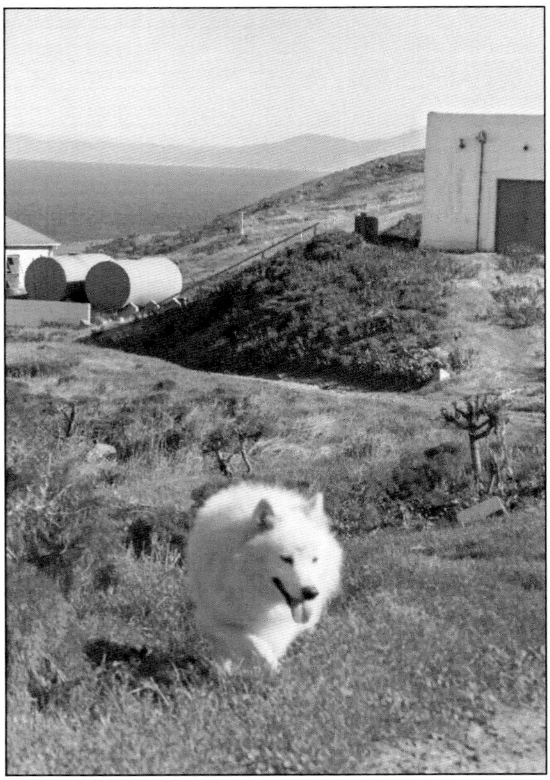

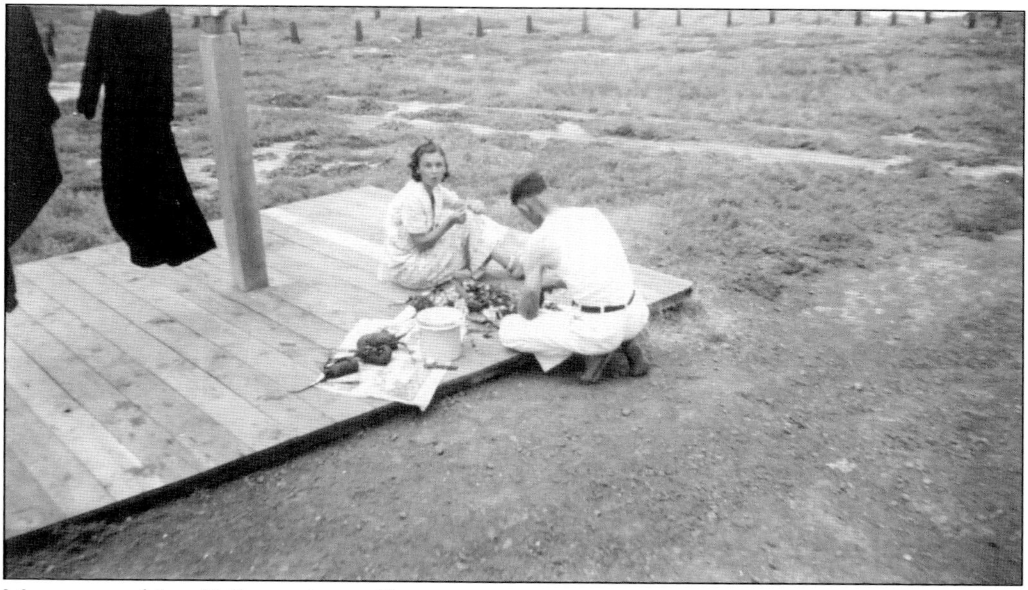

Margaret and Leo Kellogg, pictured here in the 1930s, are cleaning lobsters. The lobsters were a gift given to them by Charlie Johnson, a hermit of the island. The families benefited from Charlie's presence, as he was an avid fisherman and would also routinely set and catch abalone. The keepers would also share their catch, usually of sheepshead, a large whitefish that was plentiful in the area. (Courtesy Margaret Kellogg-Anderson.)

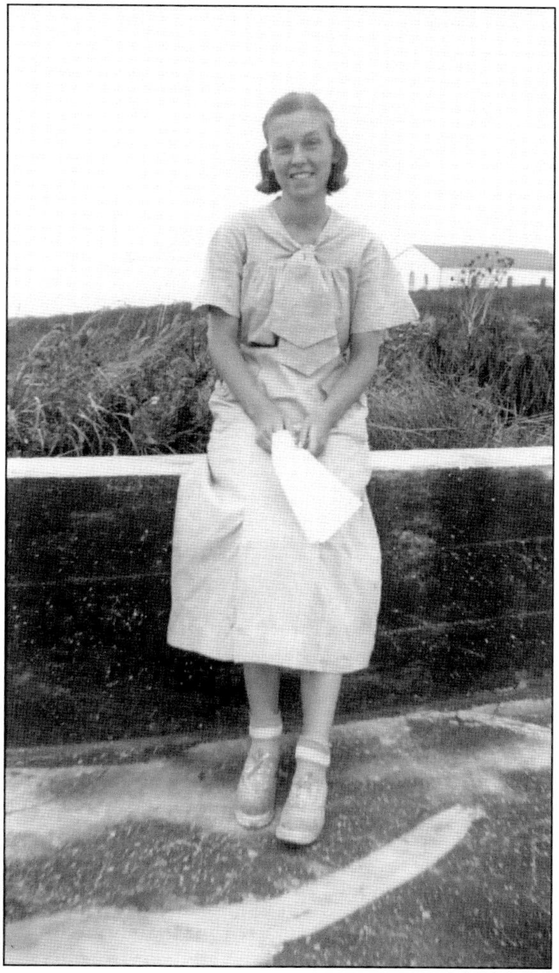

Margaret Kellogg poses inside the watershed. This is where the water was caught and put into tanks. The tanks were scrubbed and readied for the winter rain. If they were low on rainwater, a tender was sent from San Pedro with a supply of water. (Courtesy Margaret Kellogg-Anderson.)

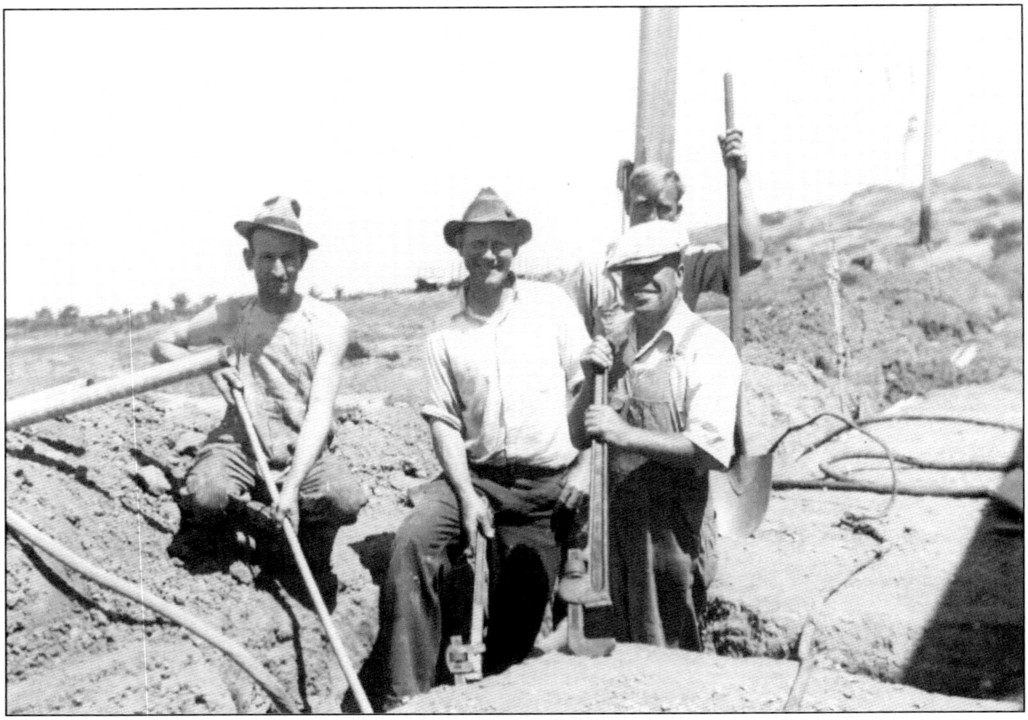

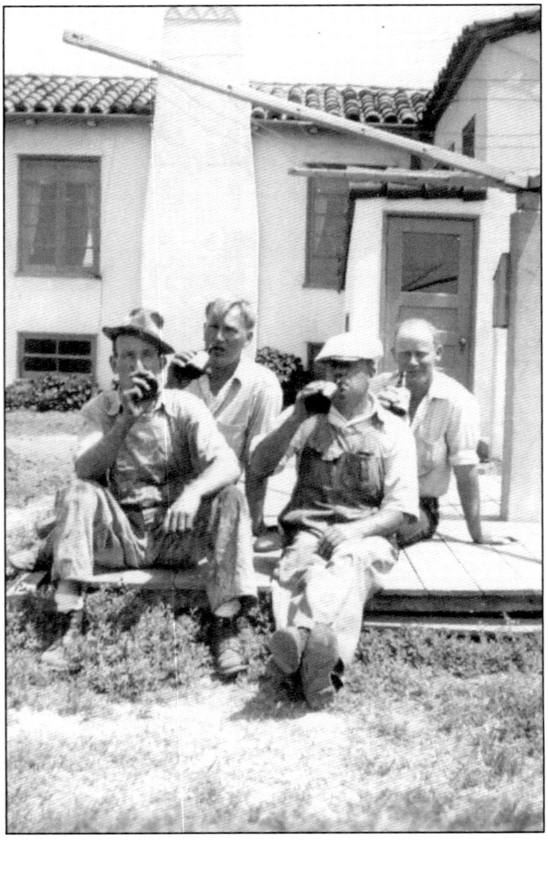

From left to right are Leo Kellogg, Howard Fawcett, George Livesoy, and Joe May. They are hard at work digging a trench. In addition to minding the light and fog signal, the men had plenty of chores on the island to keep them very busy. They also made time for rest and relaxation. The picture at left shows the men sitting outside together following their long day and enjoying a cold beverage. (Both courtesy Margaret Kellogg-Anderson.)

Due to the ocean spray of salt water, erosion and rust are constant threats to the building and lighthouse. As seen here, a serviceman is washing and hosing down the buildings, which was a regular necessity. (Courtesy Port Hueneme Historical Society.)

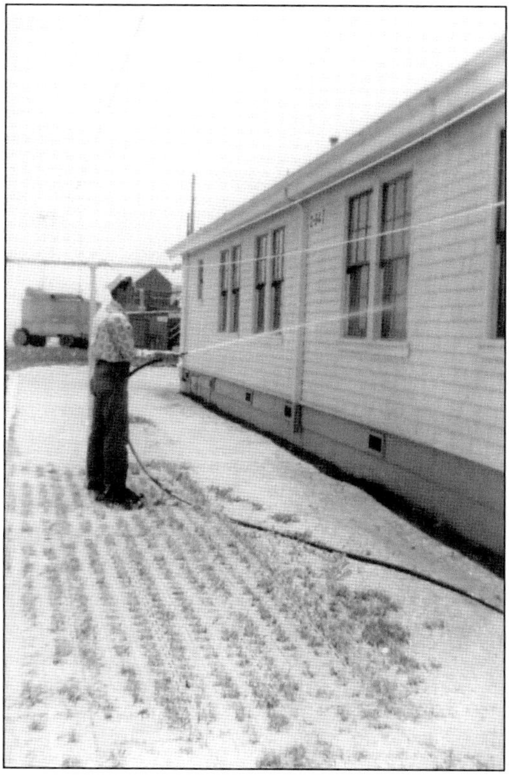

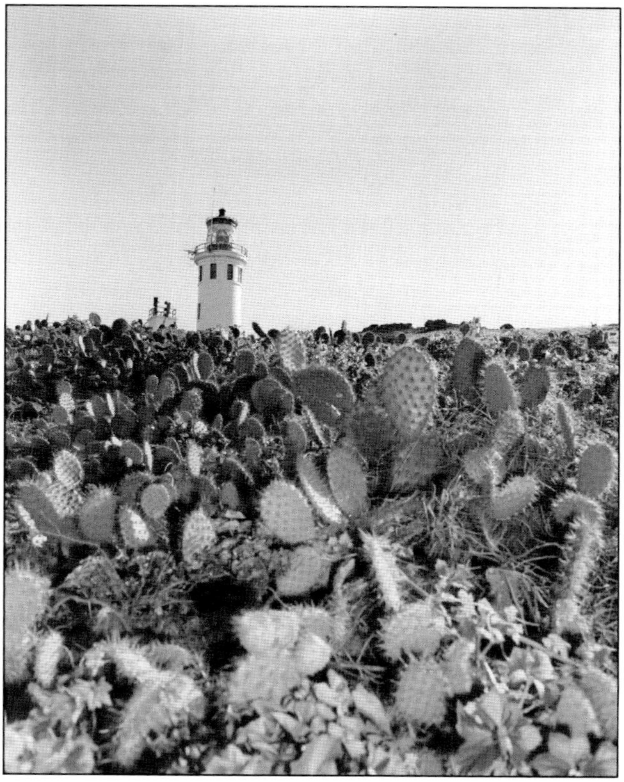

Cacti, pictured here in the 1950s, were once abundant on Anacapa. It is a nonnative plant of the island and can no longer be found here. Introducing nonnative plants and animals to the island has always been a problem. A pair of rabbits left behind or brought to the island as food created a large rabbit population, and they ate up many of the plants. Later the black rat arrived on the island via a ship, causing problems for many of the seabirds and their eggs. (Courtesy U.S. Coast Guard.)

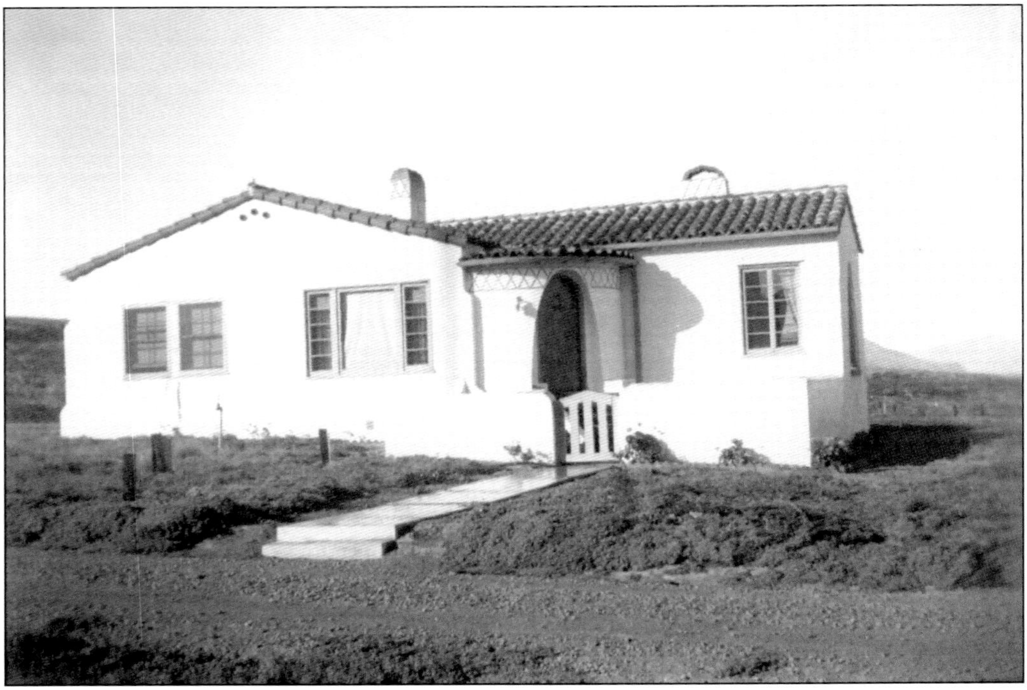

Located on the island are four beautiful, large Spanish-style homes with two or three bedrooms apiece and red tile roofs. Each home had a naturally cool temperature in the basement, making them ideal for keeping a good supply of food. During bad weather, if the boat could not make it into town, the families would rely on their basement supplies, sometimes for extended periods of time. Two of the houses are pictured here in the 1930s. (Both courtesy Margaret Kellogg-Anderson.)

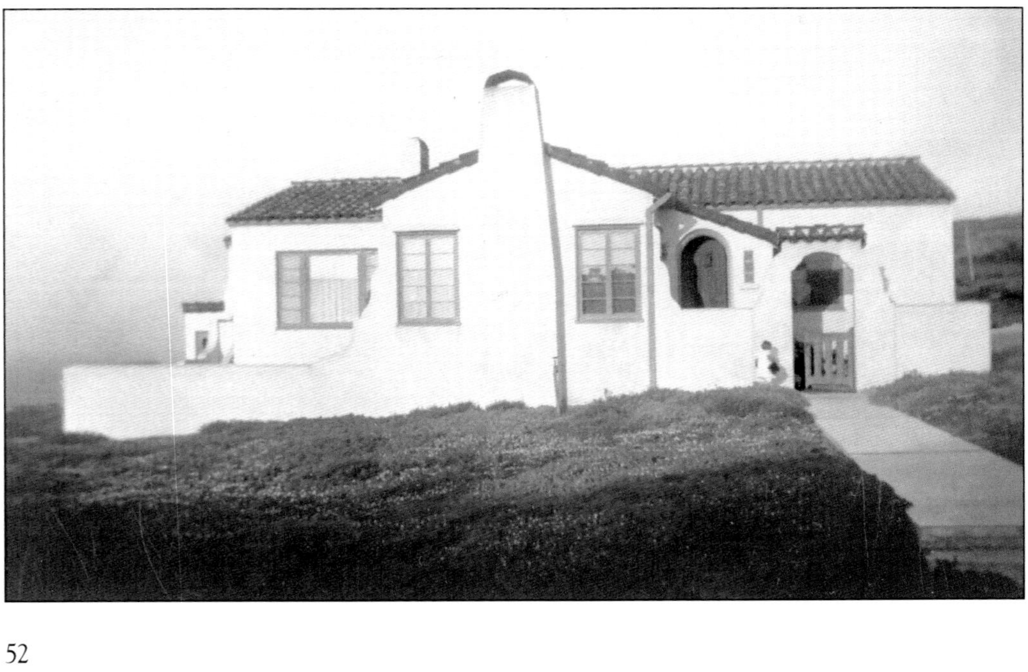

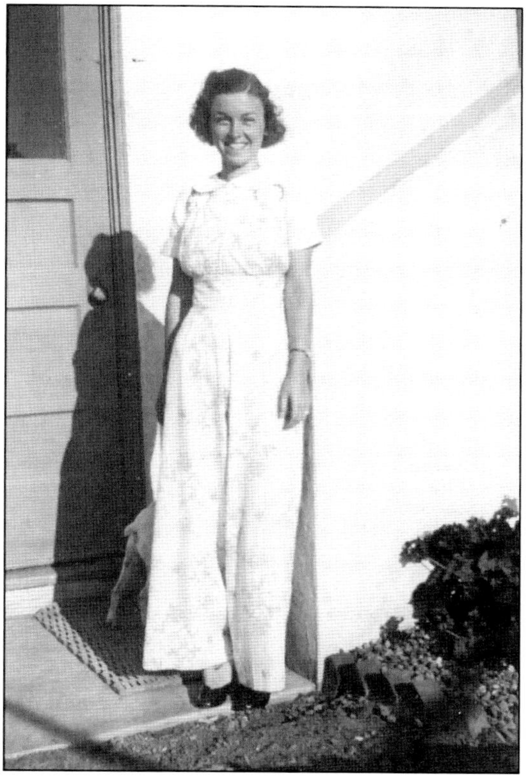

Standing in front of the building's main door are Margaret Kellogg (right) and an unidentified member of the Coast Guard (below). Surprise visits were made to check on the maintenance and cleanliness of the homes and shops, which, as a result, were always kept clean. Margaret recalls that the island was a lovely place to live, and the families enjoyed each other's company. They would routinely share delicious baked breads, cakes, and cookies prepared on iron coal-burning stoves. (Right, courtesy Margaret Kellogg-Anderson; below, Port Hueneme Historical Society.)

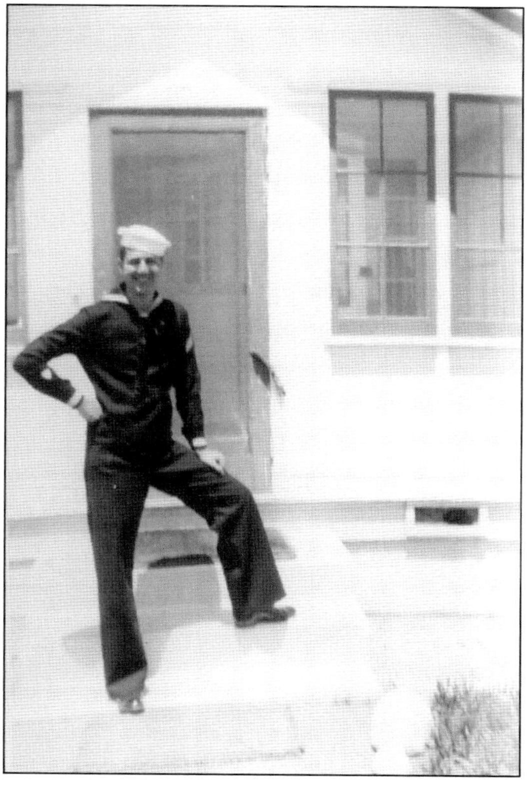

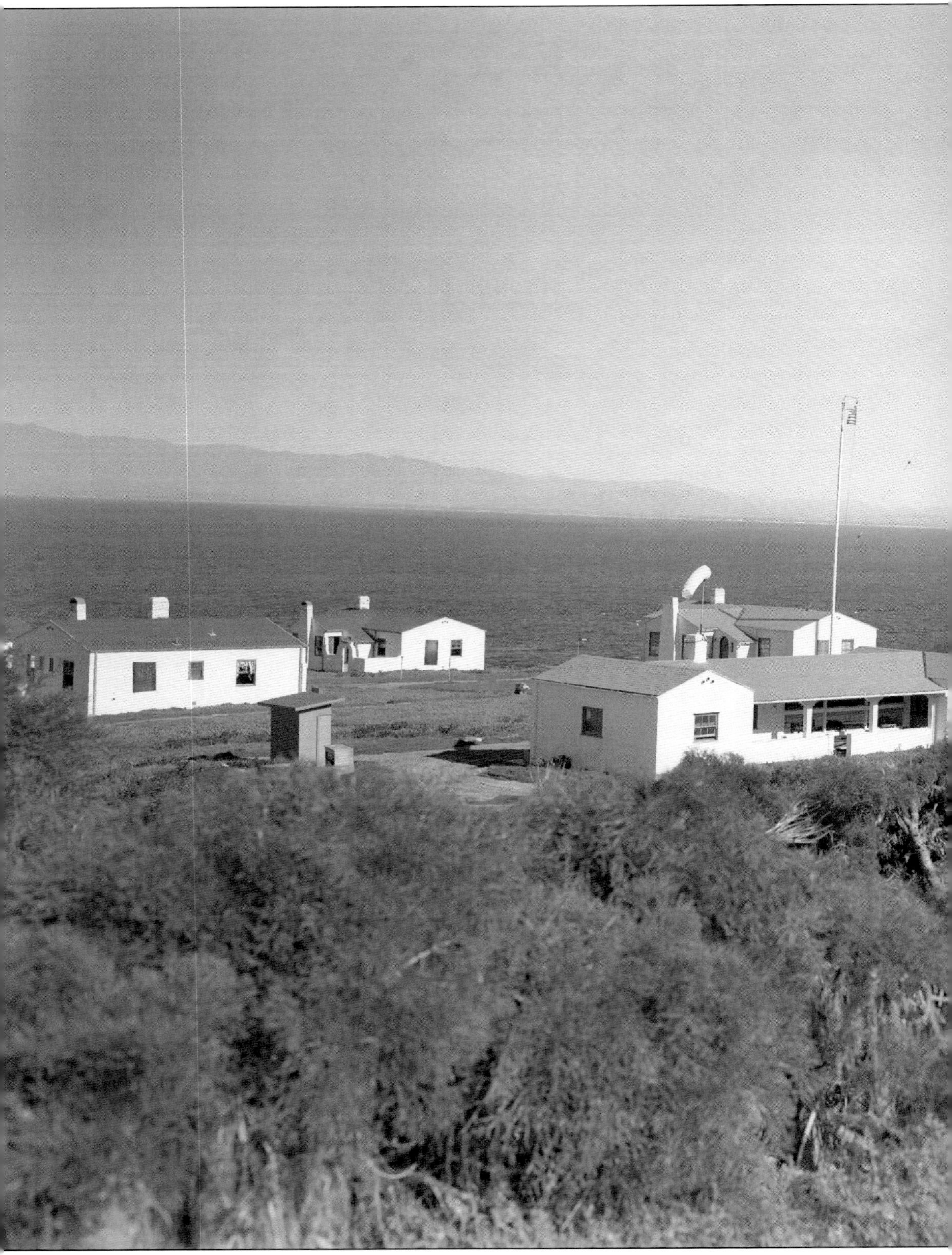

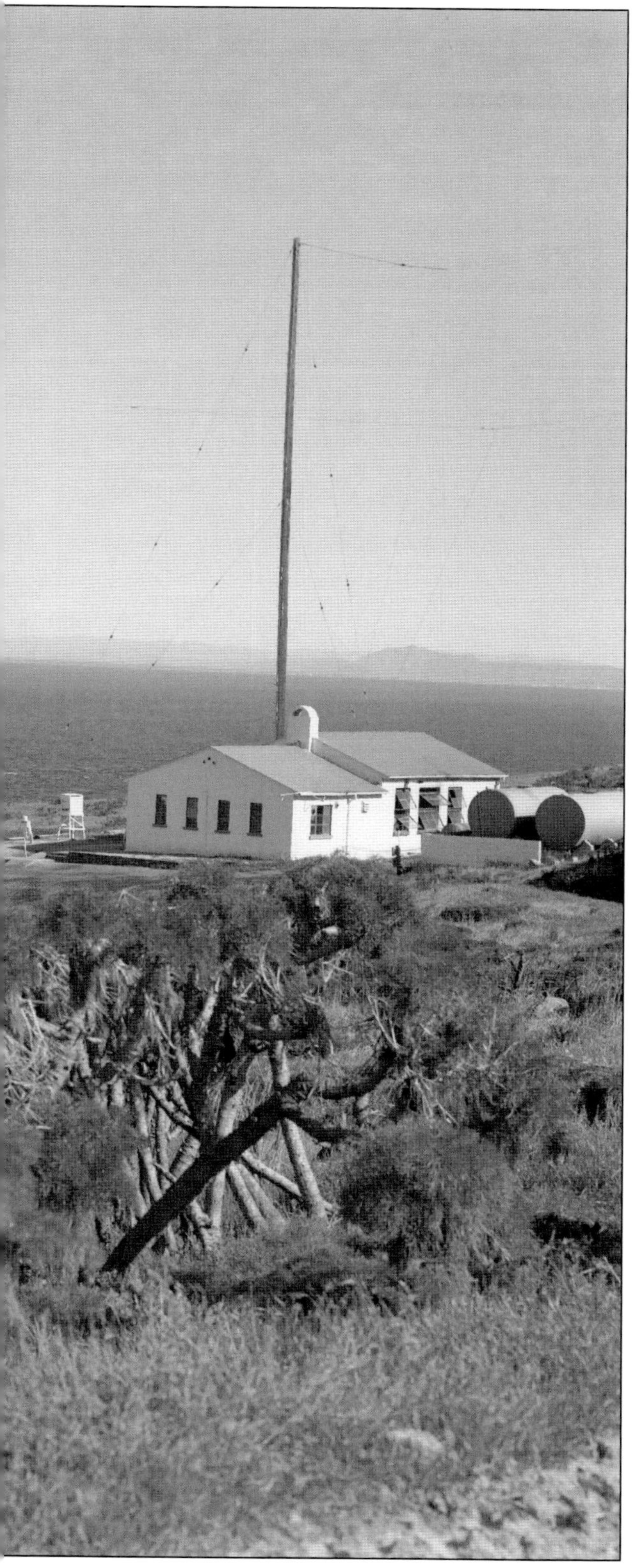

This panoramic view shows the light station grounds c. 1960s. Since the photograph was taken, three of the buildings have been razed. (Courtesy U.S. Coast Guard.)

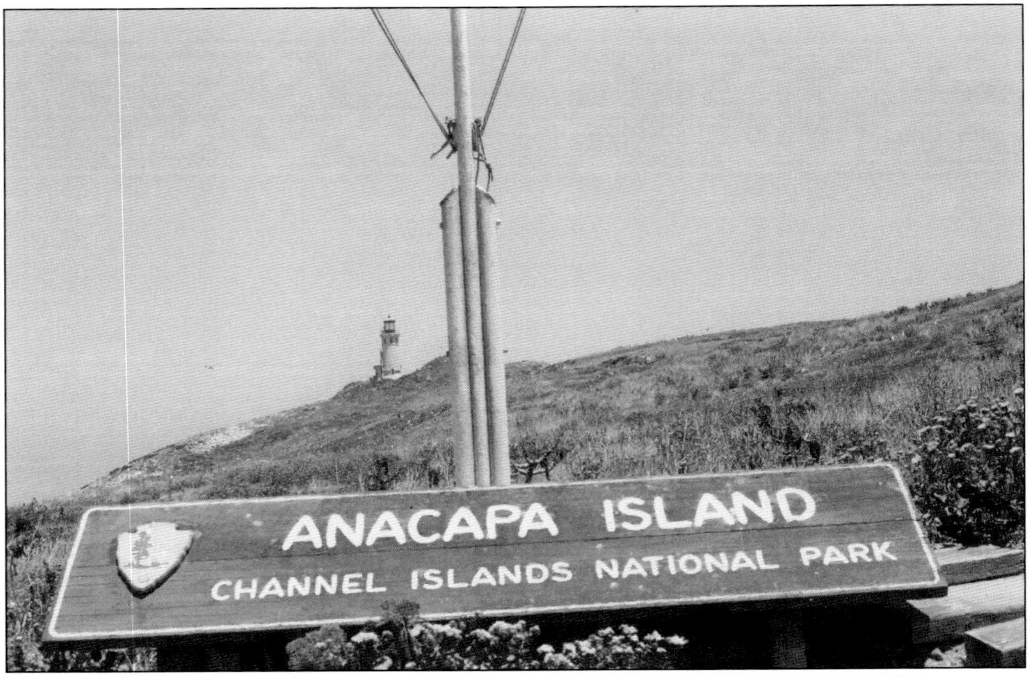

In 1938, Anacapa and Santa Barbara Islands became Channel Islands National Monument, allowing for the protection, preservation, and restoration of the islands. It was March 5, 1980, when Pres. Jimmy Carter signed the law that designated the five islands now known as the Channel Islands, their submerged lands, and waters within 1 nautical mile of each island as Channel Islands National Park. Thirty years later, the National Park Service has made great strides in protecting the natural ecology and restoring plants native to the island. A park ranger (below) assists in operating the crane, greets visitors to the island, and educates visitors on the history and how to be good stewards during their stay. (Both courtesy author's collection.)

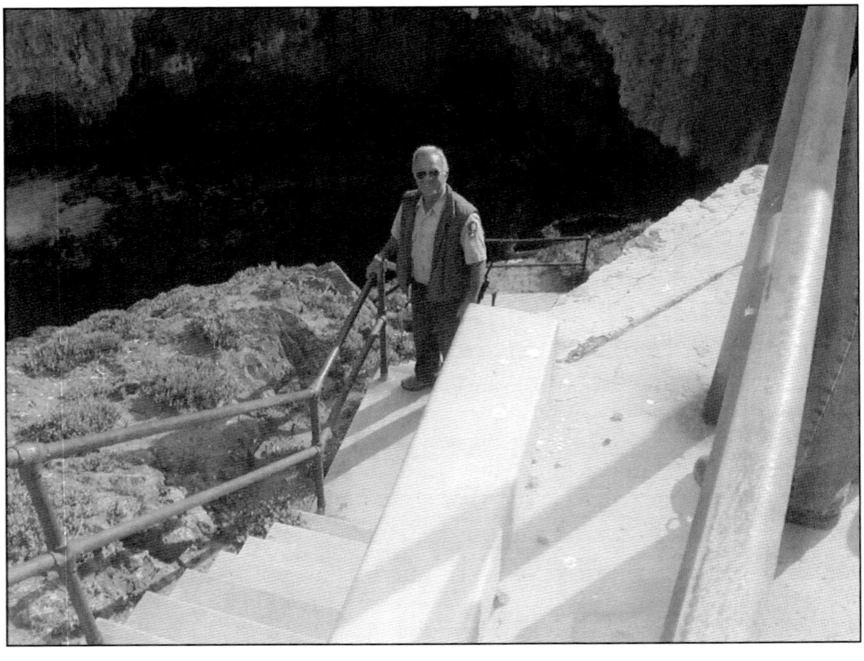

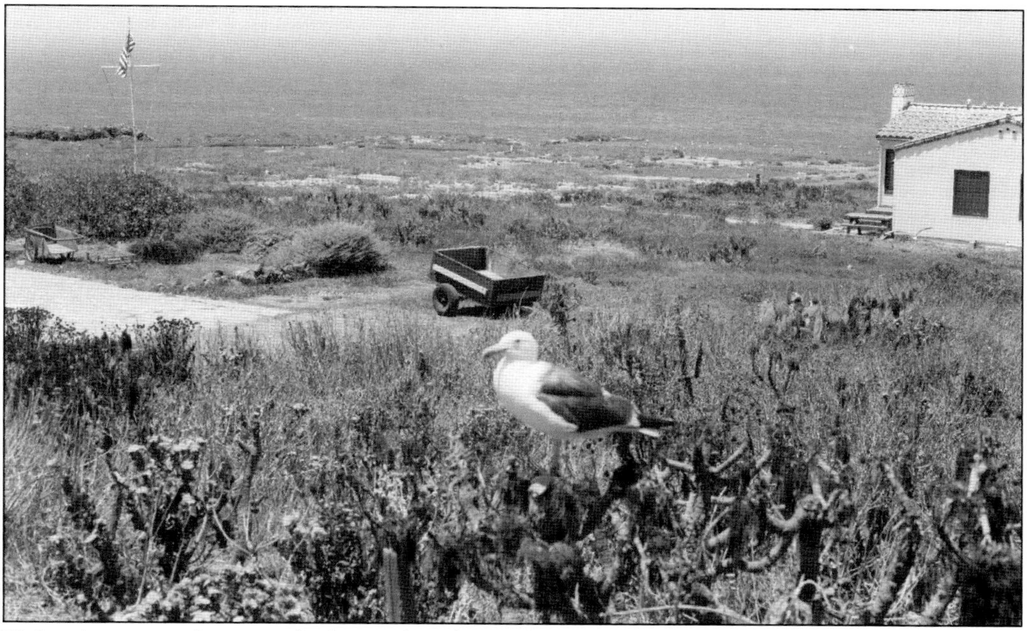

Today Anacapa is home to the largest breeding colony of western gulls in the world. The isolation of these islands creates an important absence of predators during nesting and reproductive periods. It is a primordial island protected from human habitation. The birds cover the area in the spring. Pulling up to the island, it is obvious that the birds are the majority. During nesting periods, there is a loud squawking that seems to come to a crescendo when passing the nesting area, another indication that man is only visiting. The mother birds protectively watch their chicks to be sure they do not become flustered and enter the wrong nest, which could result in deadly consequences. (Both courtesy author's collection.)

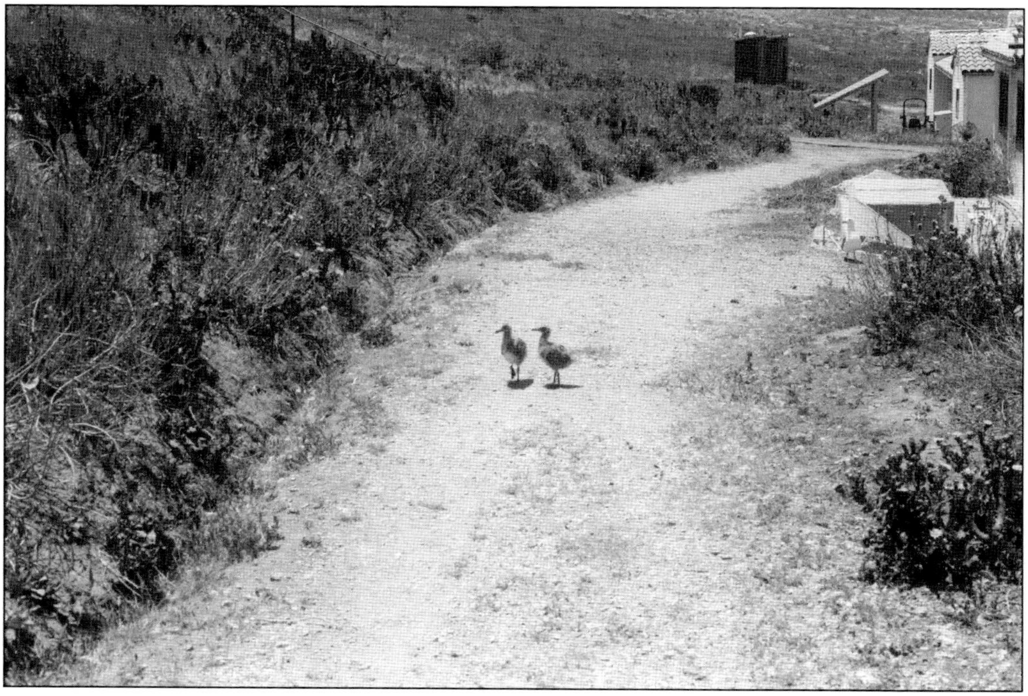

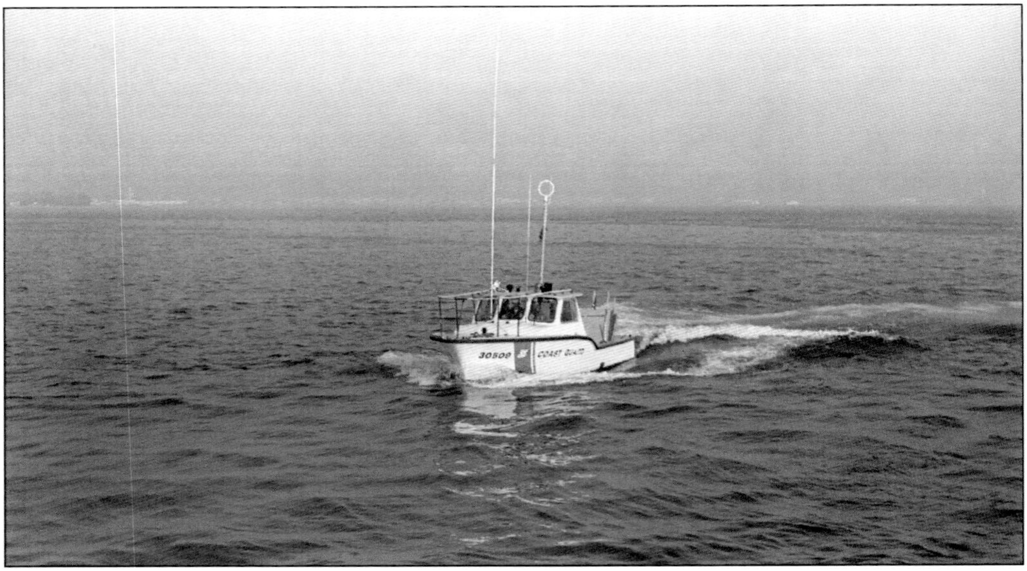

U.S. Coast Guard tender crews living on Anacapa Island were phased out in the early 1960s. By 1967, the light was fully automated, and in 1970, the Coast Guard and National Park Service signed a cooperative agreement. The lighthouse and foghorn will continue under Coast Guard jurisdiction. The other facilities are to be maintained by the National Park Service. As seen in the *c.* 1950 photograph above, a team is heading out by boat to work on the light. On rare occasions, a helicopter is used by the Coast Guard to reach the island. In 1992, it was deemed that the lighthouse required repairs, and a total of $325,000 was allocated for a complete lighthouse renovation. Petty Officer Bruce, pictured below in 2002, is seen taking in the view atop the recently renovated lighthouse. (Both courtesy U.S. Coast Guard.)

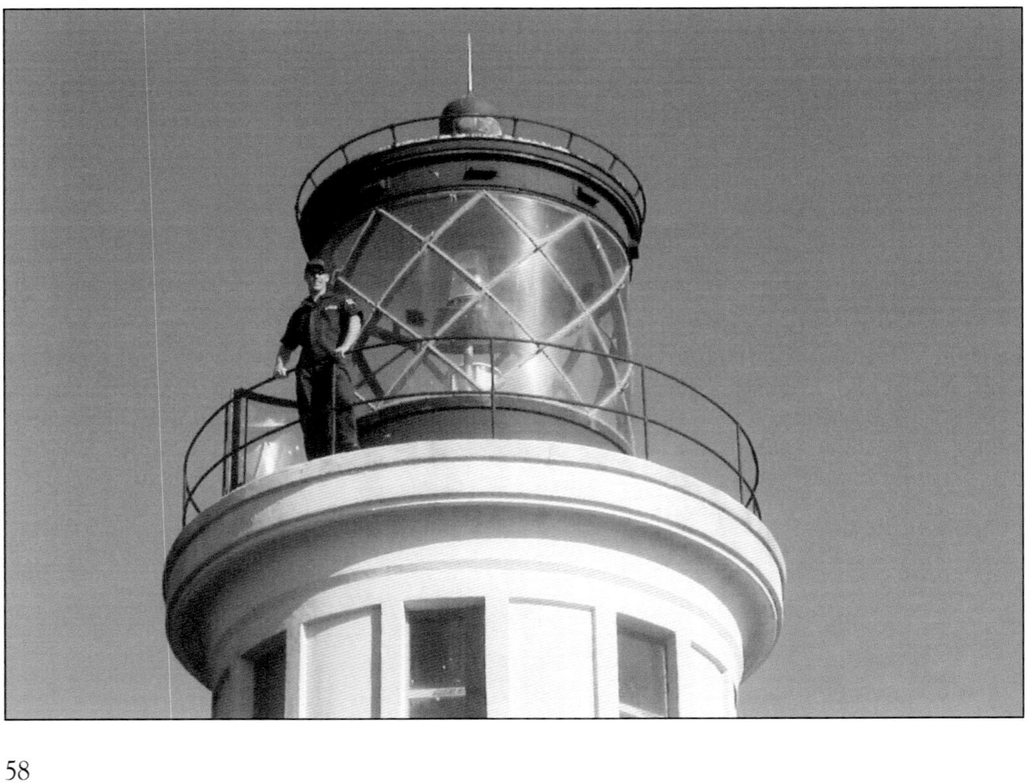

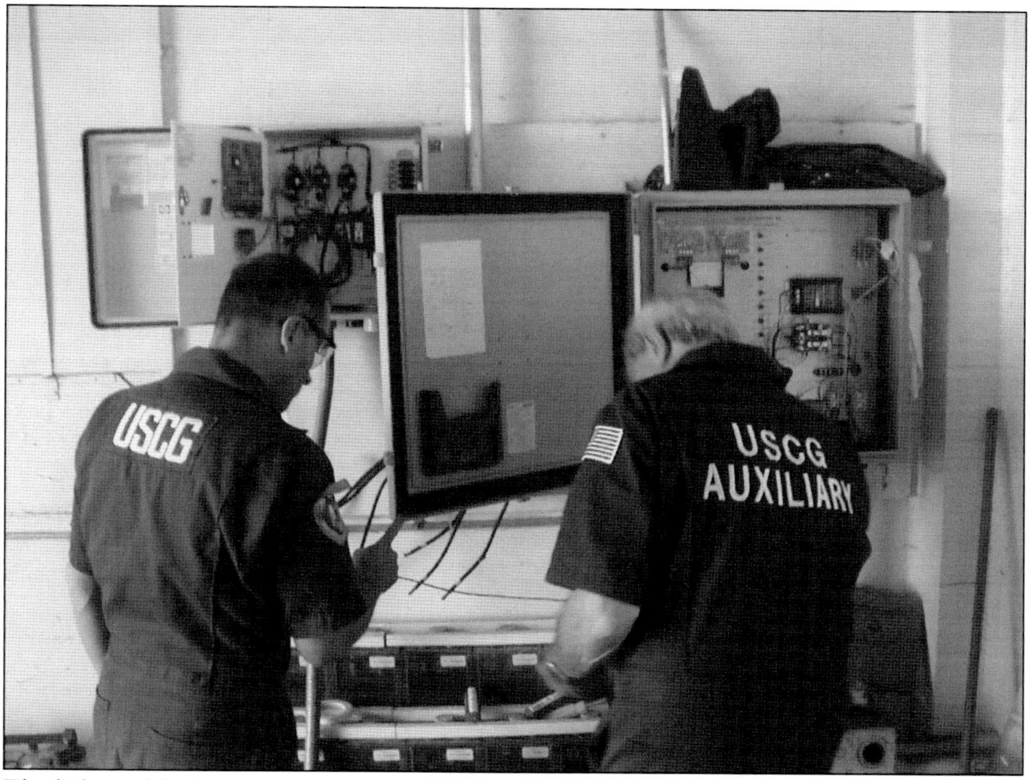

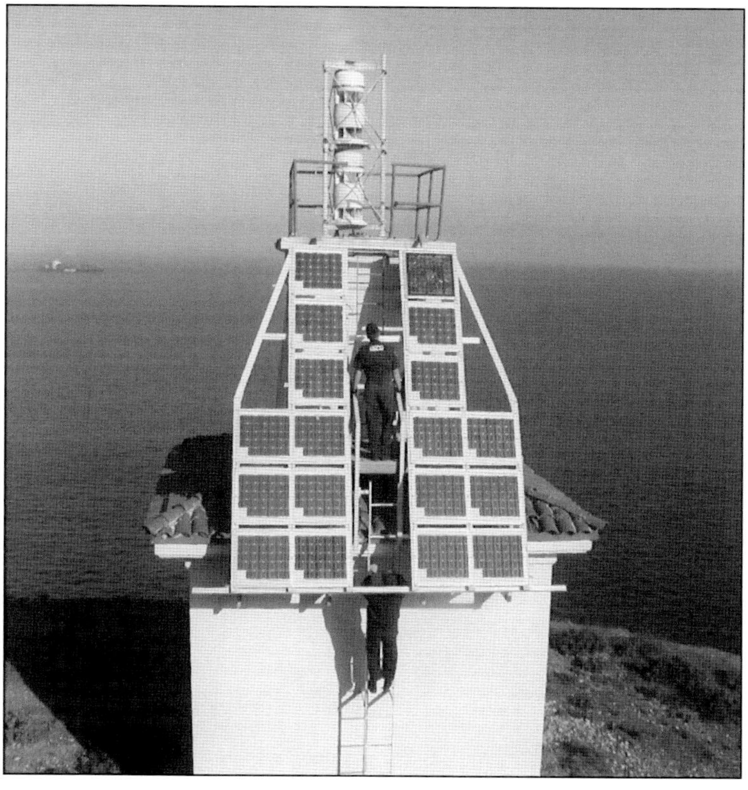

The light and foghorn were converted to solar power in 1989. In 1993, the USCGC *Conifer* embarked on a large solarization project. The U.S. Coast Guard and Coast Guard Auxiliary spent a week rewiring the lighthouse on Anacapa in February 2002. U.S. Coast Guard Chief Petty Officer John Stercks and U.S. Coast Guard auxiliarist professor Fred Allen are seen above working side by side. The large solar panels (right) allow the light to operate by the power of the sun, with only periodic maintenance (Both courtesy Eric Castro-Bran.)

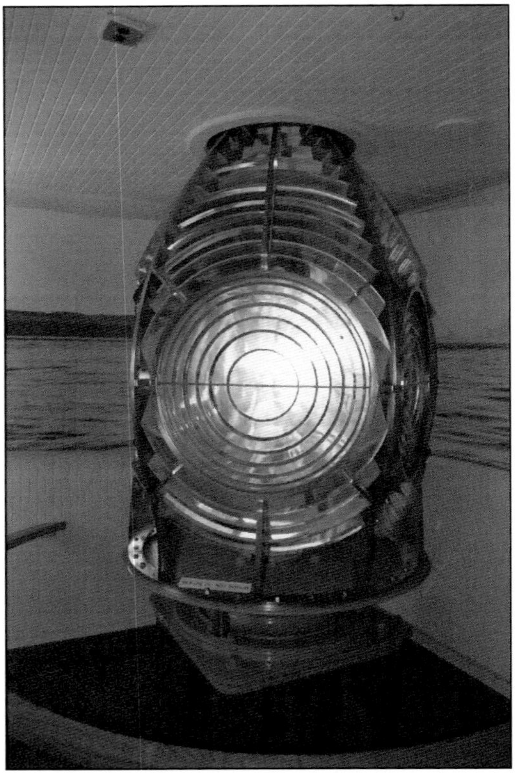

In 1932, a third order Fresnel lens lit up Anacapa, shining over 20 miles out to sea. During World War II, the light was extinguished when the facilities became a coastal lookout station for the U.S. Navy. It served for 57 years. Today the Fresnel lens is on display and beautifully preserved by the Park Service in the Anacapa Visitor Center. (Author's collection.)

U.S. Coast Guard Auxiliarist Eric Castro-Bran, lighthouse keeper of Point Vicente Lighthouse in Palos Verdes for 18 years, was part of the team that spent a week on the island in 2002. He is working on the modern lightweight beacon. Although not as attractive or historical as the Fresnel lens, the modern beacons are incredibly affordable and easy to maintain. For better or worse, this is the future of lighthouses. (Courtesy Eric Castro-Bran.)

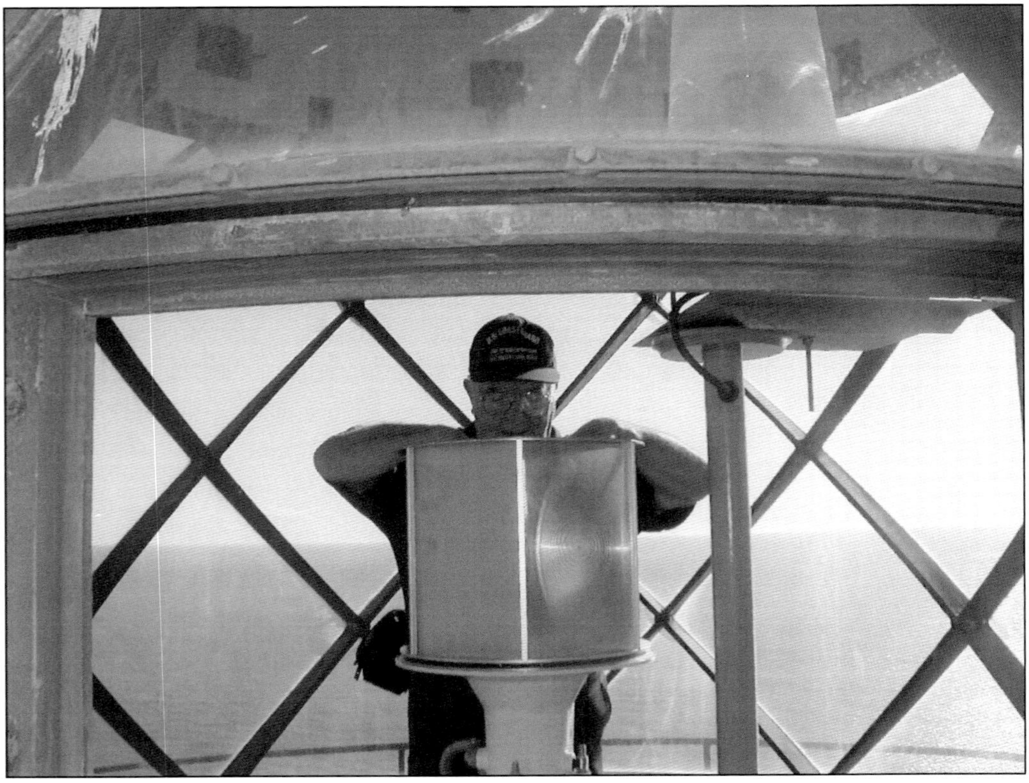

Four

PORT HUENEME

VISION OF A HARBOR

Without relying on a penny from the federal government, the new harbor was quickly becoming a reality. It would be Thomas Bard's son, Richard, who would see the dream come to fruition. Richard Bard, along with area farmers and merchants, attempted to procure the funding necessary to build the port. Several attempts were made to secure federal funding, but to no avail.

The harbor commission arranged a $1.75 million bond issue to finance construction of the port. The discovery of a natural deep-sea canyon brought with it unlimited possibilities for large vessels. The port was officially completed on July 4, 1940. The Oxnard Harbor District was created as an independent agency, which was instrumental in the creation of the port. It continues to operate the commercial side of the port to this day.

A harbor offered shelter and protection not found in bays or even within breakwaters. Referred to as a "sportsman's mecca," the harbor was designed to offer varied recreational advantages that were in closer proximity to any other yacht basin in California at that time.

The port was originally heralded as a destination for recreational boating and commercial shipping. During World War II, the U.S. Navy assumed control of the port, and the majority of the vessel traffic supported the war effort.

With peacetime came a new chapter, one of developing trade and growth. Today the port serves international businesses and oceangoing carriers from the Pacific Rim and Europe. The Port of Hueneme ranks among the top seaports in California for general cargo and is also home to the U.S. Naval Construction Battalion. The benefits of Thomas Bard's vision were realized across generations.

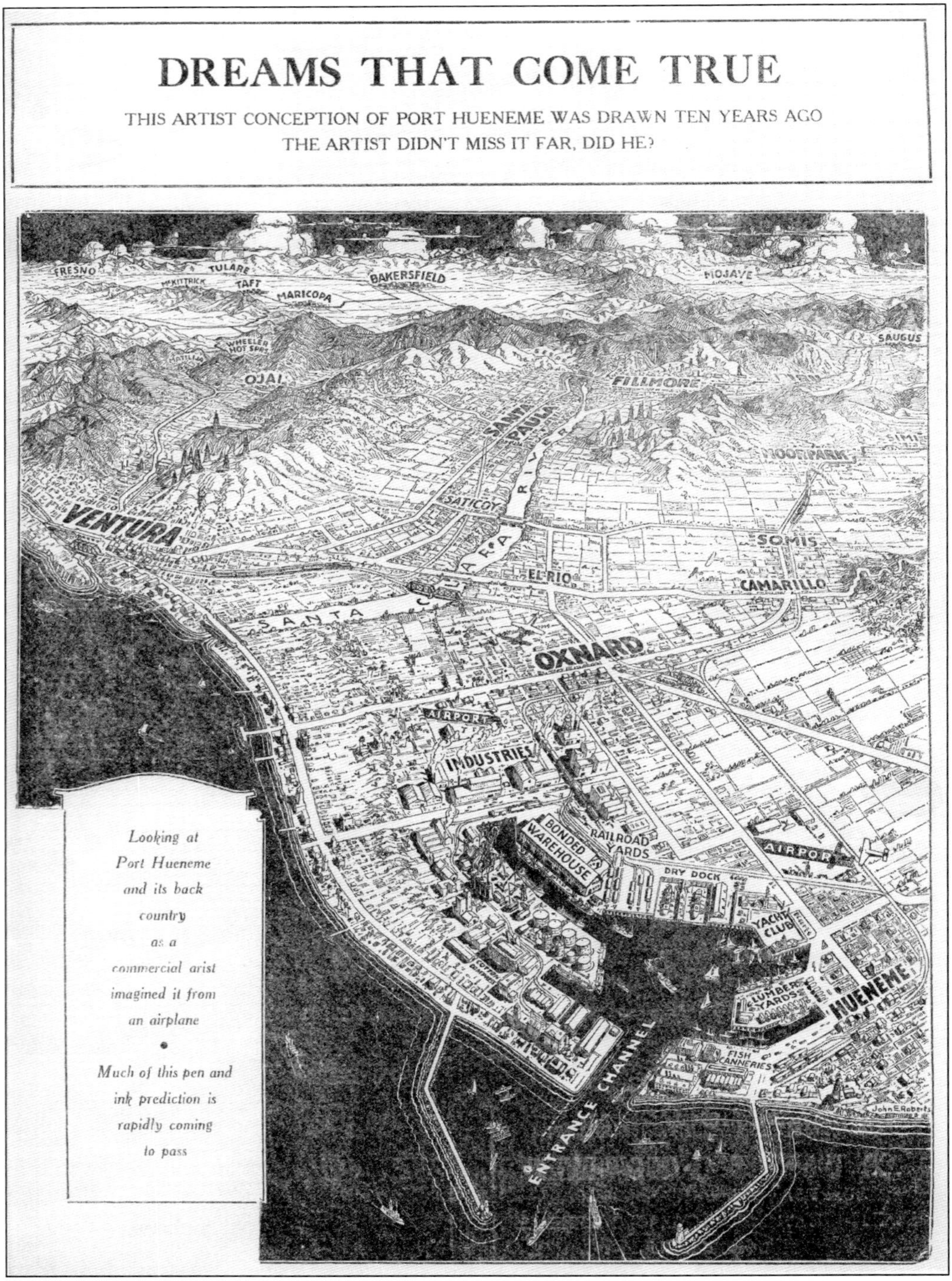

This 1929 artist's sketch envisioned the future of the Port Hueneme area. (Courtesy Laverne White-Dornbeger.)

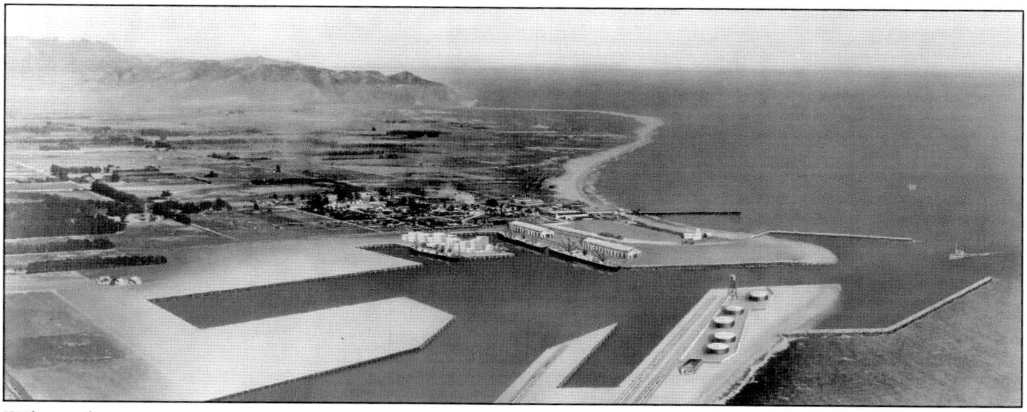

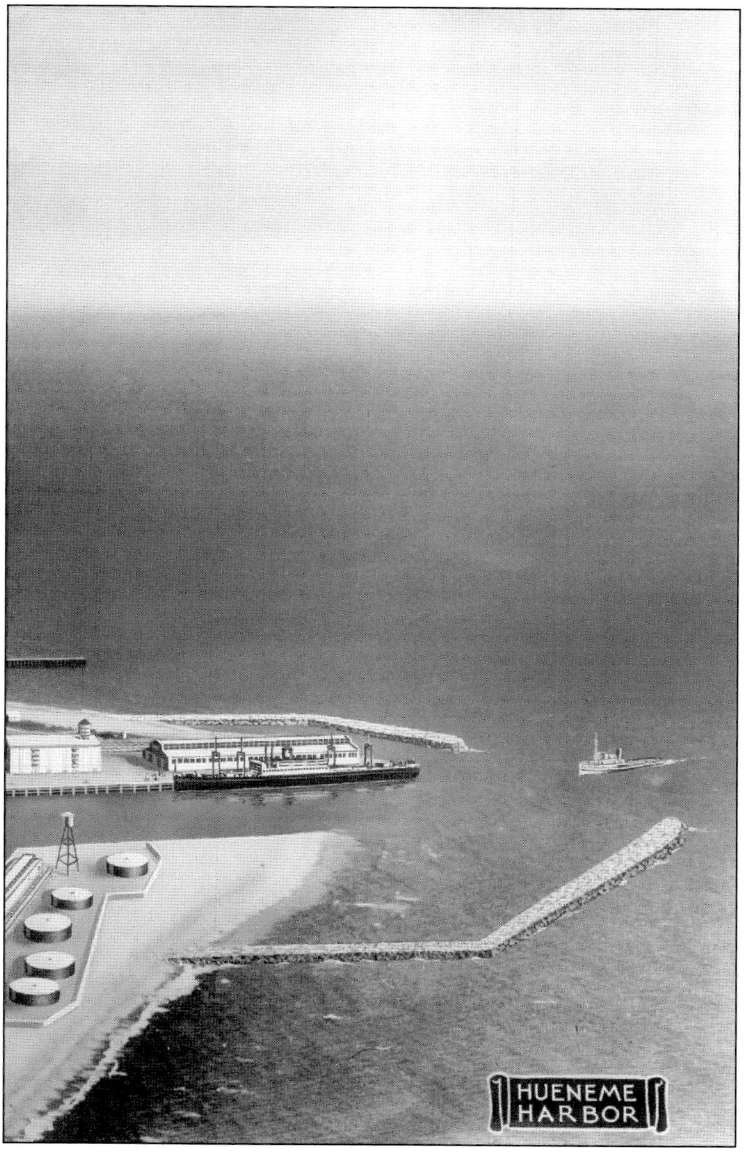

When the artist conceived these illustrations, it was still but a dream. This dream of Thomas Bard's was about to be brought to reality with the help of his son Richard Bard. (Both courtesy Port Hueneme Historical Society.)

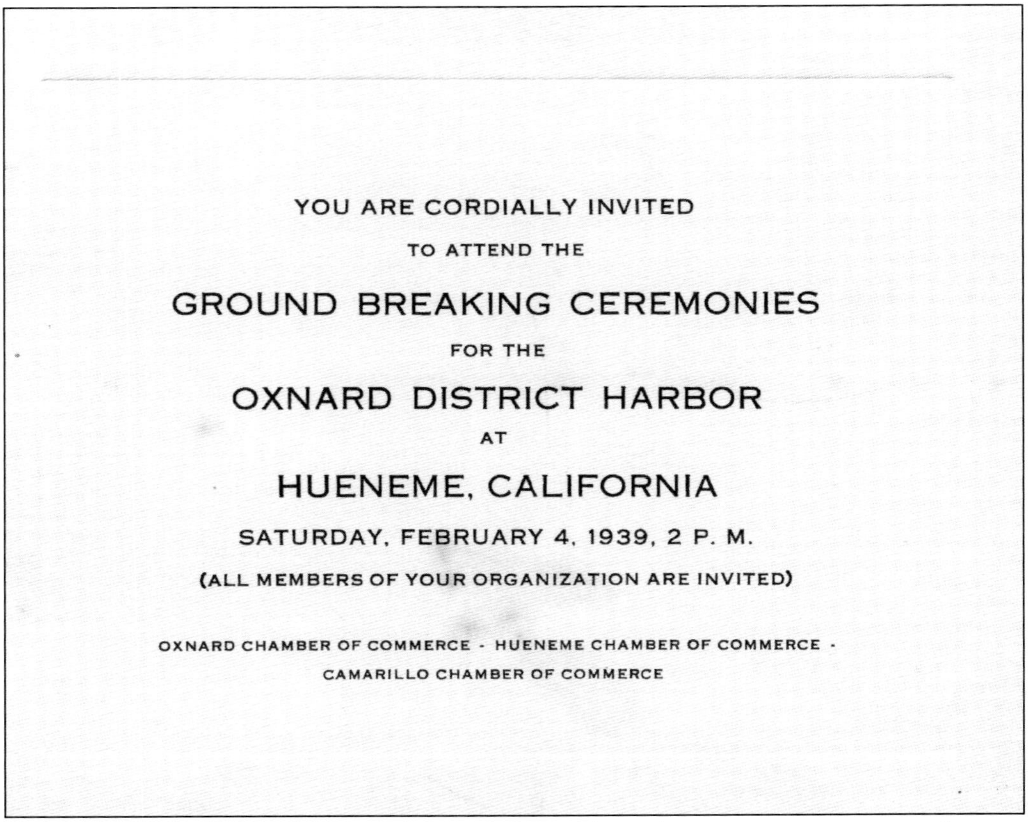

YOU ARE CORDIALLY INVITED
TO ATTEND THE
GROUND BREAKING CEREMONIES
FOR THE
OXNARD DISTRICT HARBOR
AT
HUENEME, CALIFORNIA
SATURDAY, FEBRUARY 4, 1939, 2 P. M.
(ALL MEMBERS OF YOUR ORGANIZATION ARE INVITED)

OXNARD CHAMBER OF COMMERCE - HUENEME CHAMBER OF COMMERCE -
CAMARILLO CHAMBER OF COMMERCE

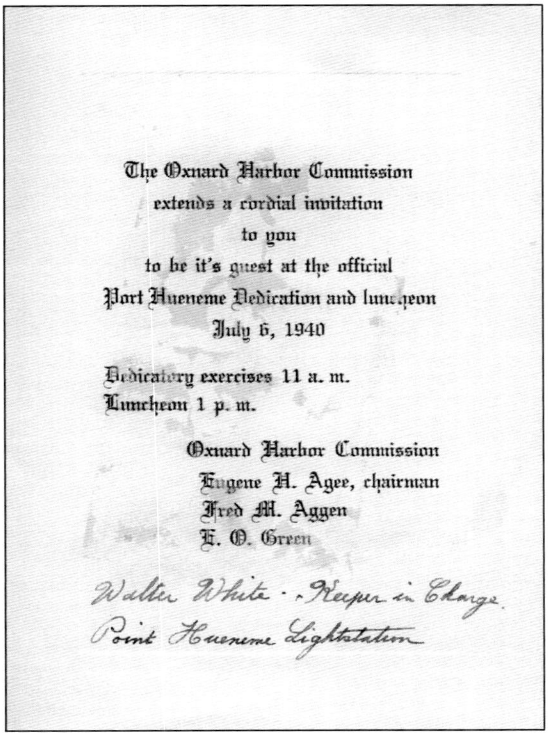

The Oxnard Harbor Commission
extends a cordial invitation
to you
to be it's guest at the official
Port Hueneme Dedication and luncheon
July 6, 1940

Dedicatory exercises 11 a. m.
Luncheon 1 p. m.

Oxnard Harbor Commission
Eugene H. Agee, chairman
Fred M. Aggen
E. O. Green

Walter White - Keeper in Charge.
Point Hueneme Lightstation

Shown here is an invitation to and announcement of the "Ground Breaking Ceremonies" for the creation of the harbor. (Both courtesy Laverne White-Dornberger.)

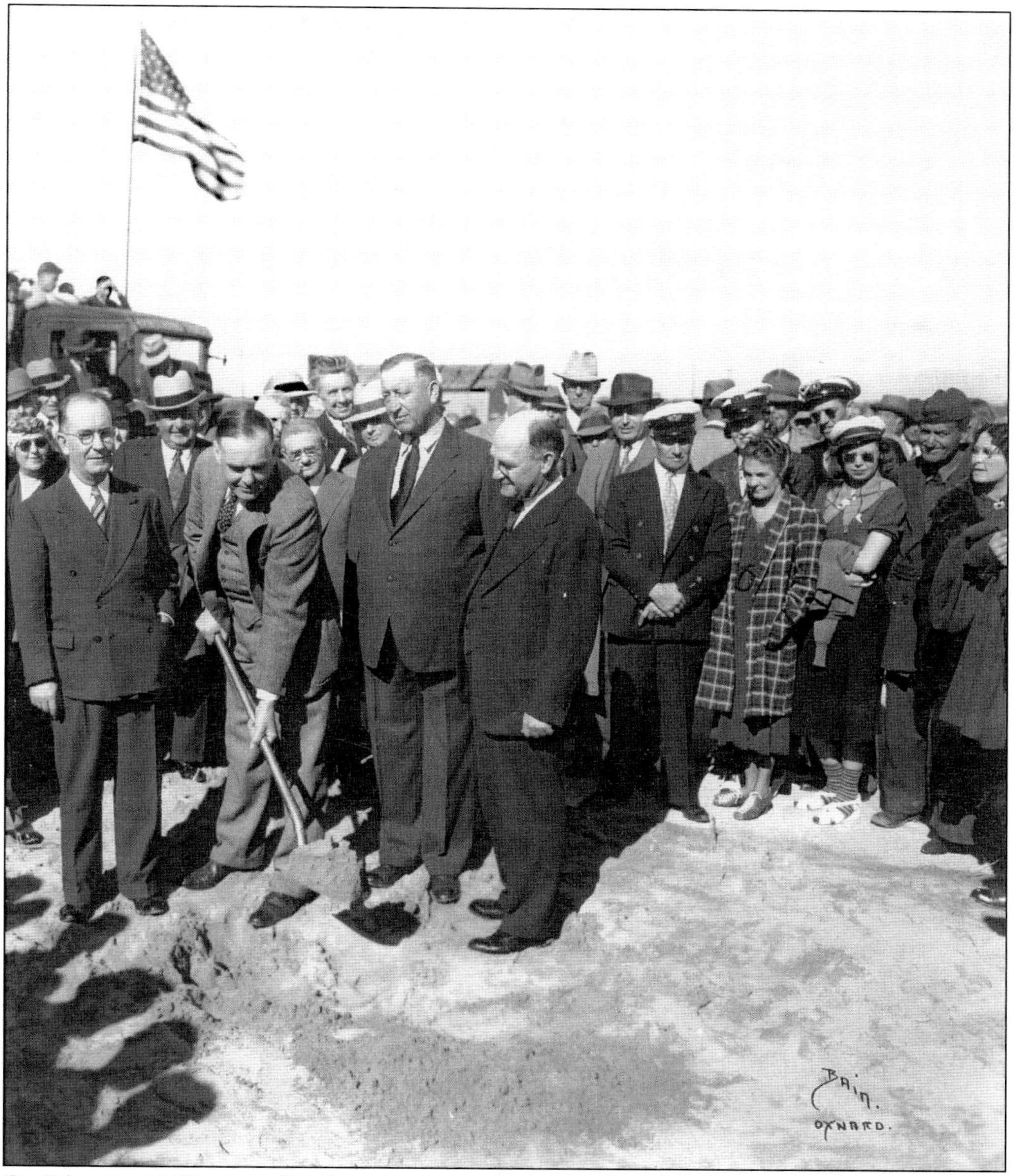

On February 4, 1939, groundbreaking commenced as Richard Bard, pioneer resident of Hueneme and prime motivator of the harbor movement, turned the first shovel of earth for harbor construction. Lighthouse keeper Walter White can be seen toward the right of the photograph wearing his white keeper hat (to his left is his wife, Francis White, and daughter Laverne; Helen and Leroy White are directly behind them). (Courtesy Laverne White-Dornberger.)

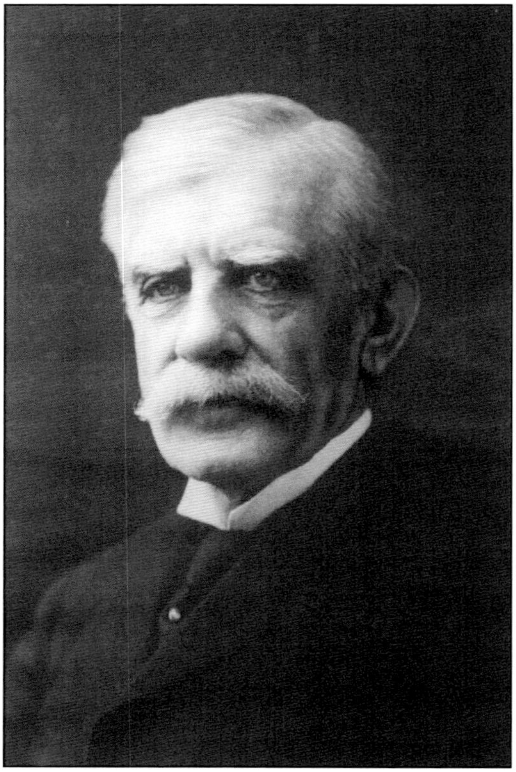

Thomas Robert Bard passed away on March 5, 1915. Though he did not live to see this momentous occasion, his work of assisting to organize Ventura County, representing the state in the U.S. Senate, and his legacy of "Father of Port Hueneme" denotes the sheer determination of one person, but in this case his perseverance for a better tomorrow was passed on to his son Richard Bard and brought to fruition. (Courtesy Joanna Bard Newton.)

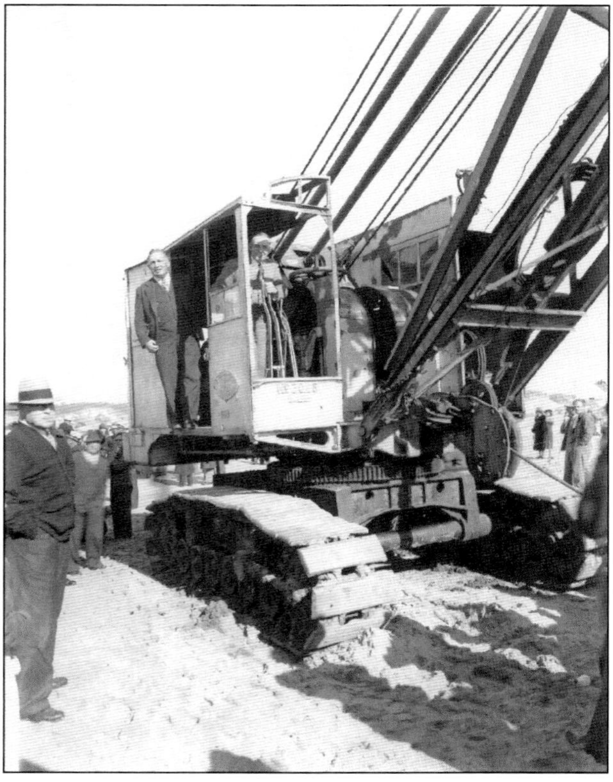

Perhaps the most spectacular moment of the entire ceremony was when Richard Bard took over the controls and broke ground again, this time using a giant excavating tractor. With great anticipation, construction had begun and years of gridlock were left behind. (Courtesy Port Hueneme Historical Society.)

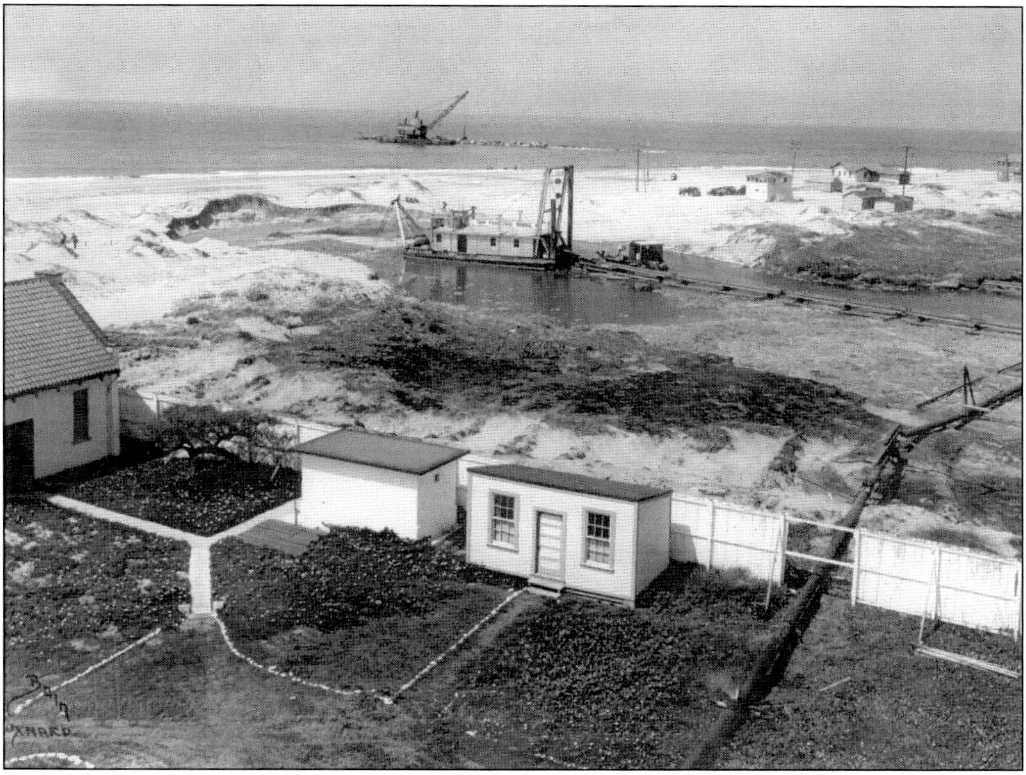

The Standard Dredging Company had a jump-start on the harbor, as they had already begun operations prior to the official groundbreaking ceremonies. With construction underway on July 21, 1939, contractors were actually ahead of schedule. A dredger was brought in by truck and assembled in the hole. After sufficient depth was obtained, a larger dredger was able to come by sea and dig the channel, thus allowing the ocean water to rush in and provide enough space to work the big dredger, which came in as it dug the channel. (Courtesy Laverne White-Dornberger.)

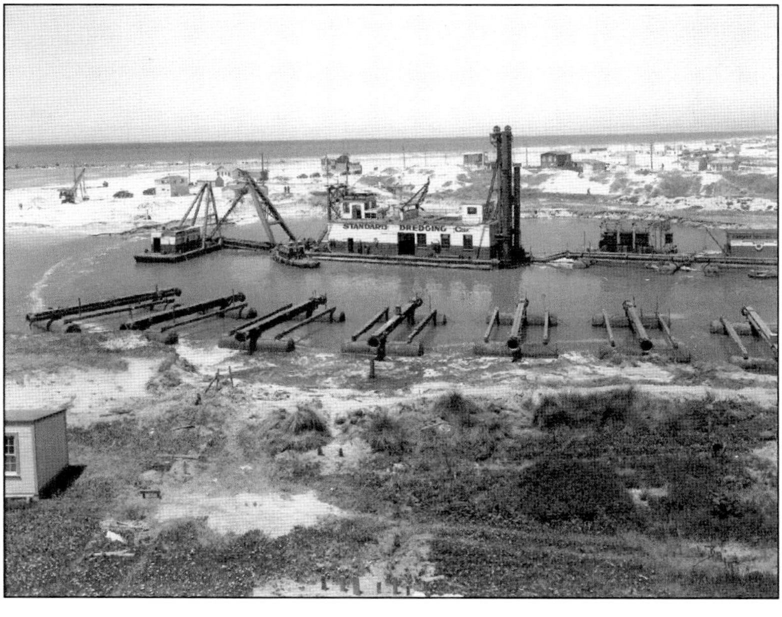

The large dredger, pictured in July 1939, is enlarging and deepening the channel to the sea. (Courtesy Port Hueneme Historical Society.)

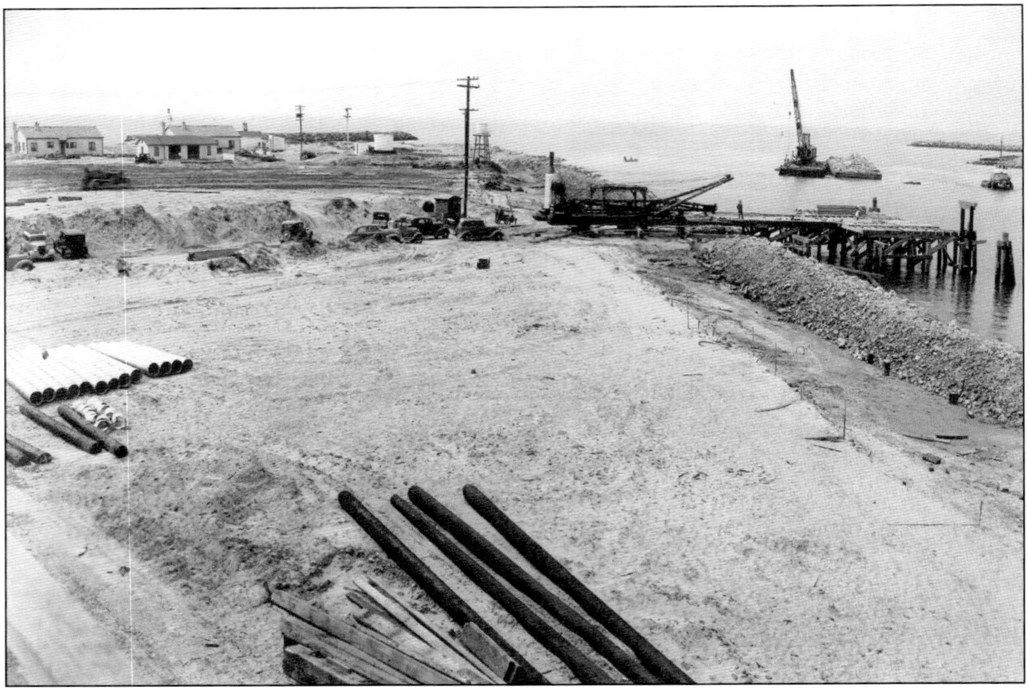

The construction was under the direction of Capt. W. R. Osgood, superintendent of the first unit of construction, who described how "workmen rolled up their sleeves and went to work." Residents recall massive progress continually taking place from one day to the next. The area was transforming right before their eyes, and equipment was constantly being delivered and set in place. Large amounts of supplies, including timber, were brought in. (Both courtesy Port Hueneme Historical Society.)

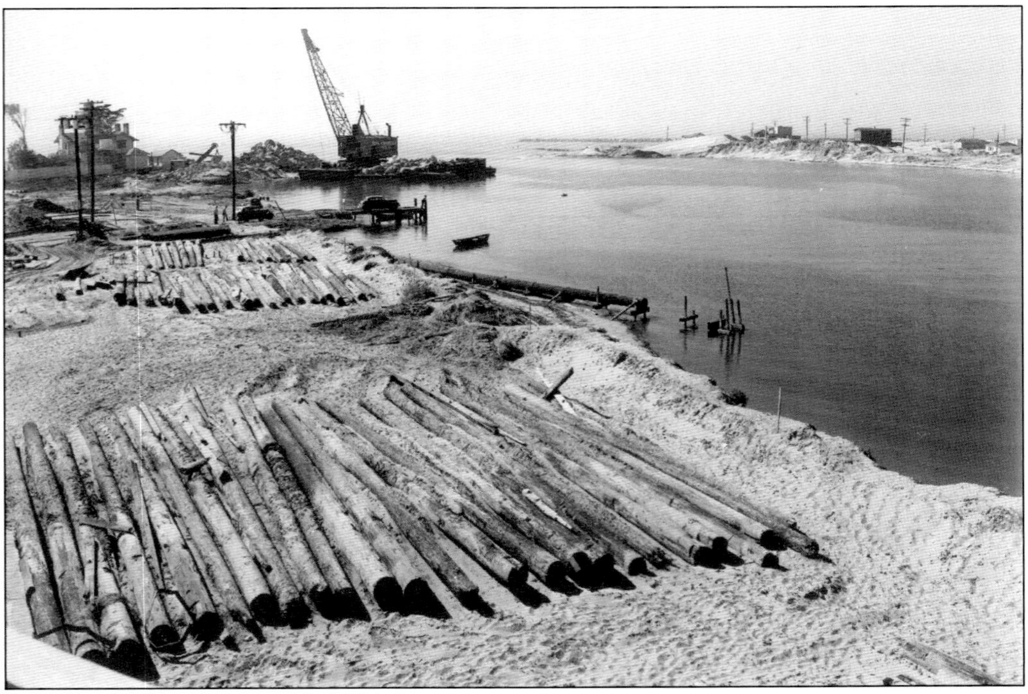

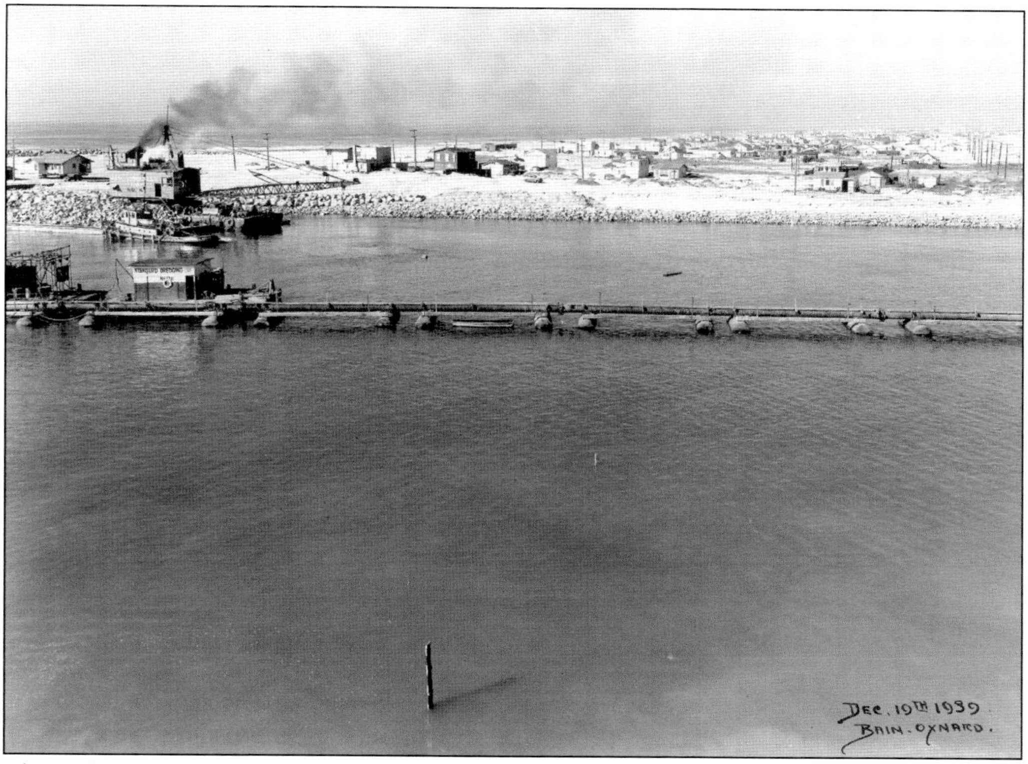

This is the site of the future turning basin. The turning or maneuvering basin occupied 40 acres (45 acres including slips), with a depth of 30 feet. The yacht slip, at that time, was 950 feet long and 200 feet wide, with a depth of 16 feet. The entire harbor site was 350 acres. (Both courtesy Laverne White-Dornberger.)

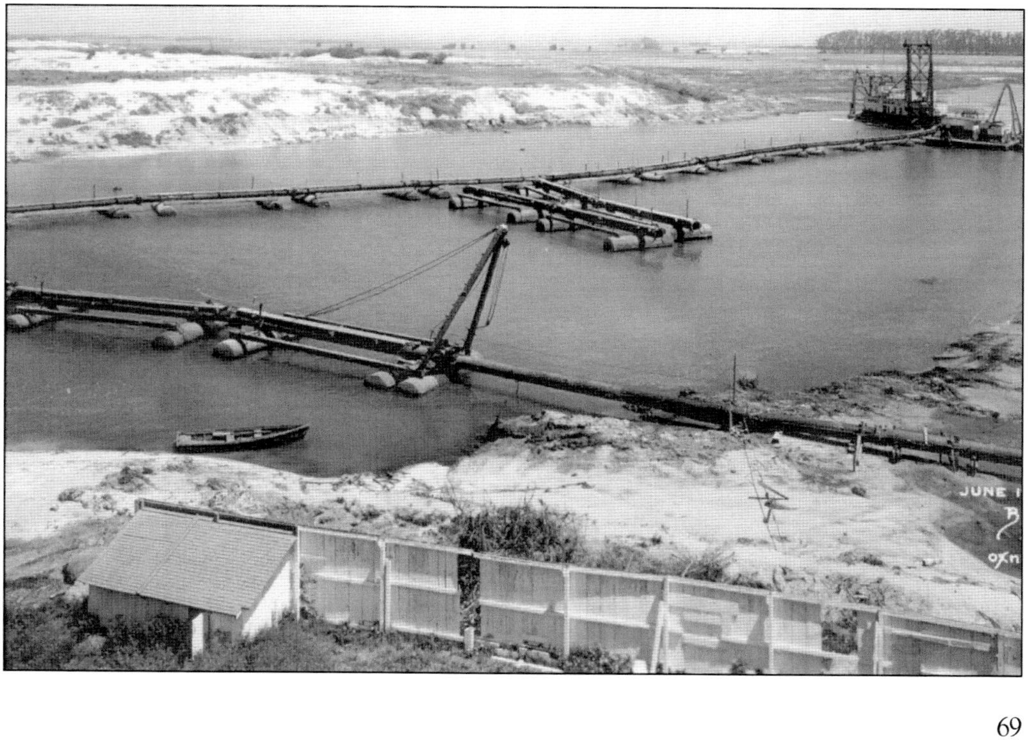

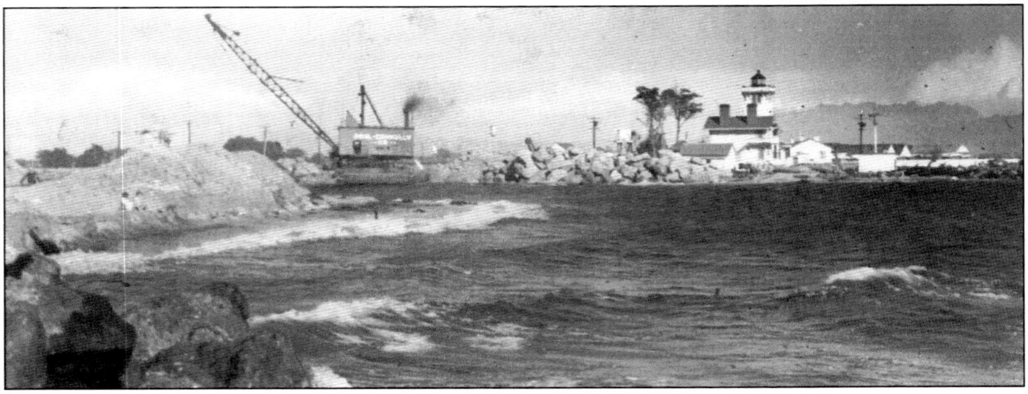

The Rohl-Connolly company of Los Angeles is hard at work in the 1939 photograph above. The lighthouse can been seen in the background as the edge of the new harbor gets closer and closer to its door. The Rohl-Connolly company (below) was commissioned as subcontractors for the rock work. Over 1,400 tons of rock were dumped and piled off Silver Strand Beach before the breakwater was finished. (Above, courtesy Ventura County Museum; below, courtesy Laverne White-Dornberger.)

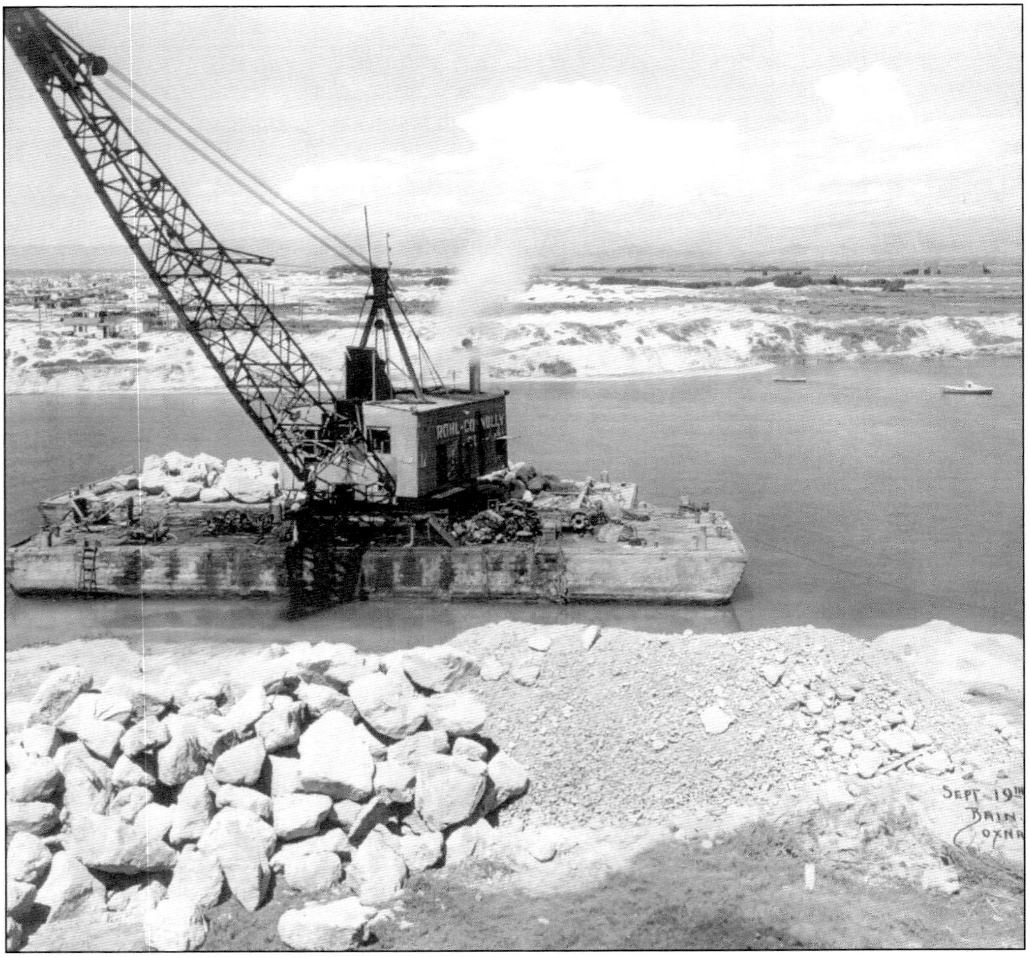

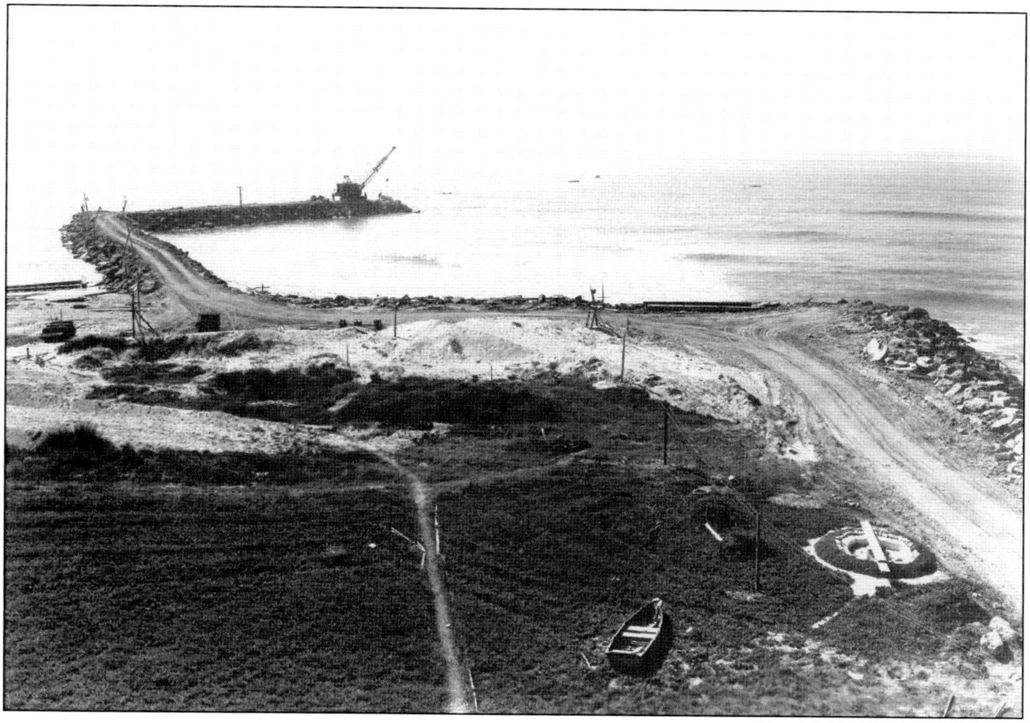

The new breakwater (above) can be seen nearing completion, and the edge of the new harbor (below) is almost completed. With progress unimpeded, the channel to the sea was dug by July 1939. This is the point where earlier engineering studies found a natural underground river. Large volcanic rocks were ejected from dredger pipes. (Both courtesy Port Hueneme Historical Society.)

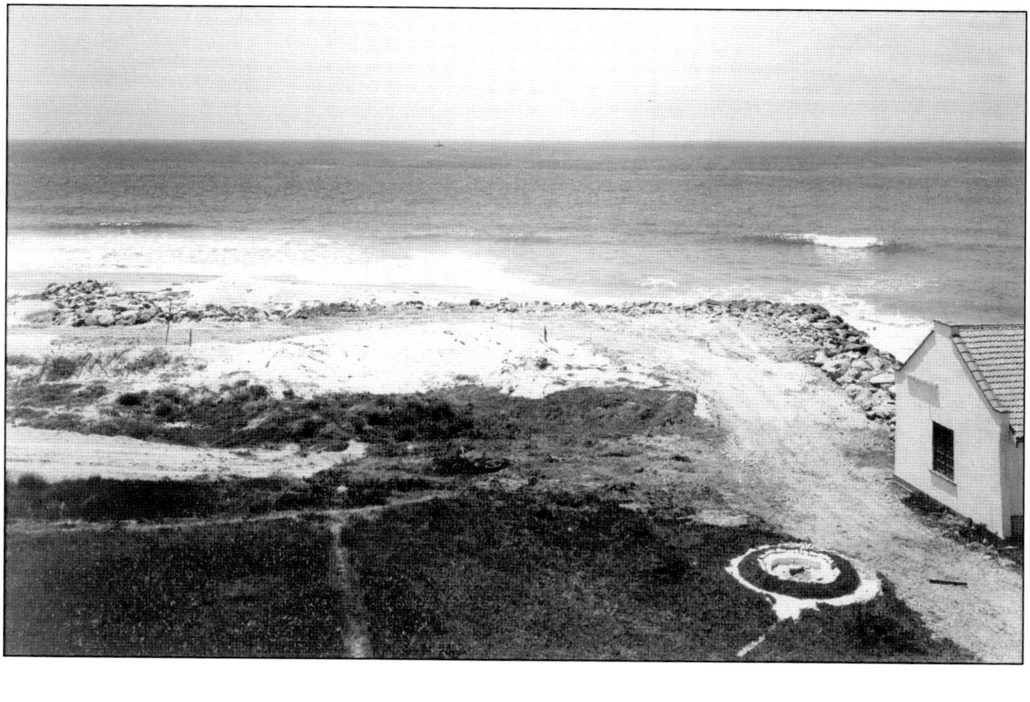

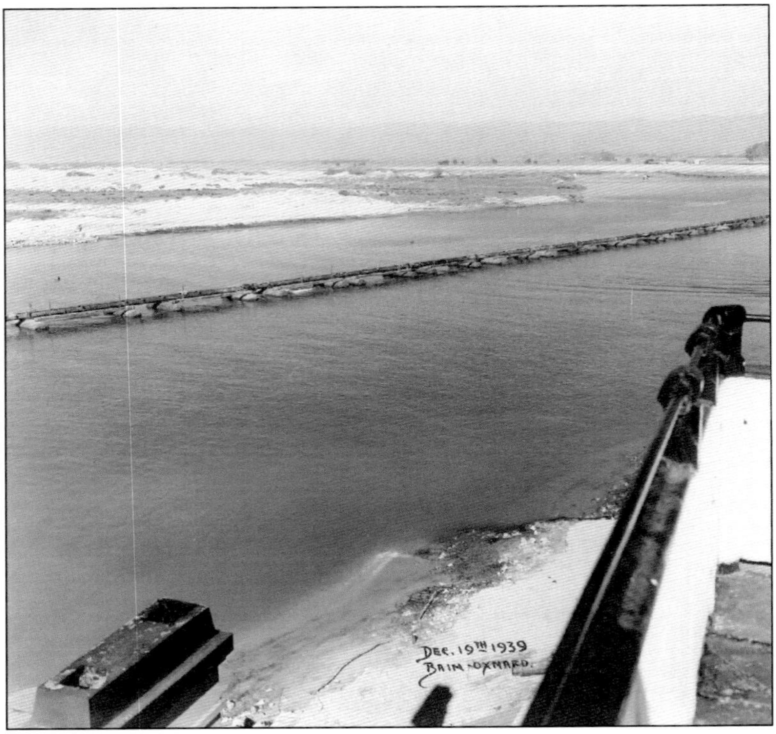

Here are views from the catwalk of the lighthouse. From the white railing of the lighthouse, the view shows just how close the lighthouse came to the edge of the new harbor. As a result, the lighthouse that served 65 years, guiding mariners to safety, could no longer be utilized as a beacon. It would, however, become the first lighthouse in history to be relocated by a barge across the harbor. (Both courtesy Port Hueneme Historical Society.)

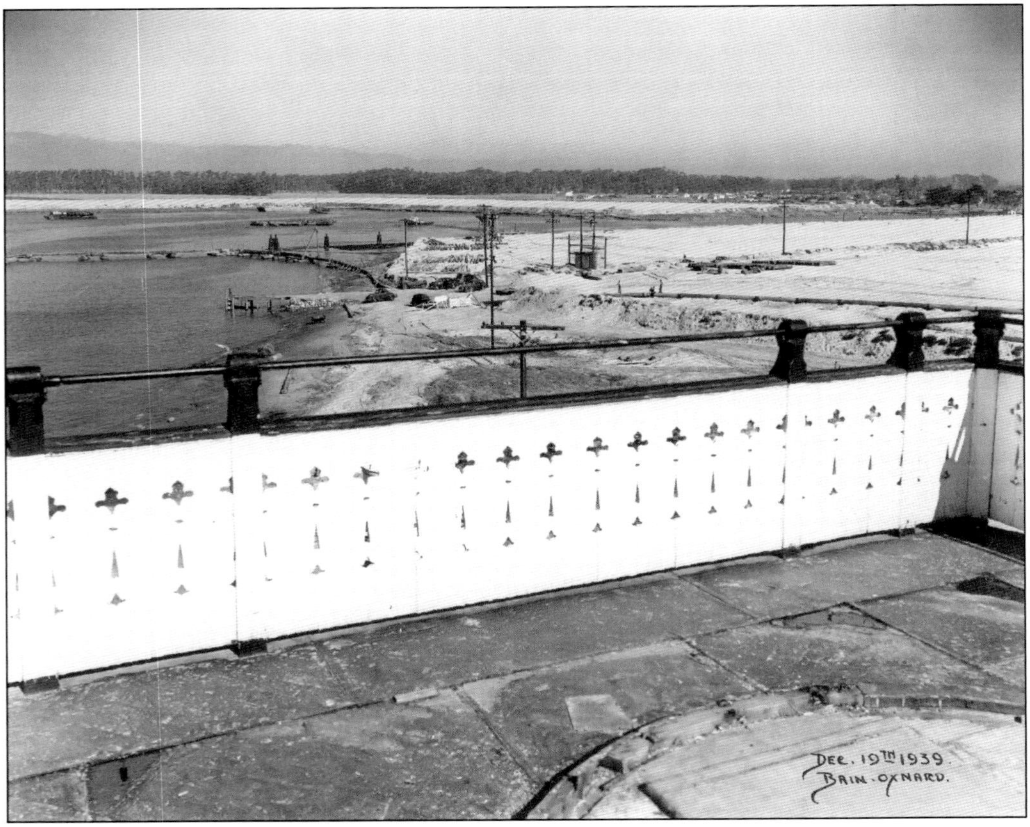

A small crowd gathered atop the lighthouse to witness the raising of the Hueneme Yacht Club flag. One report is that the yacht club had purchased the lighthouse for what was to be their future headquarters. (Courtesy Port Hueneme Historical Society.)

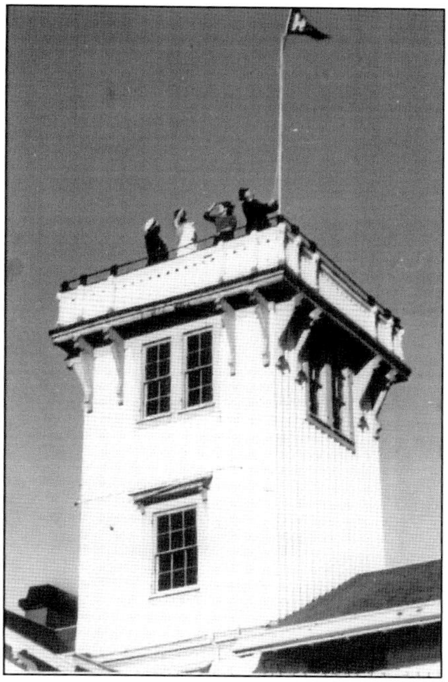

Keeper Walter White poses for what would be his last watch on the original Point Hueneme Lighthouse following its move to the Silver Strand side. (Courtesy Laverne White-Dornberger.)

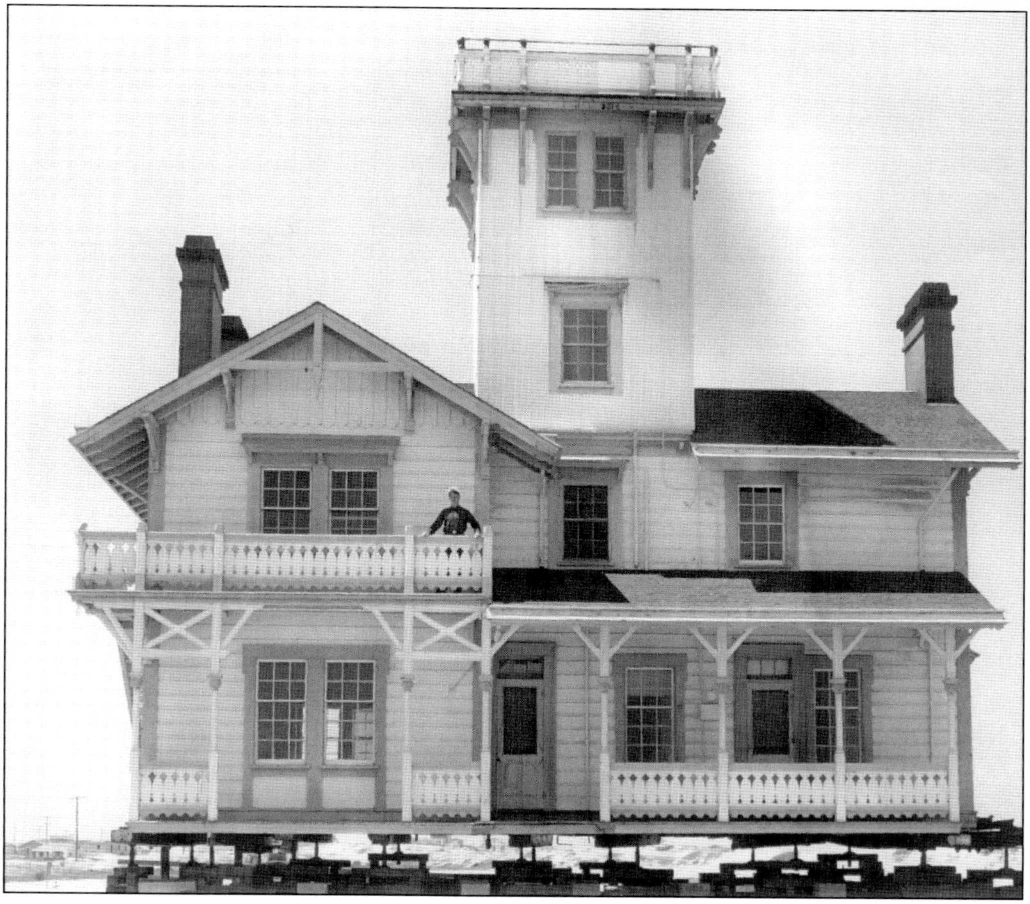

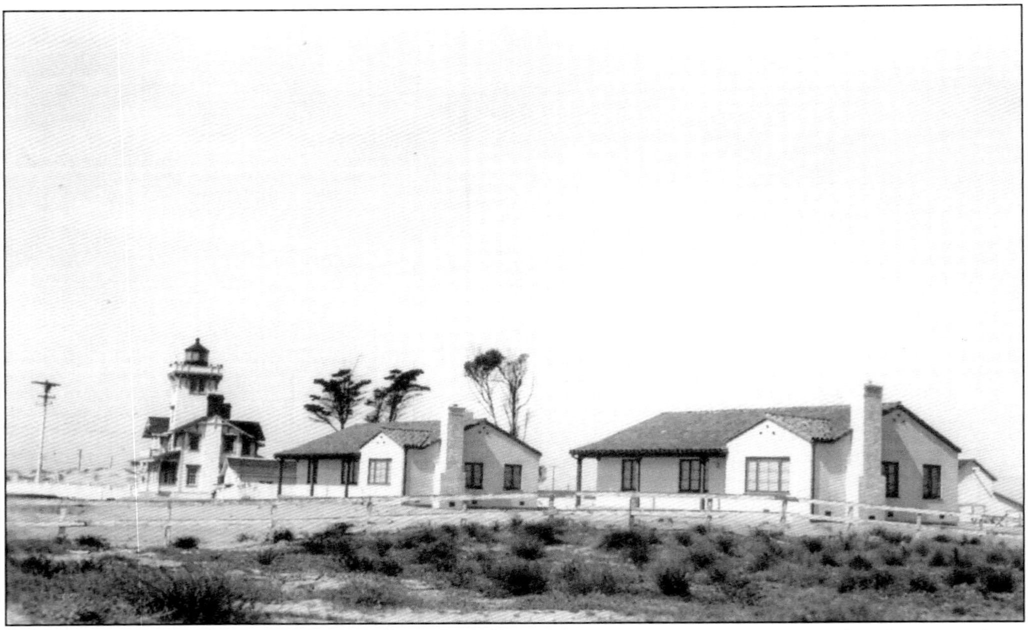

The lighthouse keeper's quarters and assistant keeper's quarters were constructed and put in place prior to the completion of the harbor. As seen here in 1939, the lighthouse is in the background. (Courtesy Ventura County Museum of History and Art.)

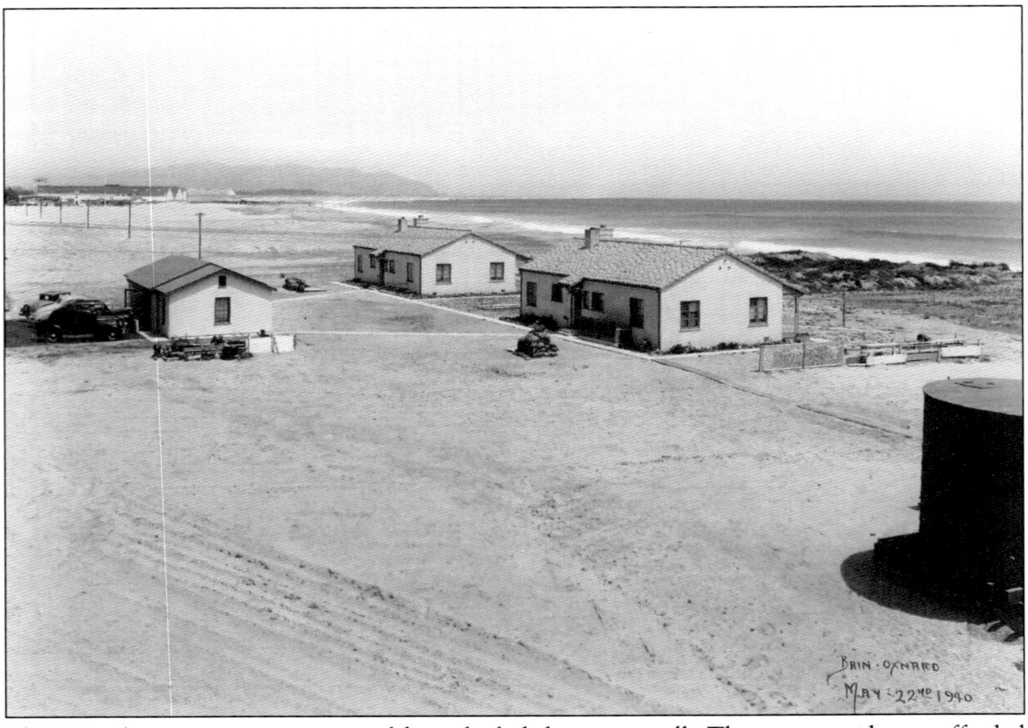

These are the new cottages as viewed from the lighthouse catwalk. These new residences afforded the keeper and assistant keeper families more privacy than they were accustomed to in the original, but unfortunately also offered less space. The shoreline in front of the cottages was extended when additional sand was brought in. (Courtesy Ventura County Museum of History and Art.)

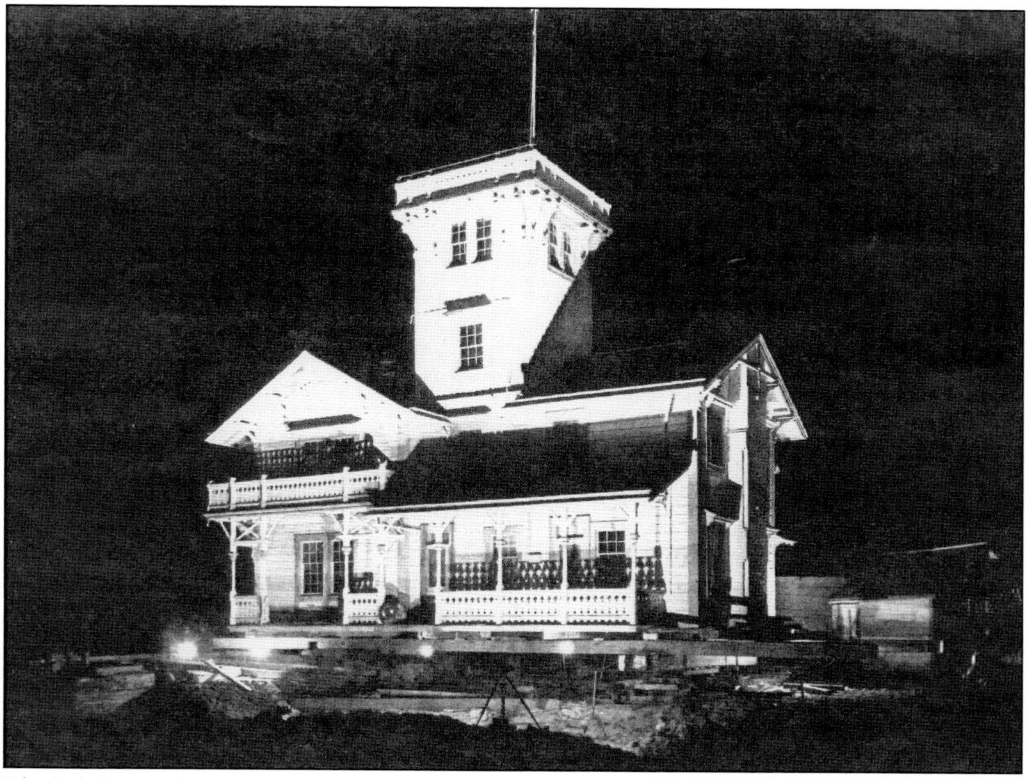

The lighthouse that once shone into the darkness finds itself the focus of the light. With its lantern room removed along with the Fresnel lens, the lighthouse is undergoing final preparations for its transport across the harbor. (Courtesy Laverne White-Dornberger.)

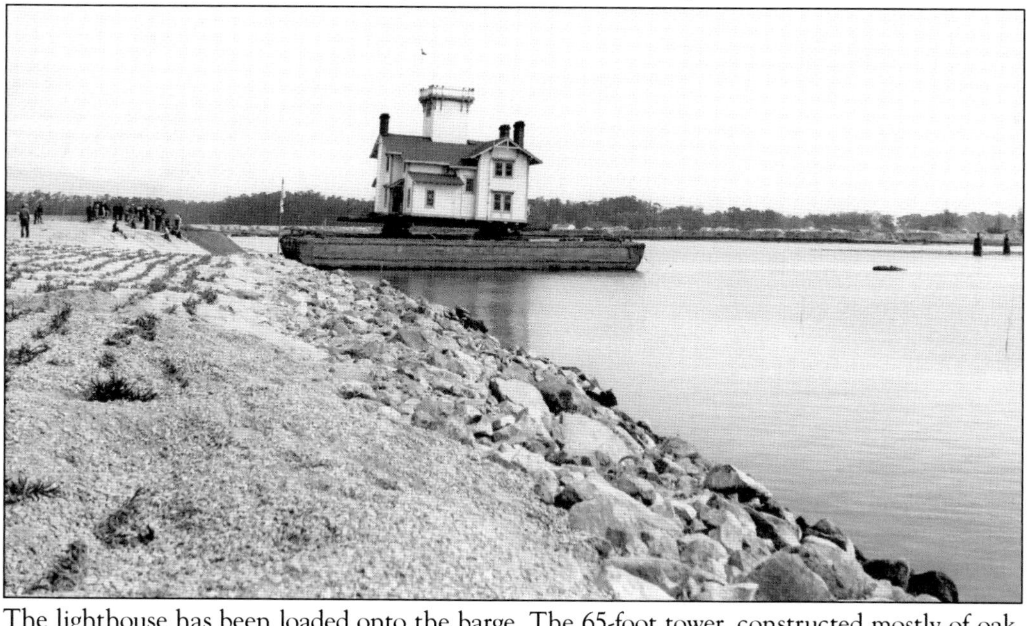

The lighthouse has been loaded onto the barge. The 65-foot tower, constructed mostly of oak, weighed 100 tons and was under the supervision of the John Brakey moving company. (Courtesy Ventura County Museum of History and Art.)

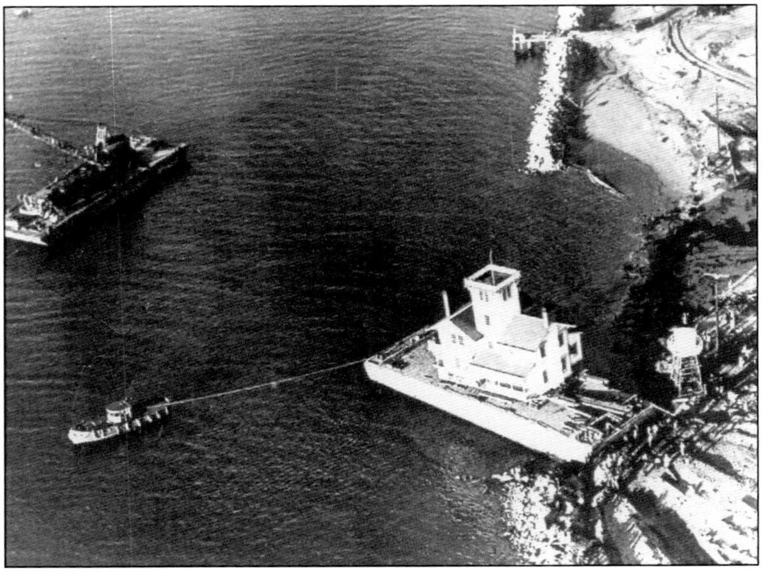

The lighthouse is on the water and being pulled by a small tugboat across the harbor to the Silver Strand side. The actual move started on February 15, 1940, and was completed on February 18, 1940. (Courtesy Ventura County Museum of History and Art.)

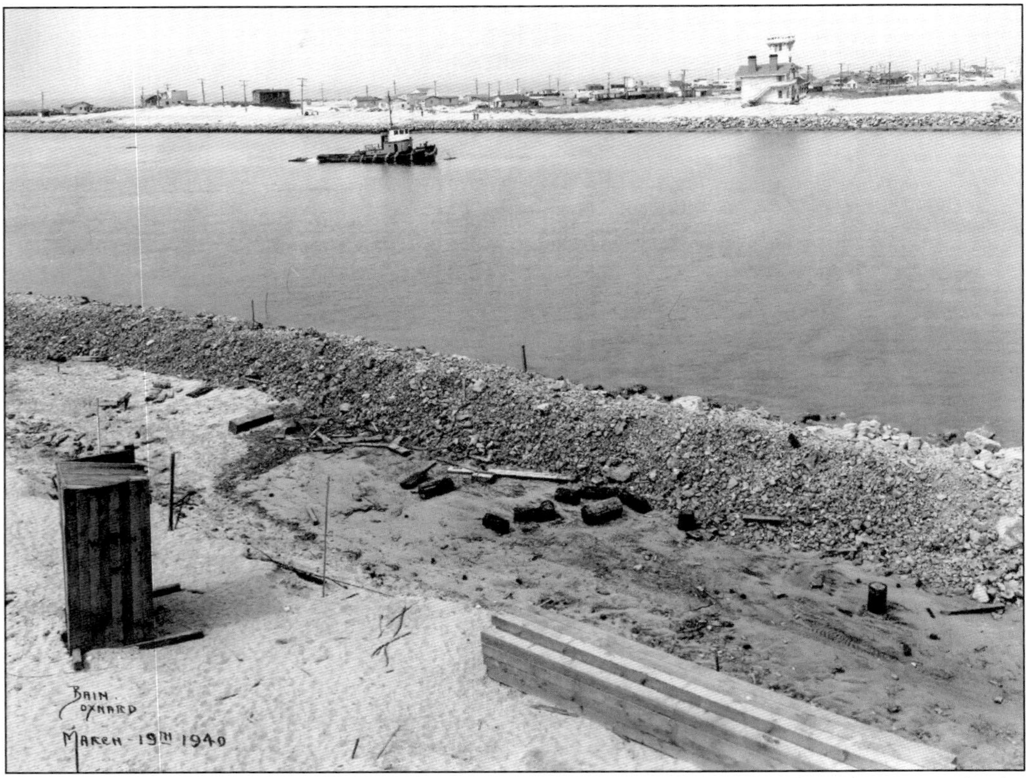

A tugboat passes by the lighthouse after it is moved to the west bank, or the Silver Strand side. One written report states that the American Legion was the only bidder at public auction and purchased it for $51. Others say it was the Hueneme Yacht Club that purchased the structure. In either case, the main problem was that it was too costly to move the structure once more (this time by truck) to its next location, in addition to the expense of securing it to a new foundation. Unfortunately, with all the effort to save this precious monument, it was eventually razed. (Courtesy Port Hueneme Historical Society.)

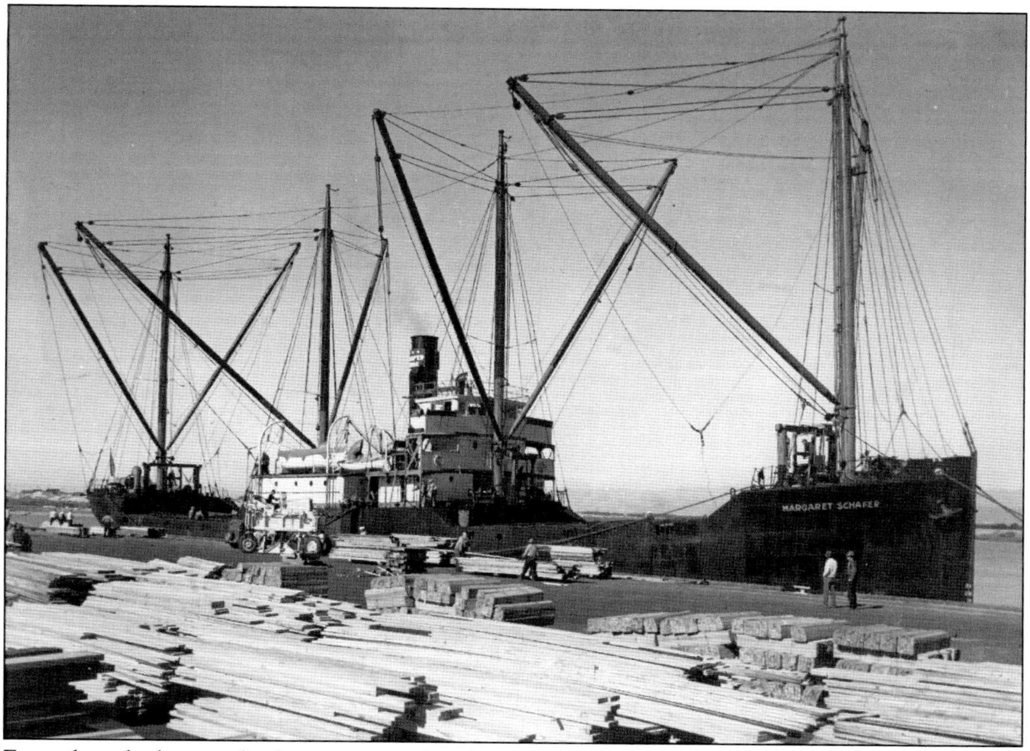

Even though the new harbor was completed in July, it went without ships until January 3, 1941, when a labor dispute from rival unions ended and 500,000 feet of lumber from the freighter *Margaret Schafer* was unloaded. Several hundred district residents, farmers, businessmen, and families gathered to watch the freighter as it entered port shortly before midnight and moved up to the new dock where it remained for the night. Early the next morning, CIO longshoremen began unloading the ship, while AFL longshoremen took the lumber from the dock and stacked it near the transit shed. That same morning, harbor authorities and civic leaders throughout Ventura paid an official visit to the first ship. The *Margaret Schafer*, after unloading, was scheduled to leave that night for Aberdeen, Washington. (Both courtesy Port Hueneme Historical Society.)

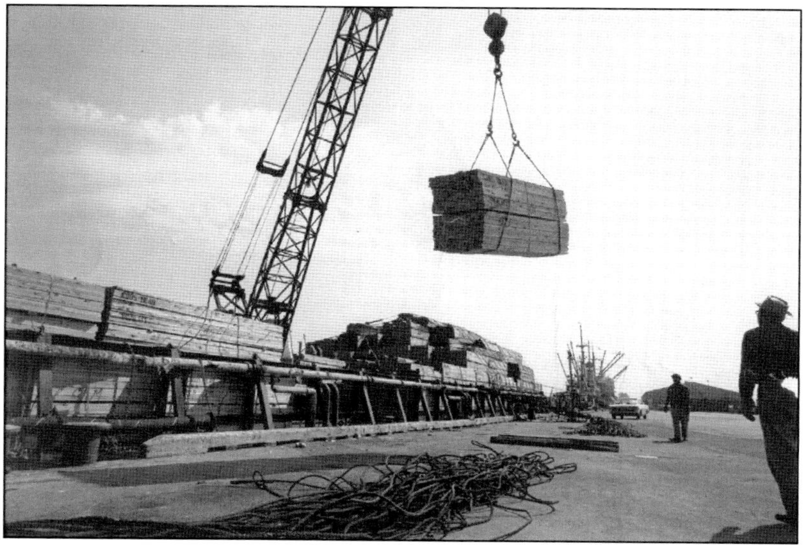

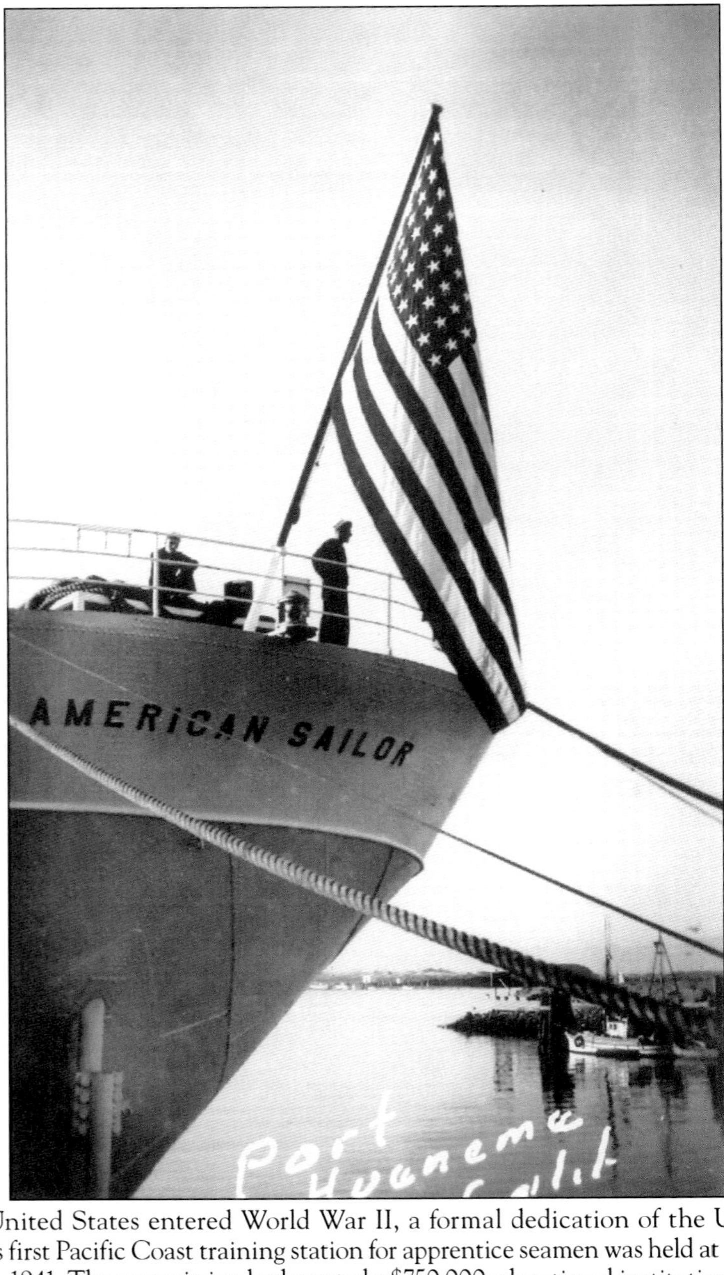

Before the United States entered World War II, a formal dedication of the U.S. Maritime Commission's first Pacific Coast training station for apprentice seamen was held at Port Hueneme on August 30, 1941. The commission had erected a $750,000 educational institution that provided seamen training for the expanding American merchant marine. *American Sailor*, formerly the 6,865-gross-ton freighter *Edgemont*, completed its 6,000-mile voyage to Port Hueneme on schedule and participated in the ceremonies. Converted at a cost of $1.75 million, *American Sailor*, which was the commission's new training ship, was assigned to the Port Hueneme station. It was converted from a freighter into one of the largest and most modern vessels and was considered to be the finest training ship in the world. On board were trainees who had already received preliminary shore training at the Hoffman Island Station at New York. The Oxnard Harbor District made docking facilities for *American Sailor* and land adjacent for recreational facilities available to the commission without cost. (Courtesy Port Hueneme Historical Society.)

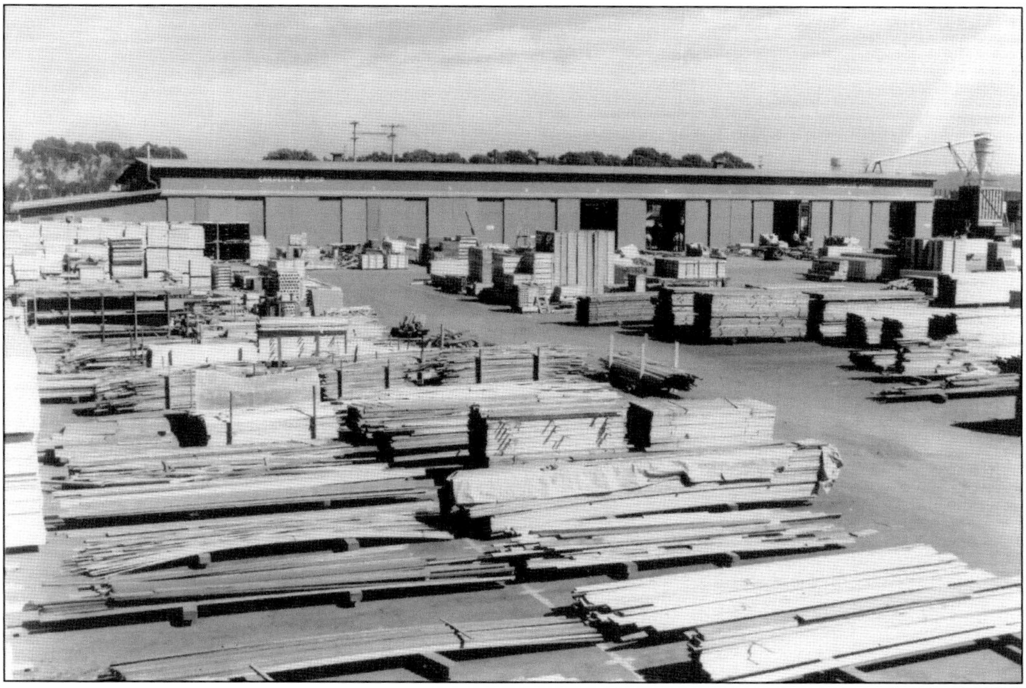

Following the outbreak of the war in the Pacific, the navy took over control of the port on March 5, 1942. The new lumberyard (above) at the Advance Base Depot became the largest lumberyard in the world. A Seabee advance base and an amphibious-landing training school were also constructed. By the end of the war, Hueneme's wharves where handling 150,000 tons of cargo a month. (Courtesy Port Hueneme Historical Society.)

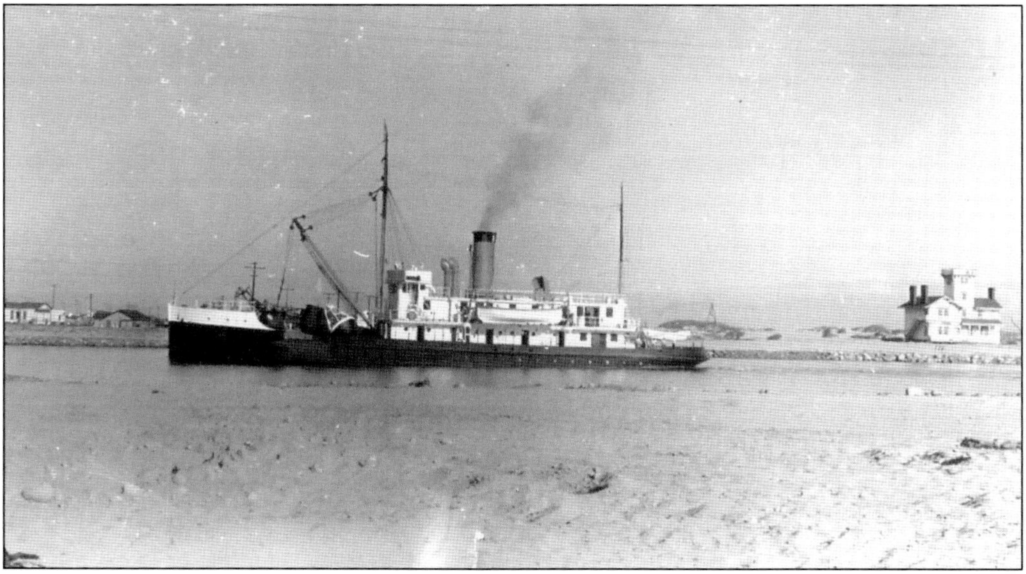

The lighthouse tender *Lupine*, originally assigned to the 18th Lighthouse District, was transferred to the Naval District in 1943, taking it from San Francisco to San Pedro, California. Here it is sailing out of the newly constructed Port Hueneme. The lighthouse, shown on the far right, has already been moved to the west bank. (Courtesy Charles Johnson, Ventura County Museum of History and Art.)

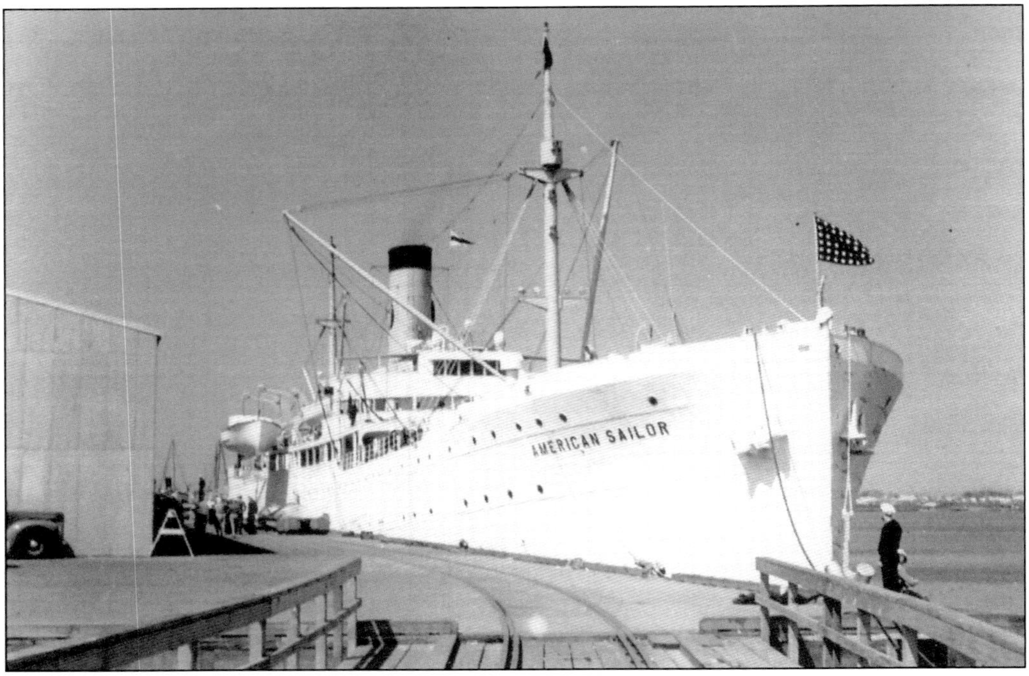

American Sailor docks at Port Hueneme while a young boy (below) is taking in its splendor. (Both courtesy Port Hueneme Historical Society.)

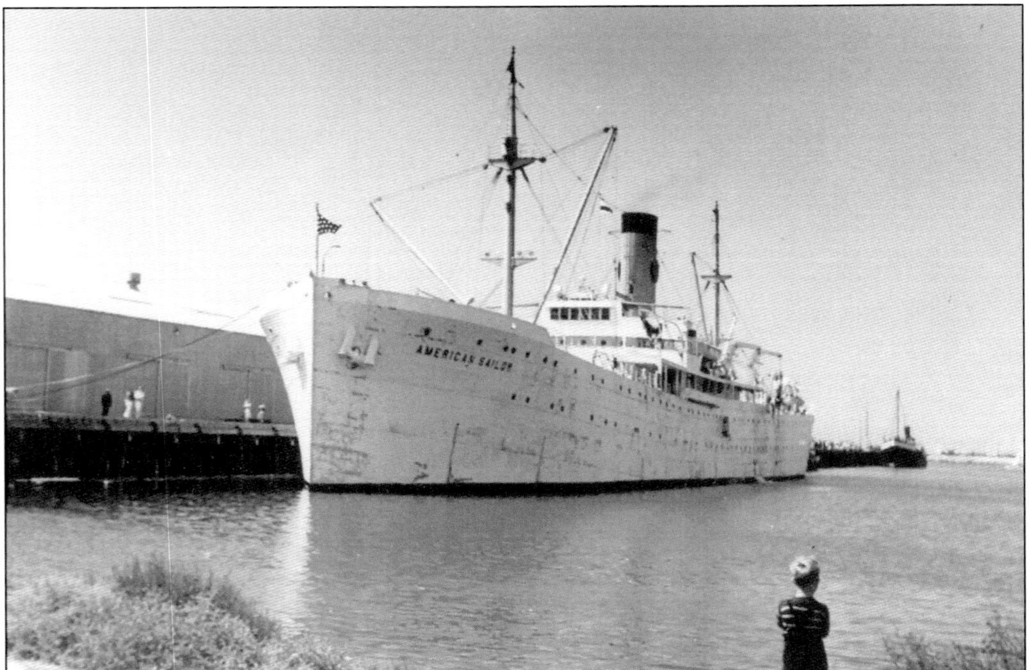

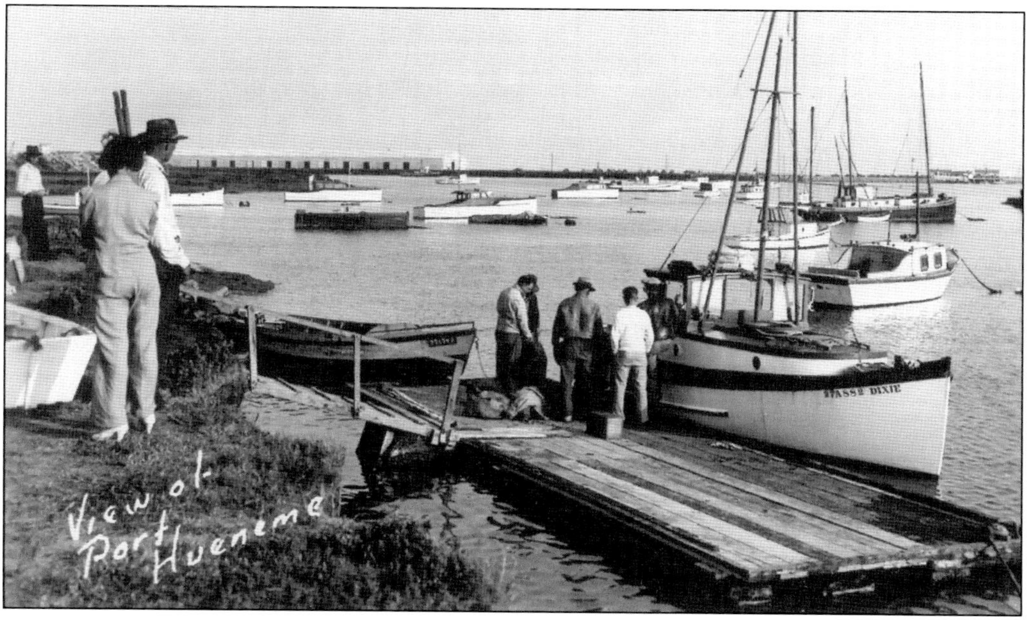

Boats are shown here in the late 1940s. With the new harbor, recreational boating increased as well. As advertised, "From sea to mountains, practically every form of outdoor recreation can be enjoyed. Boating, swimming, surf and deep sea fishing, hiking, hunting, relaxation in beach or mountain cottages is constantly increasing." (Both courtesy Port Hueneme Historical Society.)

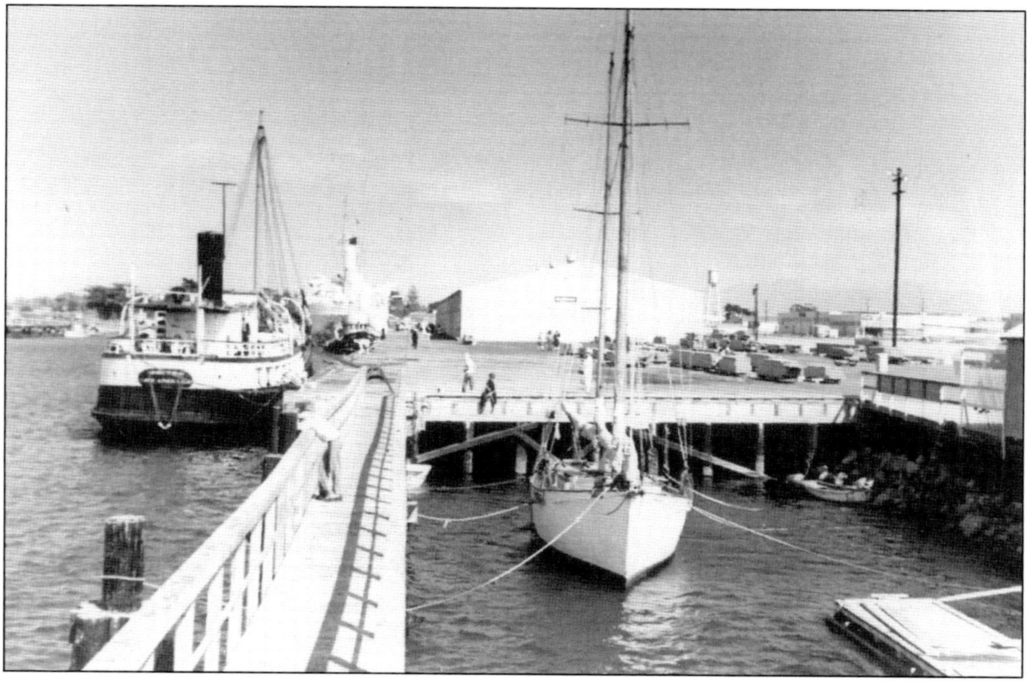

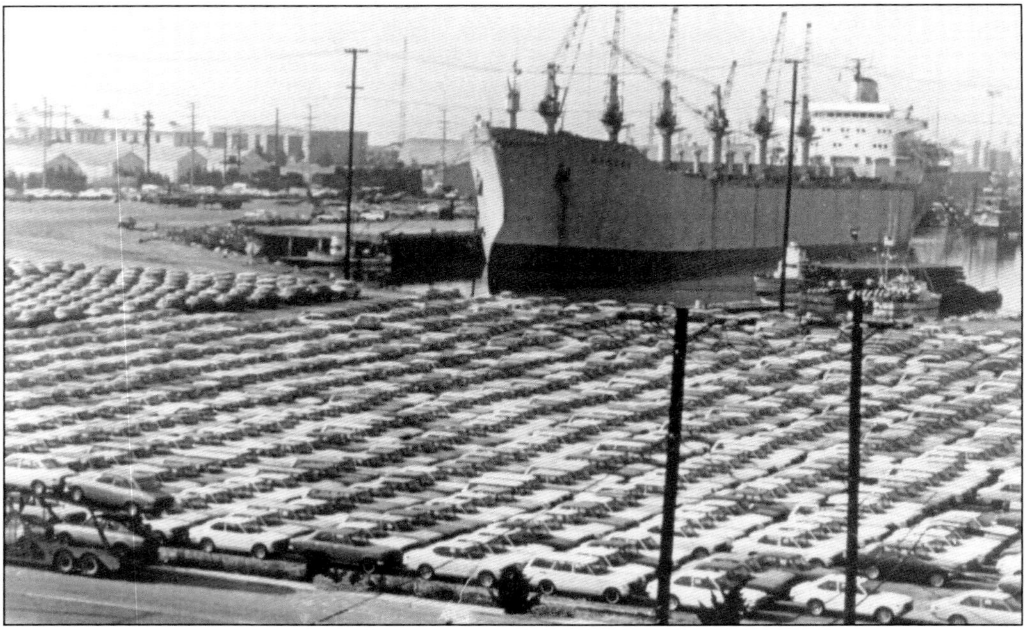

Acres of Mazda automobiles from Japan, pictured here in the 1970s, are seen on the on-dock auto terminal area. The arrival of Mazda Motors of North America in 1977 became the port's new gem, handling 17,300 automobiles from 1977 to 1978. (Courtesy Port Hueneme Historical Society.)

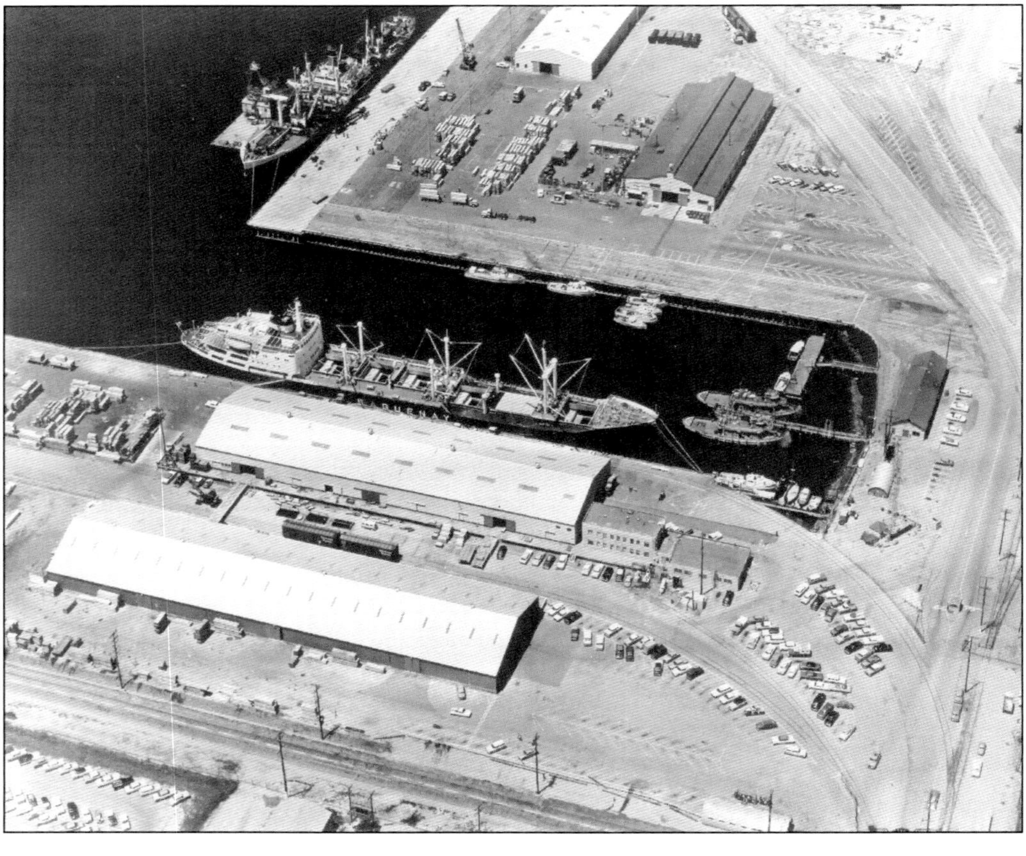

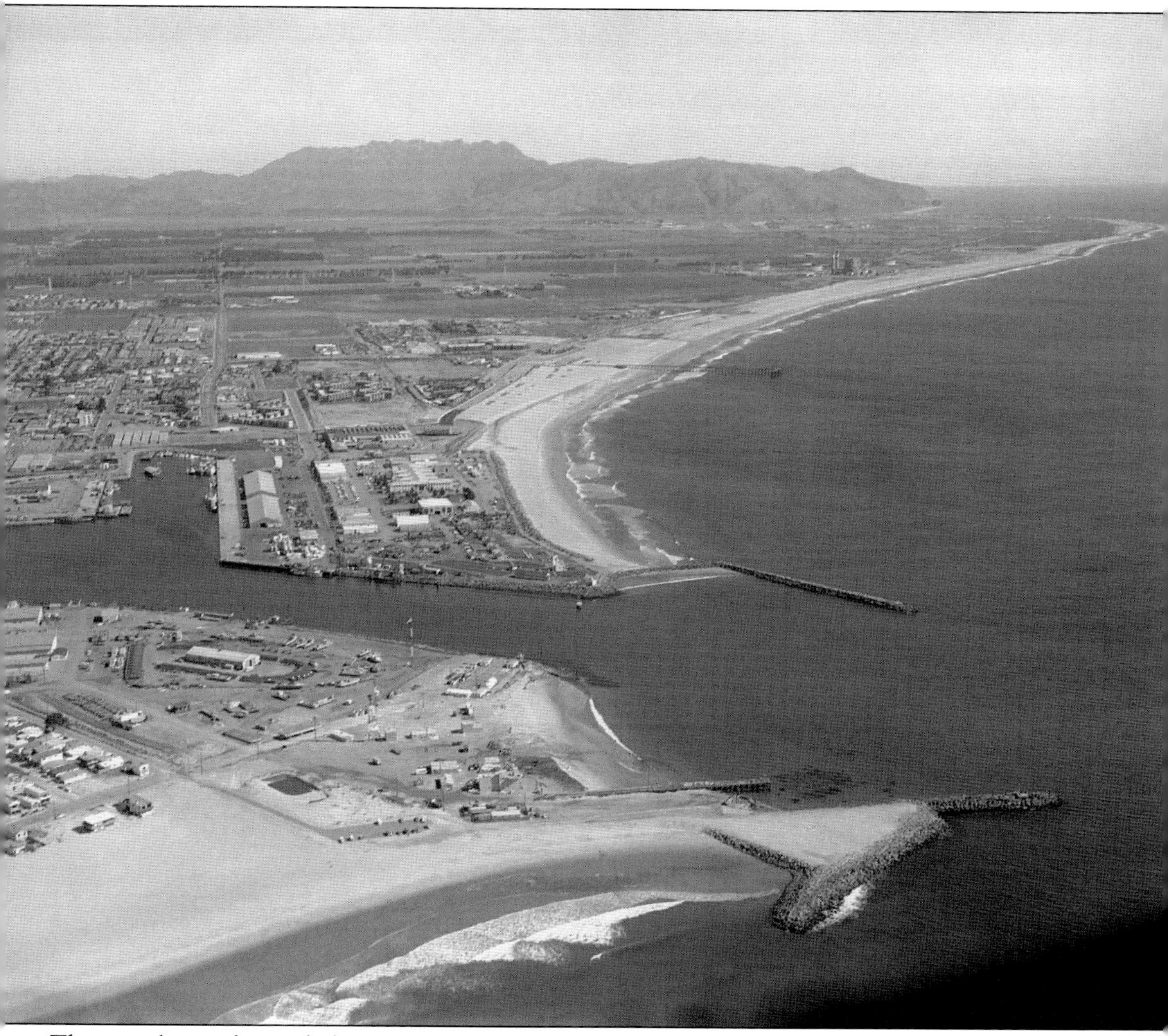

This aerial view from a helicopter shows the harbor entrance in 1950. Port Hueneme is jointly operated by the U.S. Navy and the Oxnard Harbor District. It is the only deepwater harbor between Los Angeles and San Francisco and is the U.S. port of entry for California's central coast region. It ranks among the top seaports in California for general cargo. Today Port Hueneme handles over $7 billion in cargo each year. (Courtesy U.S. Coast Guard.)

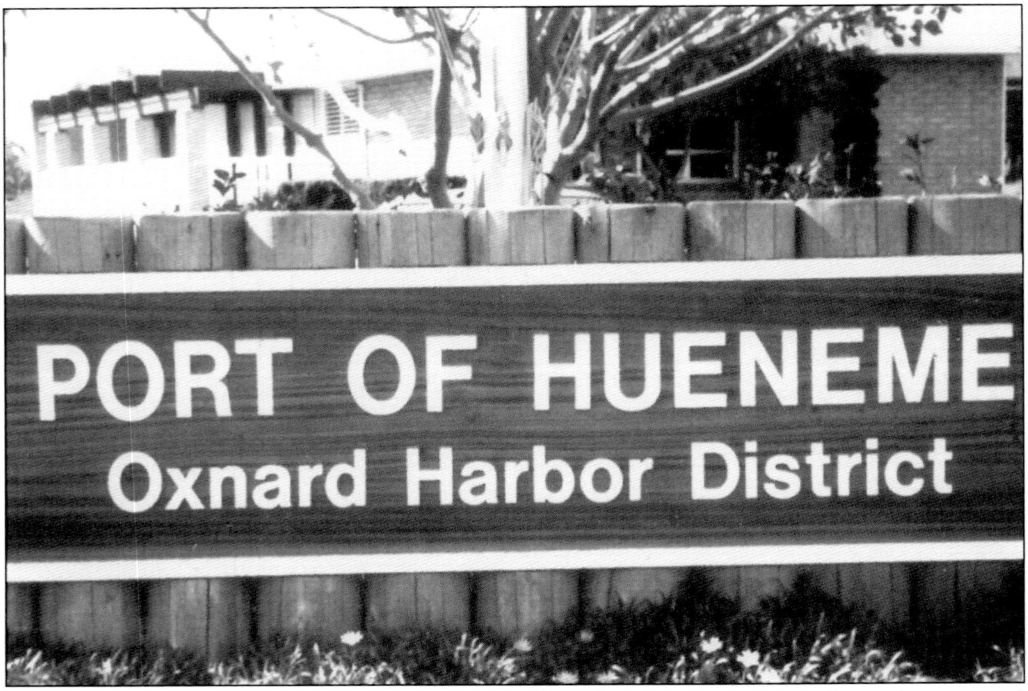

According to its own description, "The Oxnard Harbor District is an independent special district (business enterprise) a political subdivision of the State of California which owns and operates the commercial Port of Hueneme. The District was created in 1937 under authority of an act of the legislature of the State of California which provides for the formation of Harbor Districts." The Oxnard Harbor District receives no taxes for its operations, depending only on port business–generated funds. Harry Pollack and Leo Ramirez (below), are standing outside the Harbor District headquarters in the 1970s. (Both courtesy Port Hueneme Historical Society.)

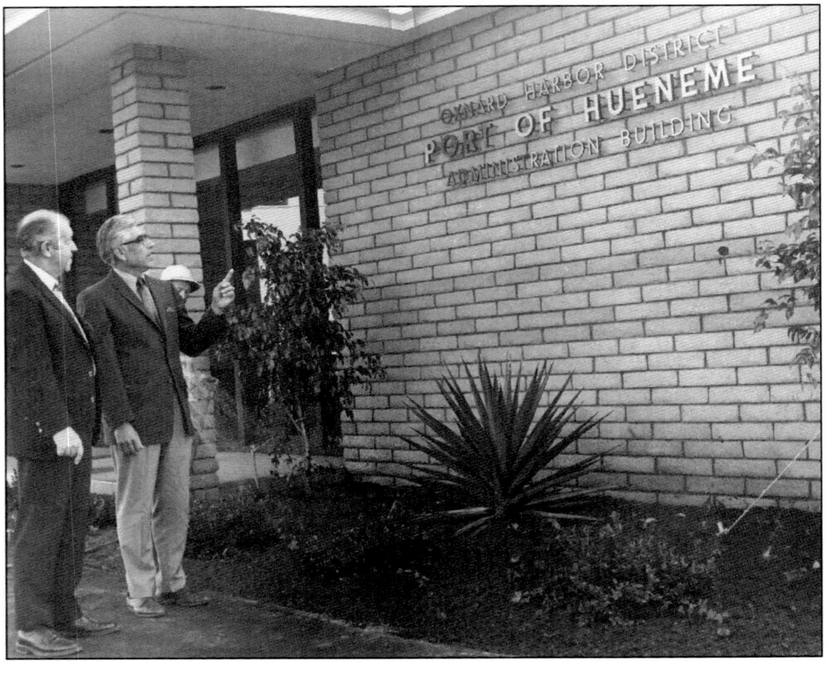

Today, the Port of Hueneme ranks among the top seaports in California for general cargo. The *Los Angeles Times* dubbed Hueneme "The Little Port That Could" in 2005, stating that "experts call Hueneme one of the nation's best examples of a niche port." The port serves import and export of automobiles, heavy agricultural equipment and industrial vehicles, fresh fruit, fresh produce, forest products, and project cargo. It is the top seaport in the United States for citrus export and ranks among the top ten ports in the country for automobile and banana imports. The sign in the photo to the right is in the South Terminal area of the port, which handles the perishable cargoes. Some of the perishable cargoes going out include citrus. Incoming cargoes include bananas and melons. (Both courtesy of Kim Castro-Bran.)

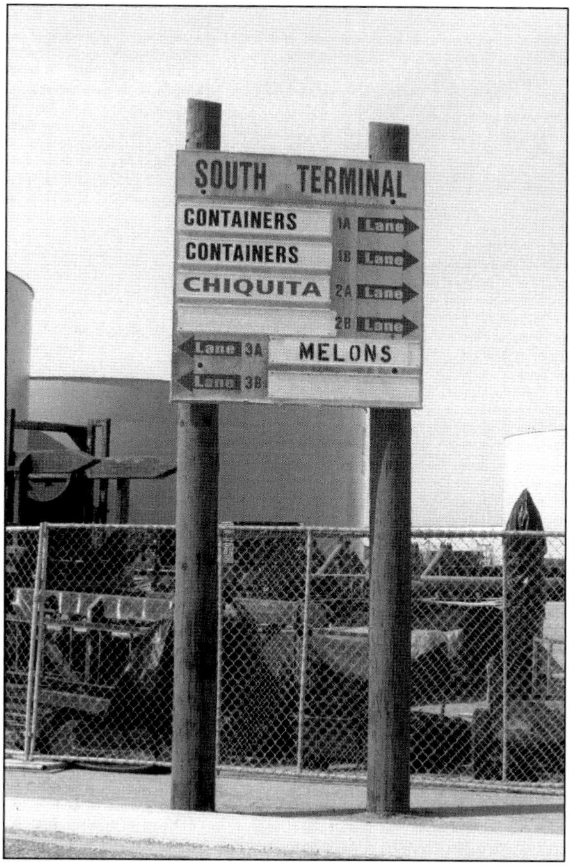

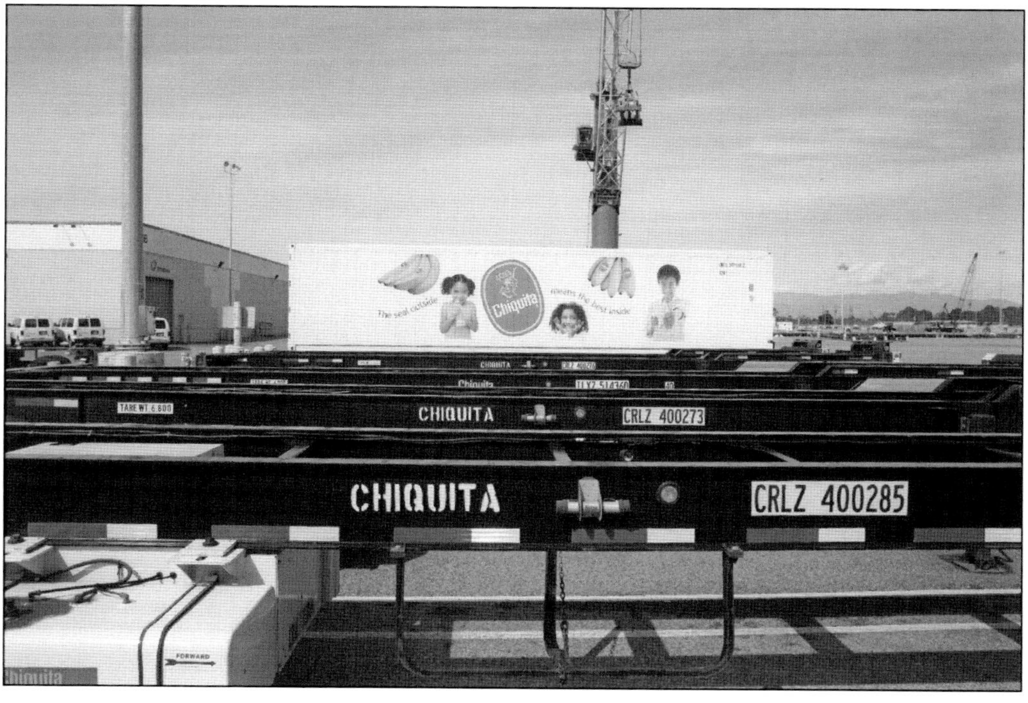

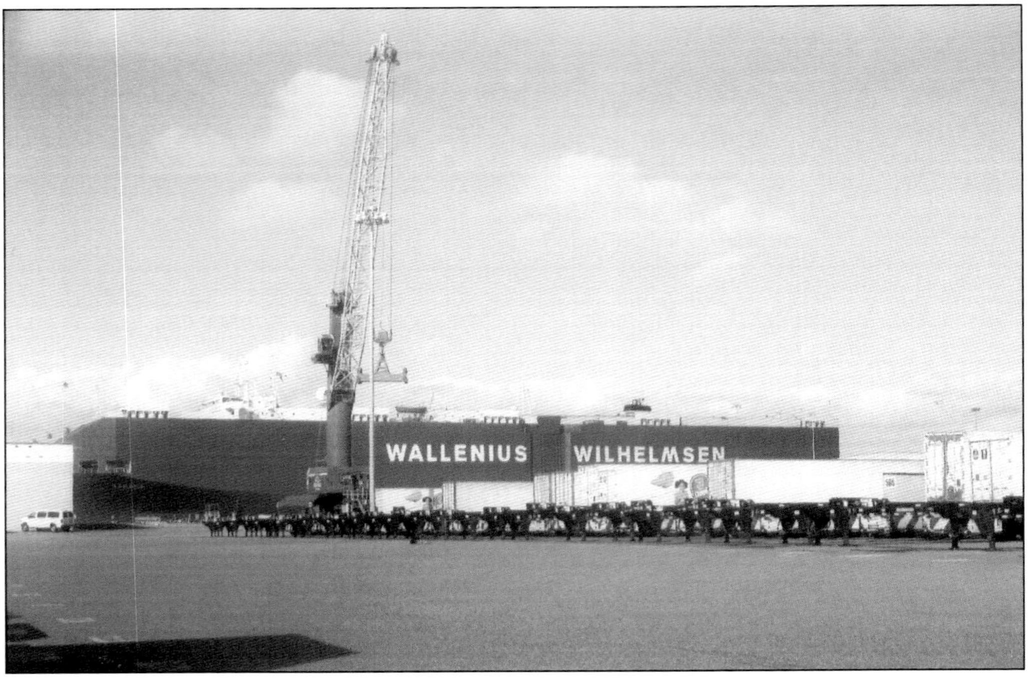

The Port of Hueneme is also one of the nation's top 10 in automobile imports, with some of its primary trading partners being Germany, Sweden, Japan, and Korea. The port has made acres of on-dock auto terminals available for automobile carriers worldwide. Port Hueneme has put emphasis on the automobile and roll-on/roll-off trade, reinforcing its continued growth. Wallenius Wilhelmsen Logistics carriers (above and below) show the size of these car carriers. (Both author's collection.)

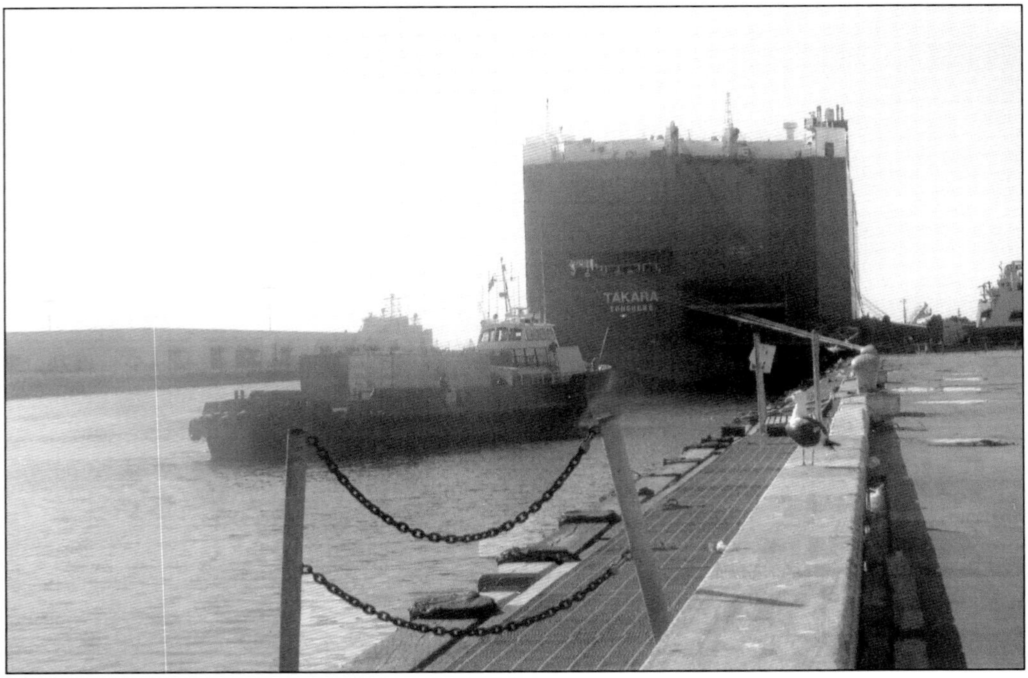

Five

Point Hueneme

A New Light

With the new port's construction, the Lighthouse Service decided that a new lighthouse structure also would be needed since the original building would stand too close to the harbor's edge to be utilized. The new structure was a model of its time. The 1920s and 1930s experienced the rise of the architectural designs of art deco and art moderne. The Lighthouse Service incorporated this design style for some lighthouses. The majority of these structures were being constructed in Alaska and the Pacific Northwest, but they included a site in Southern California: Point Hueneme.

Unlike any other lighthouse in California, this new light in Hueneme was a drastic departure from the more traditional house-like buildings or cylindrical-style structures more commonly identified with lighthouses. Nonetheless, Hueneme's new look ushered in a new chapter in the growth and development of the Ventura County area, along with the recently completed port-harbor complex of Port Hueneme in 1941.

The lighthouse is located at the entrance to Port Hueneme, the only deepwater commercial port between Los Angeles and San Francisco. This new and present-day structure stands 52 feet above sea level. There are 40 gently slanting steps that lead up to the tower, with the last 11 steps almost ladderlike. Climbing through the entrance in the floor of the top deck, one comes face to face with the jewel of the lighthouse, the Fresnel lens. The light of the Fresnel lens can be seen 12 to 15 miles out at sea, depending on the height of the observer and visibility conditions. The light is a fourth order Fresnel lens, which was manufactured in 1897, that was brought to the light station in 1899 and then relocated into the present structure in 1941.

The Point Hueneme Lighthouse continues to serve as a valuable aid to navigation to this day for both commercial shipping and recreational boaters.

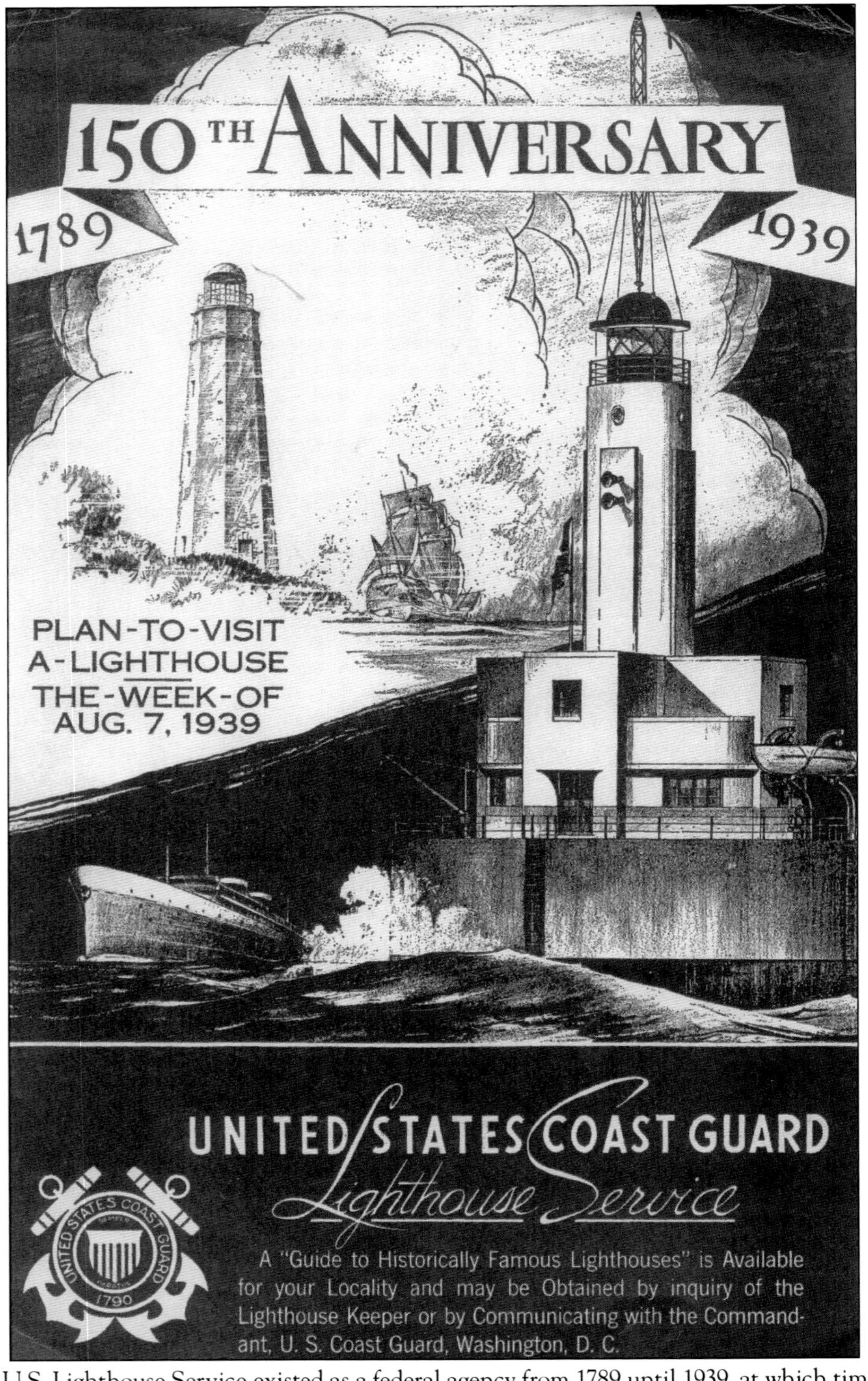

The U.S. Lighthouse Service existed as a federal agency from 1789 until 1939, at which time the Coast Guard absorbed the Lighthouse Service. During World War II, all lighthouse personnel were given the option to enlist as a military member of the Coast Guard or work as a civilian. This unique piece of memorabilia is referring to that transition. (Courtesy Laverne White-Dornberger.)

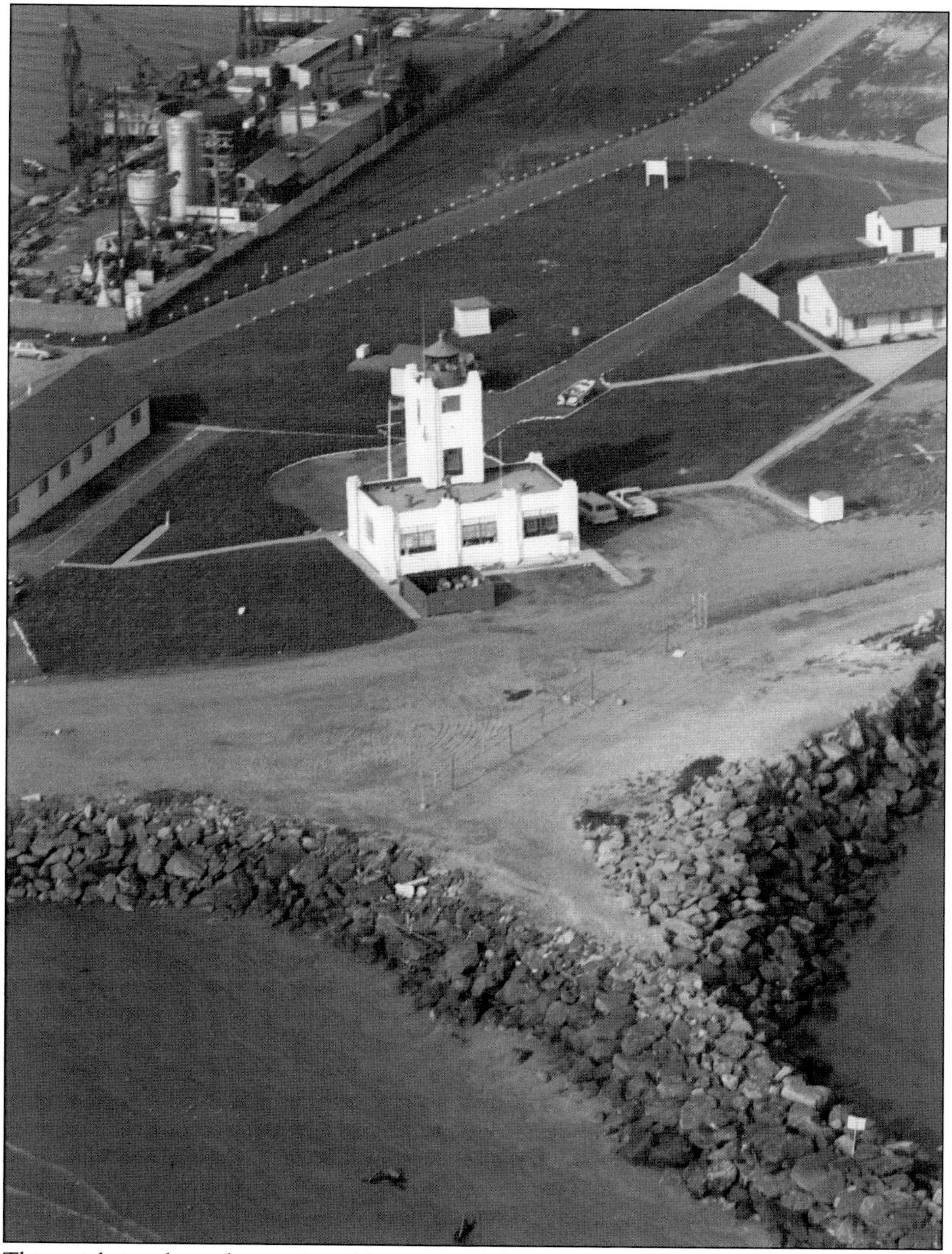

This aerial view shows the new Point Hueneme Lighthouse in 1950. The lighthouse was constructed in 1940 and first lit in 1941. It is an art moderne–style structure and today is 70 years old. The lighthouse has already served five years longer than its predecessor, and over the years, it has become an expression of architectural trends and a time capsule of its era. It is a representation of the last generation of manned lighthouses that will ever be built. Often interchangeable, both terms "Port" or "Point" are used to refer to the lighthouse. It is the Point Hueneme Lighthouse in the city of Port Hueneme. (Courtesy U.S. Coast Guard.)

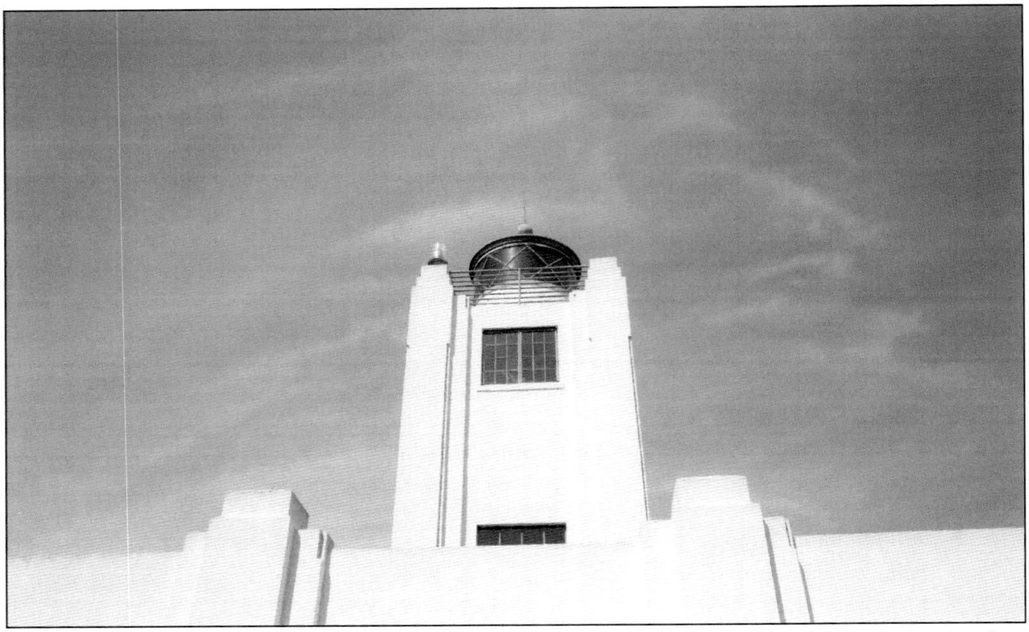

Art deco and its immediate successor, art moderne, were two of the fresh architectural styles that emerged from 1920 to 1940. The art moderne and international style have roots in the European movement that shunned the long continuum of architectural tradition that was perceived as fussy, impractical, and excessively ornate. The lighthouse was considered current, practical, and cost-effective for its time. It was a very streamlined approach to lighthouse construction. The second tier of the lighthouse (above) seems to jut out of nowhere, with very sleek lines. The structure was, however, self-contained, allowing the keeper to operate the fog signal and mind the light at the same time. (Both author's collection.)

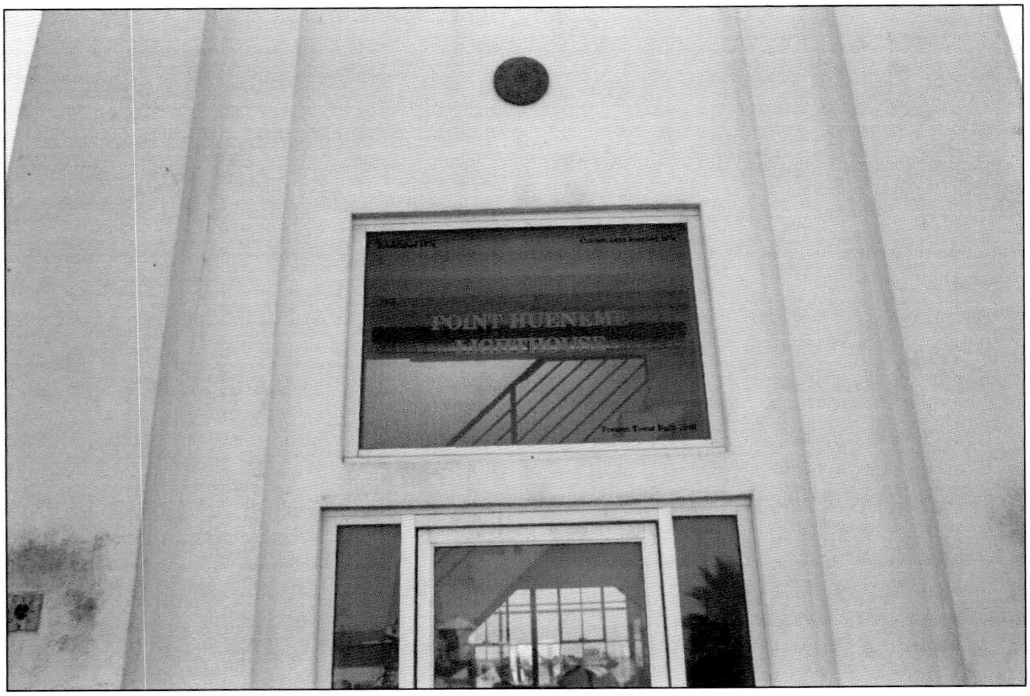

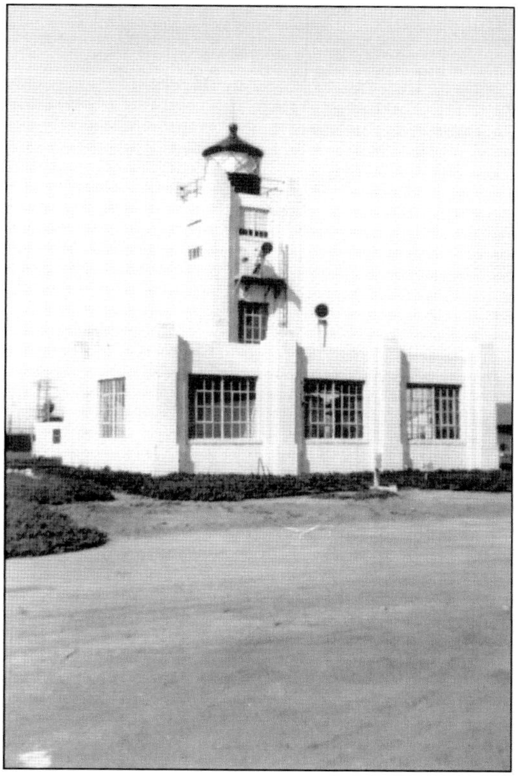

The Point Hueneme Lighthouse (right) is pictured in the 1940s with its foghorn on the outside of the building on the second tier middle window. Walter White (below) has now found himself keeper of the new lighthouse. The fog signal equipment from the first Point Hueneme Lighthouse has been relocated to the first floor of the new Point Hueneme Lighthouse. Walter White is standing next to the Crosby Automatic Signal with his hand on the steam valve and arm running vertical with the steam pipe. It was a vibrating column of air that created the audible tone. (Both courtesy Laverne White-Dornberger.)

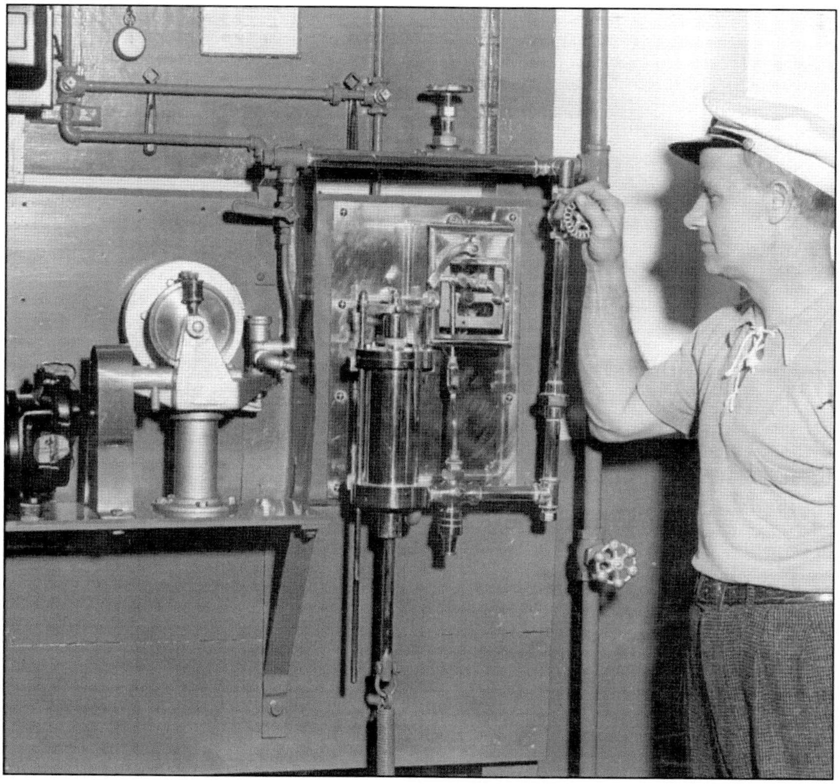

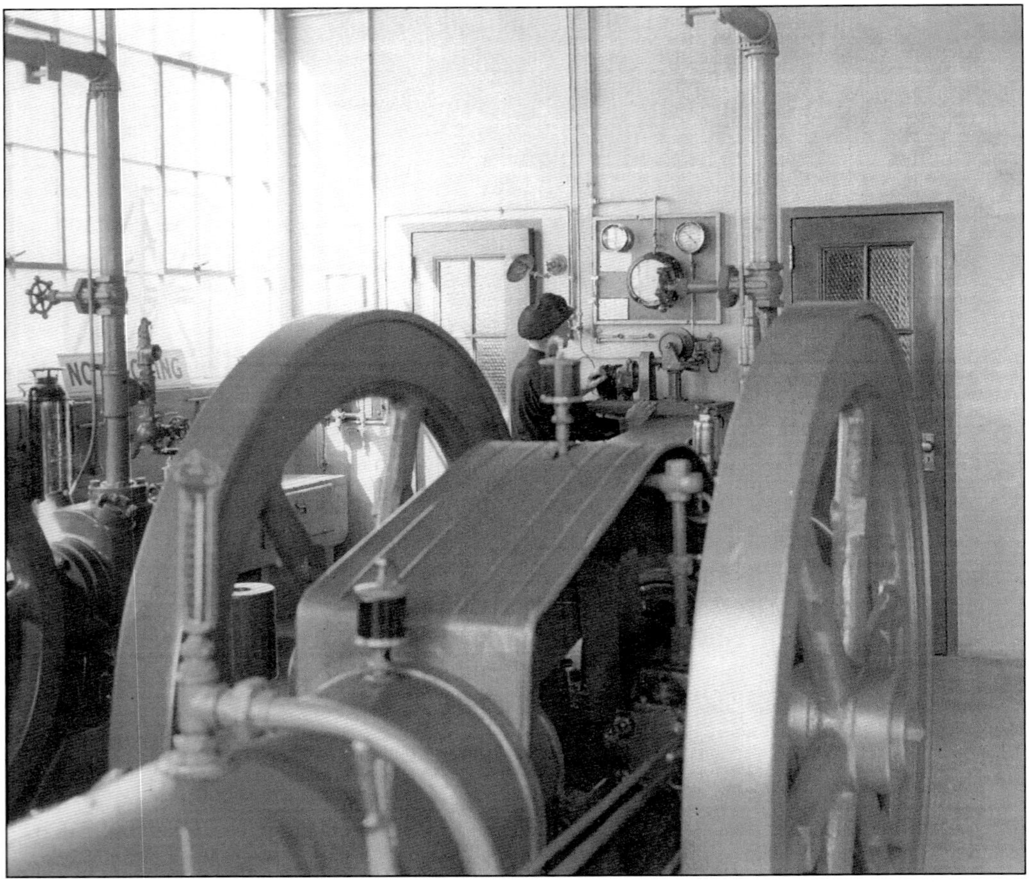

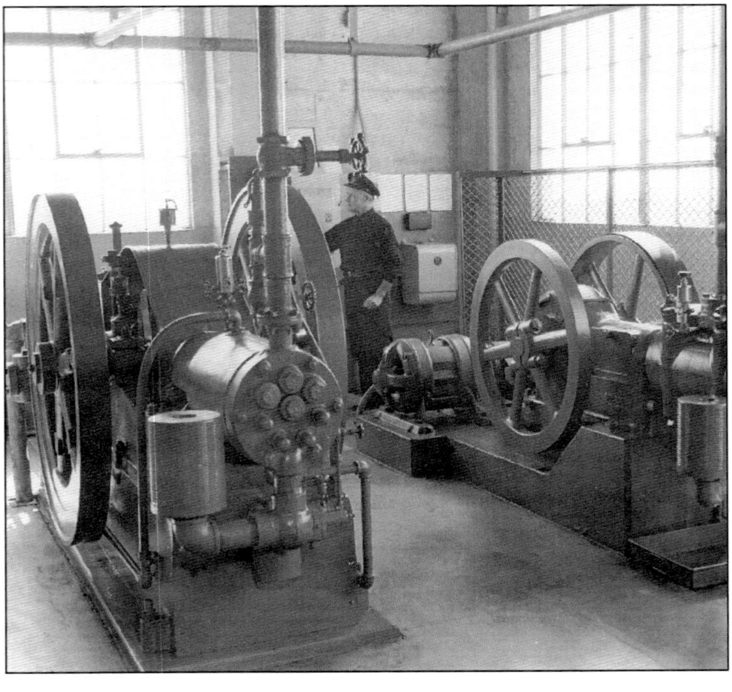

Housed on the first floor of the new lighthouse (above) is the fog signal equipment relocated from the first lighthouse. As shown, the equipment occupied much of the space. Keeper Walter White, pictured here in the 1940s, is seen in the middle of the photograph operating the fog signal equipment. The equipment consisted of a Fairbanks/Morse engine and compressor combination, along with the fog signal timing device (electric and air). (Both courtesy Laverne White-Dornberger.)

The Fresnel lens (right), pictured here in the 1940s, is the second Fresnel lens. It was constructed in 1897 and brought to the lighthouse in 1899. It is a fourth order Fresnel. Fourth orders are generally used for harbors or ports and can shine approximately 12 to 14 miles out to sea. (Courtesy Laverne White-Dornberger.)

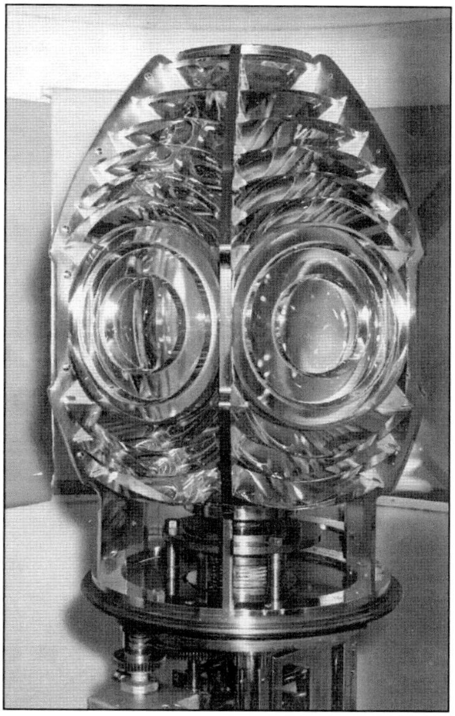

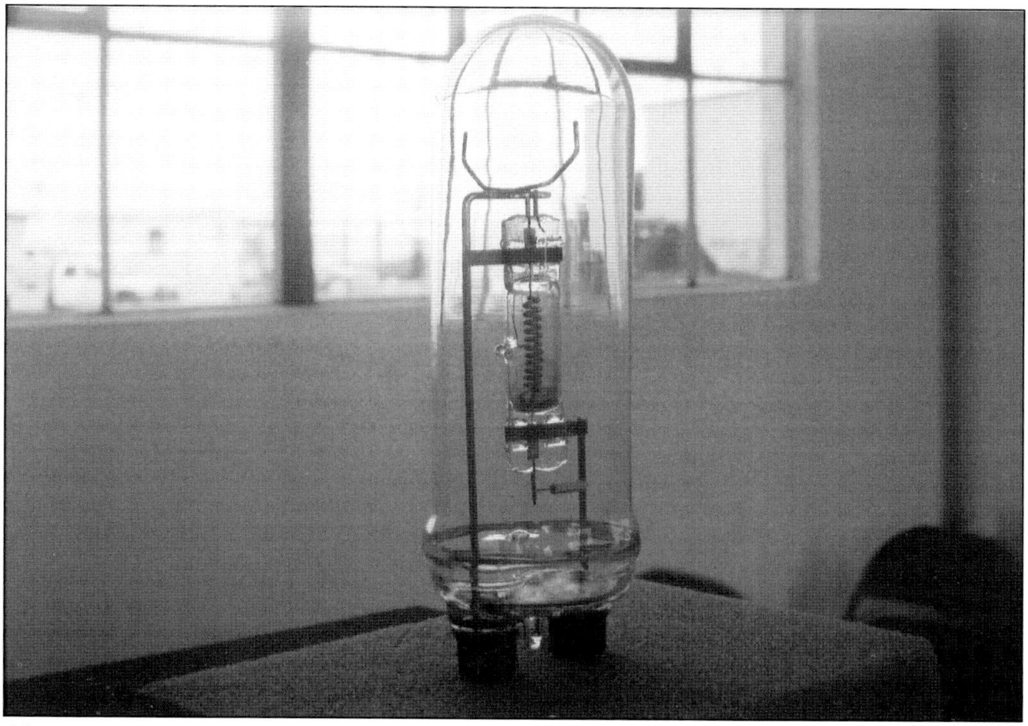

Above is a 1,000-watt lamp used to illuminate the Fresnel lens. Prior to the 1,000-watt lamp, a 500-watt bulb was used. The position of the glass prisms allow them to pick up the rays of light traveling in different directions and bend the light, sending it out in a straight beam for 12 to 14 miles. (Point Hueneme Lighthouse Collection.)

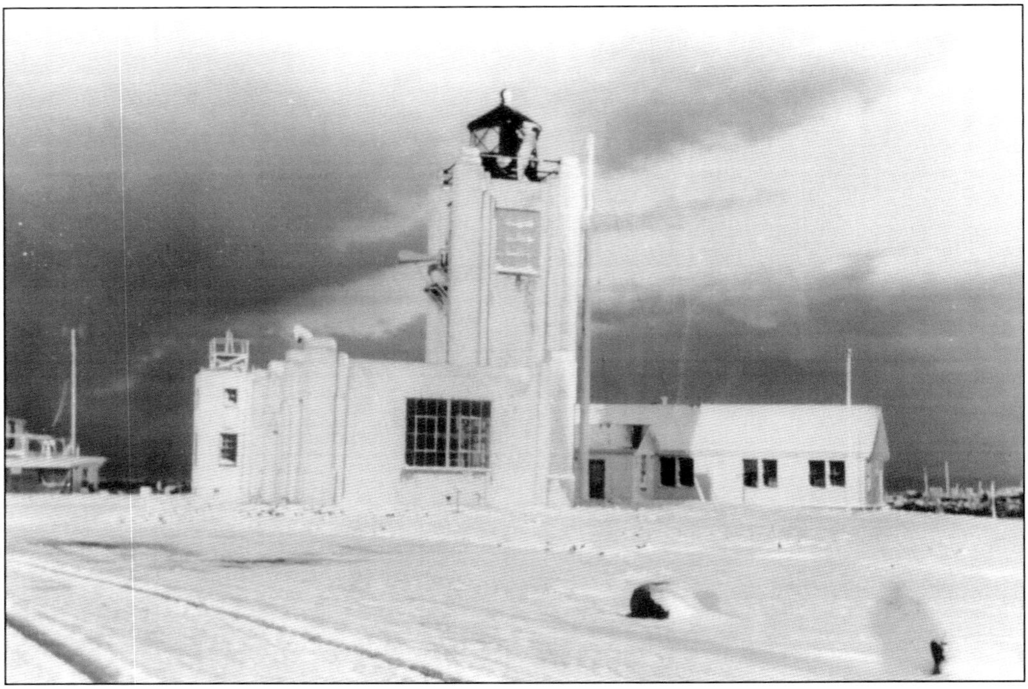

Point Hueneme Lighthouse is pictured here in the 1940s during a heavy storm. Lighthouses are known to have rapid erosion because of the harsh effects of the sea and saltwater spray. (Courtesy Port Hueneme Historical Society.)

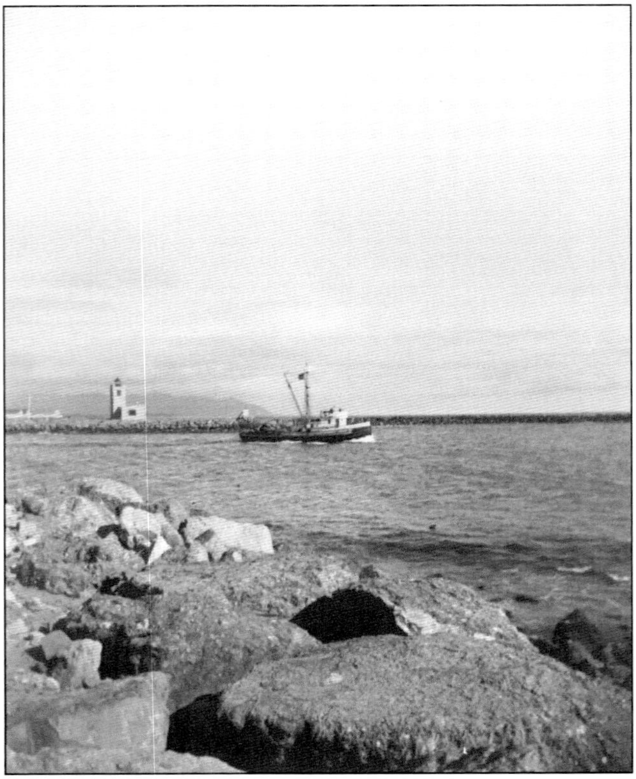

A tugboat passes by in 1940. The lighthouse can be seen in the distance. (Courtesy Port Hueneme Historical Society.)

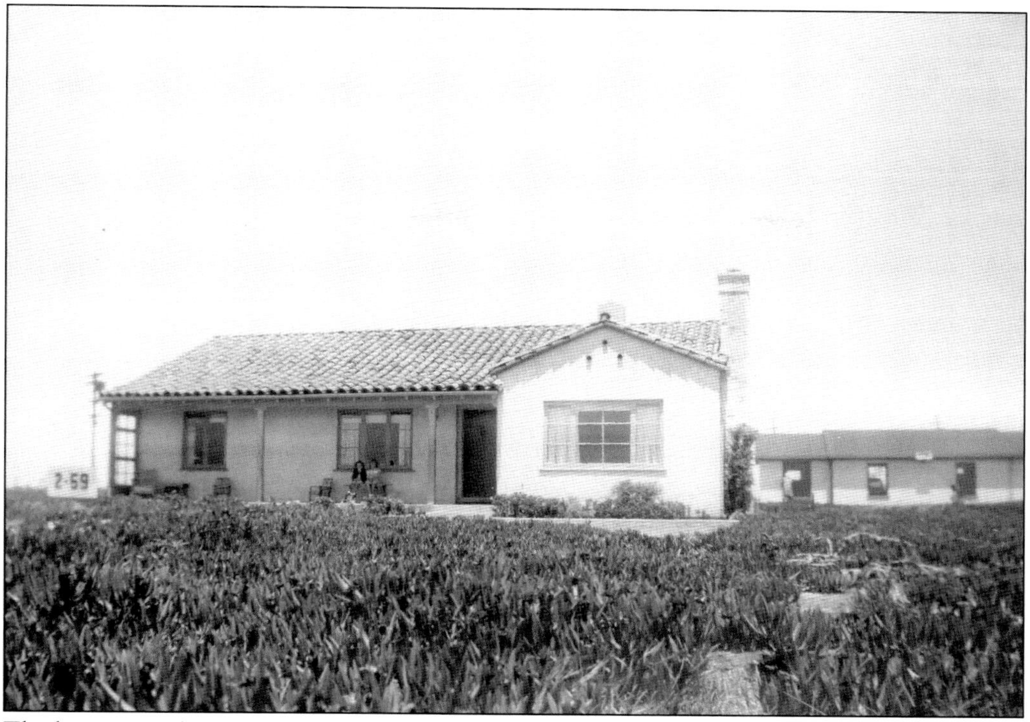

The keeper's and assistant keeper's quarters pictured above and illustrated in the blueprints at right were constructed just prior to the new lighthouse structure. They reflect a Spanish-Mediterranean style with their distinct terracotta roofs. The modest structures afforded the residents some privacy and basic comforts. Today they are leased by the City of Port Hueneme to private ventures. (Courtesy Laverne White-Dornberger.)

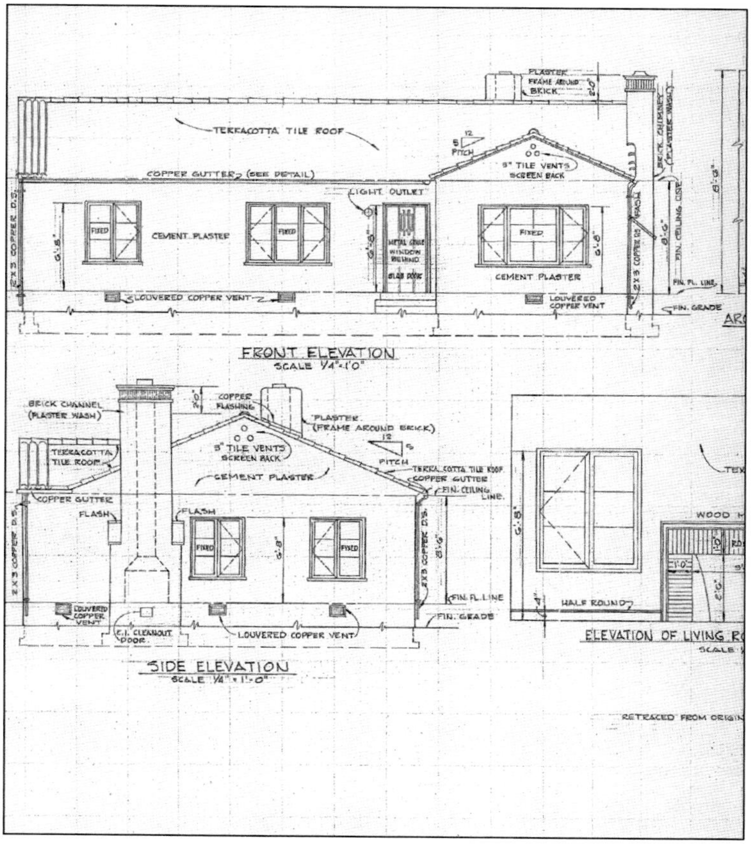

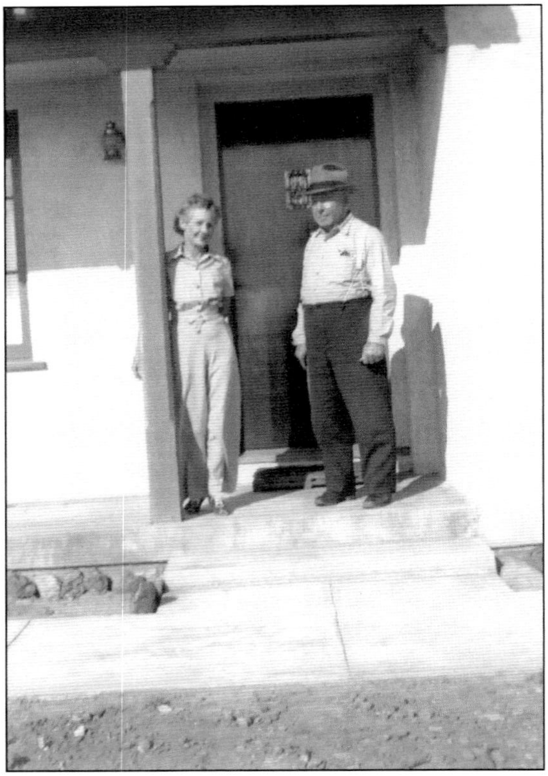

Francis White and O. L. Jenkins, assistant superintendant of the Office of the Superintendant of Lighthouses, 18th District, San Francisco, California, stand outside the keeper's dwelling. (Courtesy Laverne White-Dornberger.)

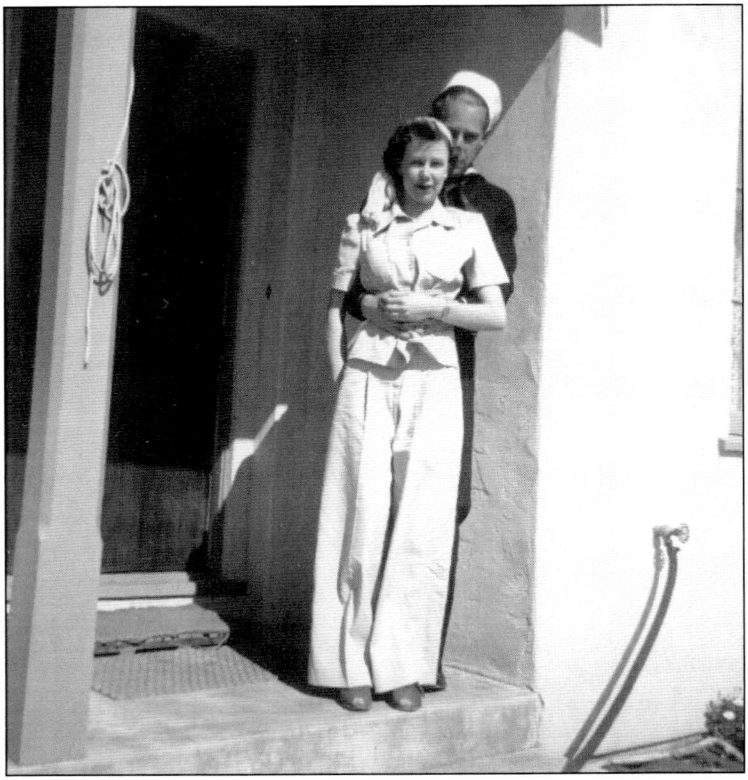

Bert Dornberger and Laverne White, pictured here in 1940 posing by the keeper's quarters, would soon marry and start a family. Laverne has happy memories of growing up in the original Point Hueneme Lighthouse and witnessing all the changes, including the new lighthouse. (Courtesy Laverne White-Dornberger.)

Bert Dornberger and Dave Powers pose for the camera in their service uniforms. (Courtesy Laverne-White Dornberger.)

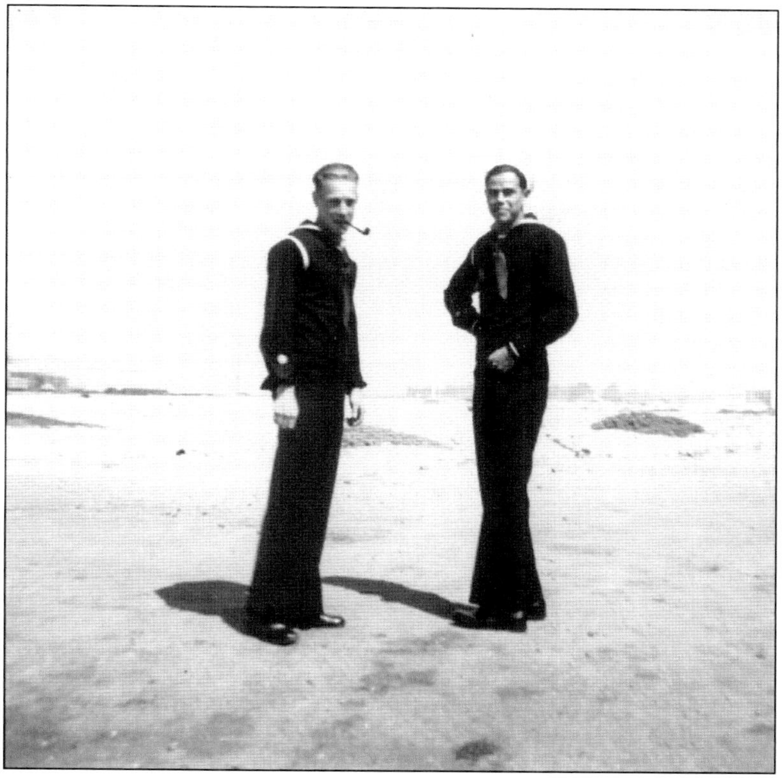

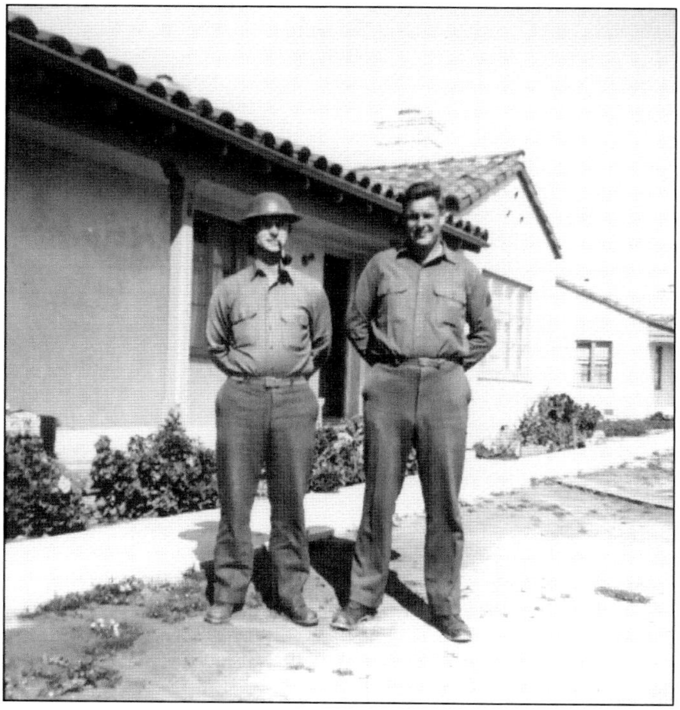

Soldiers pose in the front yard of the keeper's quarters. To the right of the soldiers, not seen in the photograph, was an anti-aircraft gun. The encompassing area was regularly monitored by servicemen. (Courtesy Laverne-White Dornberger.)

UNITED STATES COAST GUARD

ADDRESS REPLY TO:
COMMANDANT
U. S. COAST GUARD
HEADQUARTERS
WASHINGTON 25, D. C.

DEC 17 1948
FILE:

Mr. Walter White
Glen Acres Road
Vashon Island, Washington

Dear Mr. White:

My attention has been called to the fact that you have retired from the position of Keeper in the Coast Guard at the close of 30 November 1948, after rendering more than forty-one years of honorable service in the former Lighthouse Service and the Coast Guard.

I take pleasure in congratulating you upon your long and efficient service, and entertain the hope that you may long enjoy the leisure afforded by relief from active duty.

Very truly yours,

Merlin O'Neill

MERLIN O'NEILL
Rear Admiral, U. S. Coast Guard
Acting Commandant

4 years, on Lightvessel 70
total of years 45 years in the Service

During Walter White's 21-year service at Point Hueneme, where he was in charge of 32 men during the war, the Lighthouse Service was absorbed by the U.S. Coast Guard. White served the last few years in the armed forces before retirement. On November 30, 1948, White retired as lighthouse keeper. His service spanned the British Navy, merchant ships, the Lighthouse Service, and finally the U.S. Coast Guard. His service took him to four light stations: Piedras Blancas, Point Montara, Point Arguello, and Point Hueneme. He married in 1909, and he and his wife, Frankie, raised their three children at the stations (a fourth child died of diphtheria at the age of nine at Point Montera). White's career, counting four years on a lightship, actually totaled 45 years in the service. He retired to Vashon Island, Washington, where he could be surrounded by water. (Courtesy Laverne-White Dornberger.)

A woman stands in front of the Point Hueneme Lighthouse and flagpole. The flagpole was from the original Hueneme Lighthouse positioned at the current structure. The flagpole was recently donated to the lighthouse by a local Hueneme resident whose father had received it as a gift. It is made of solid wood and is currently inside the new structure. (Courtesy Port Hueneme Historical Society.)

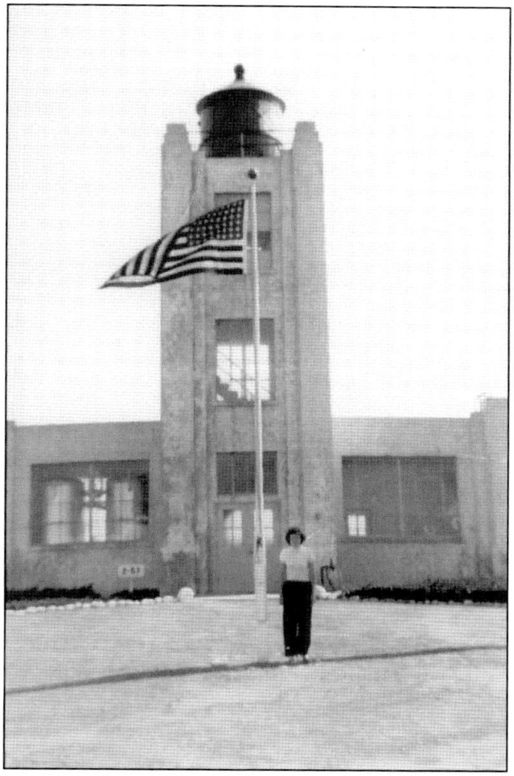

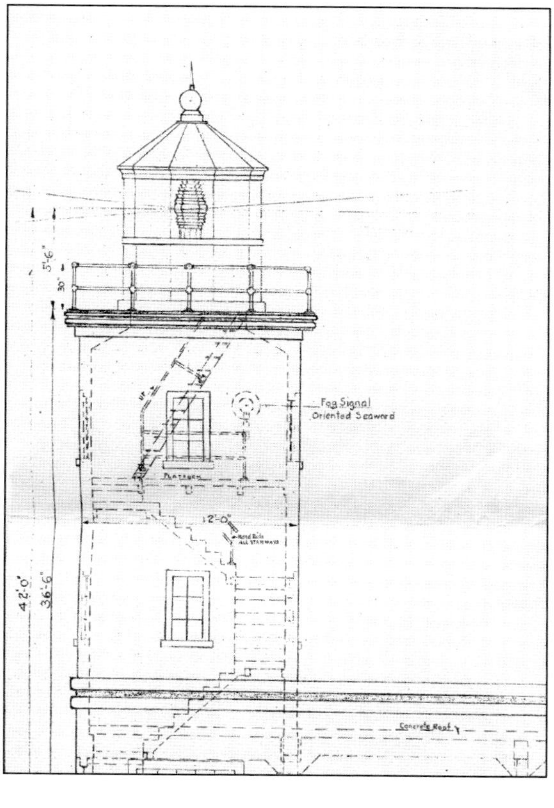

The Point Hueneme Lighthouse tower blueprints show the lighthouse stairs as they slant to the next floor. (Courtesy Laverne-White Dornberger.)

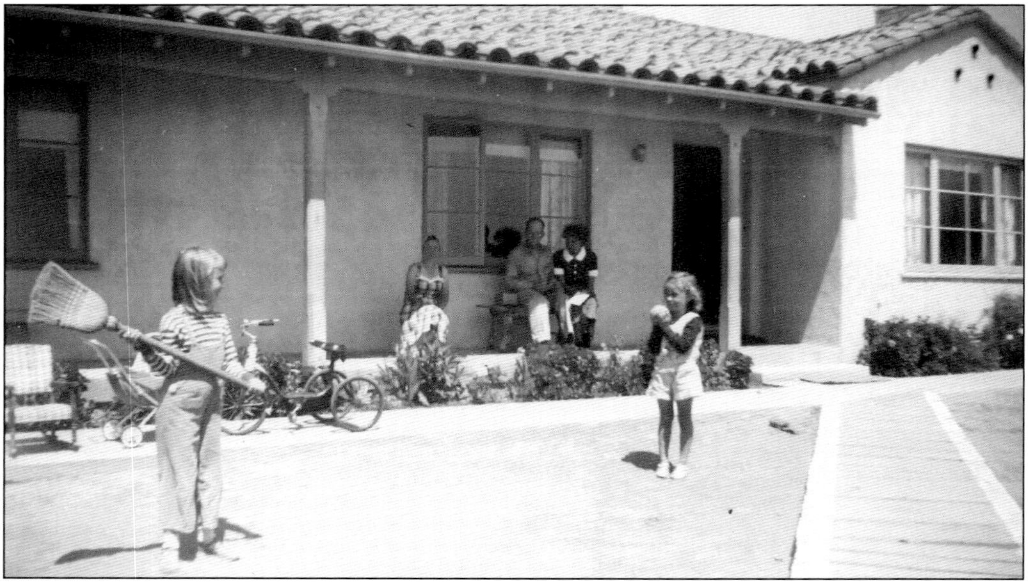

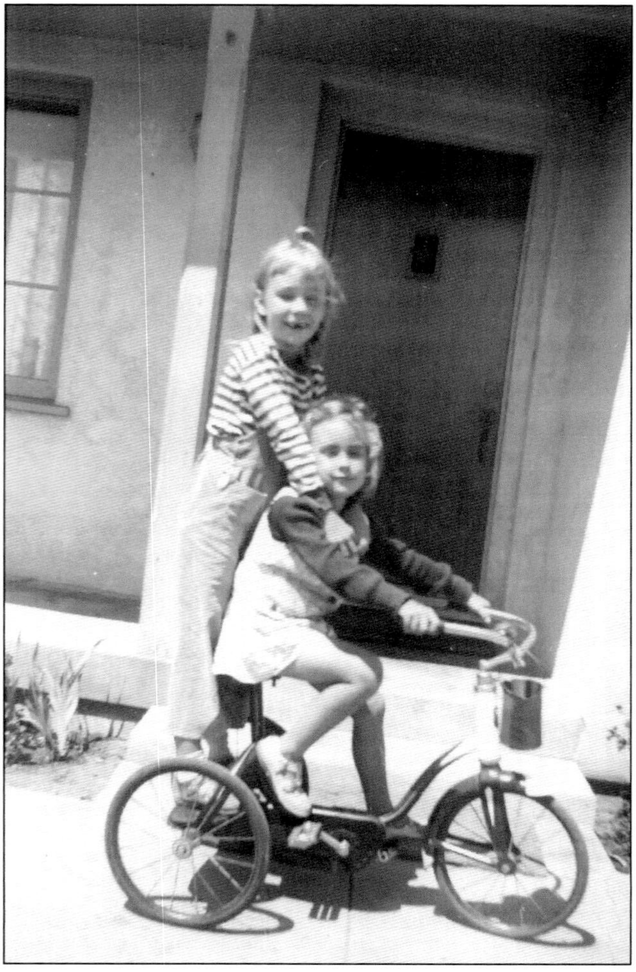

Following Walter White's retirement from Point Hueneme Lighthouse, Leo Kellogg, who once served as assistant keeper at Anacapa Lighthouse, was transferred to the lighthouse as head keeper (civilian). Sitting on the porch of the keeper's quarters is daughter Margaret. Leo Kellogg and his wife, Joan, enjoy watching Elsie and Claudia play baseball with a broom and ball. The girls (at left) had the run of the area as they rode bikes around the lighthouse grounds. Leo Kellogg passed away on November 21, 1952, at the age of 52 inside the keeper's quarters at the Point Hueneme Lighthouse. Following his death, the assistant keeper, George Ward, became the head keeper. (Both courtesy Margaret Kellogg-Anderson.)

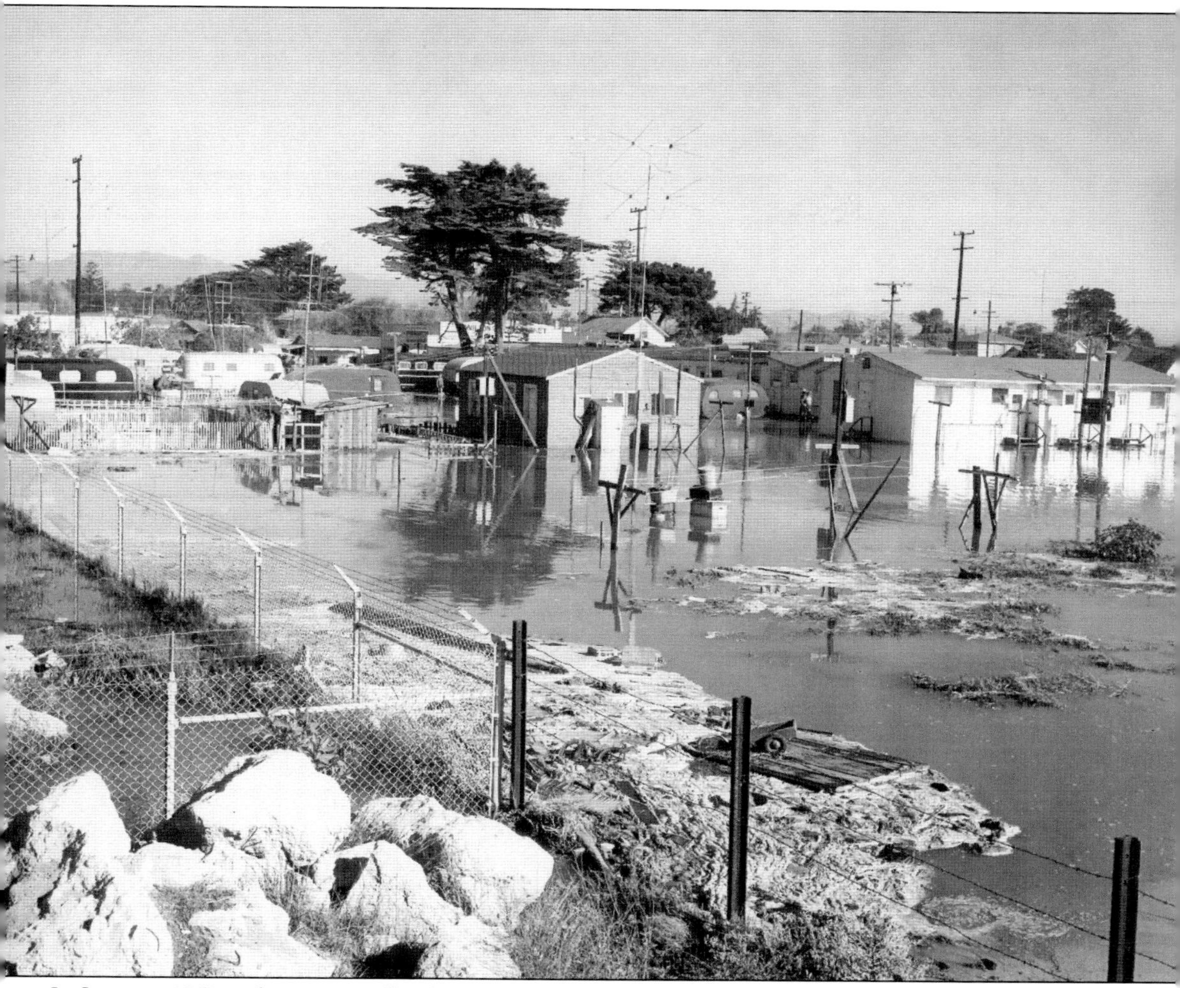

In January 1951, a devastating flood enveloped the streets of Hueneme, wreaking havoc on the city and spilling several feet of water into the community. Two years later the city employed engineer R. A. Wilson to solve the flooding situation by increasing the rapidly eroding shoreline. (Courtesy Port Hueneme Historical Society.)

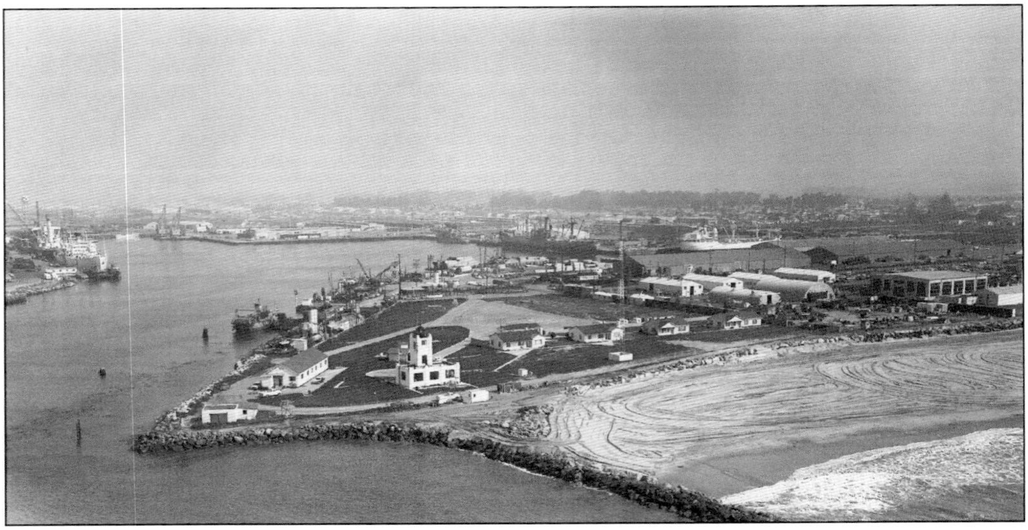

In the 1950s a U.S. Coast Guard helicopter photographed the area of Port Hueneme. The image above looks to the northeast and shows the entrance to the port, with the lighthouse to the south or east side of the channel. The image below shows an aerial view of the lighthouse compound including the radio station, keeper's quarters, and lighthouse. (Both courtesy U.S. Coast Guard.)

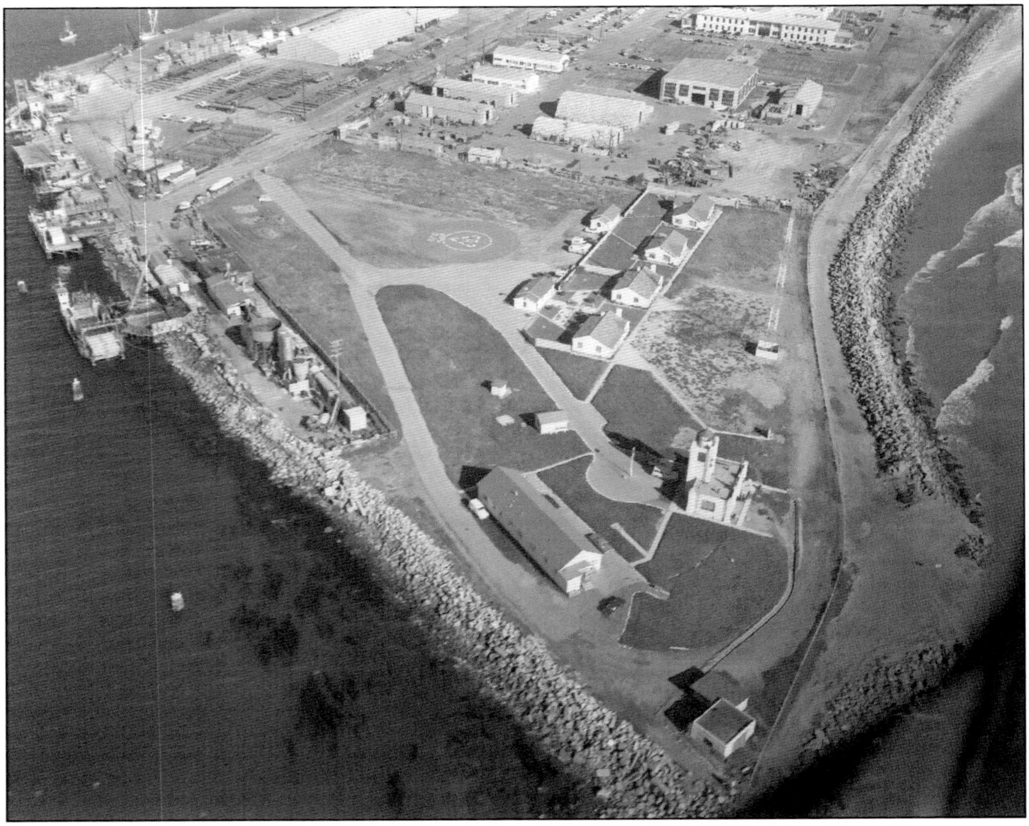

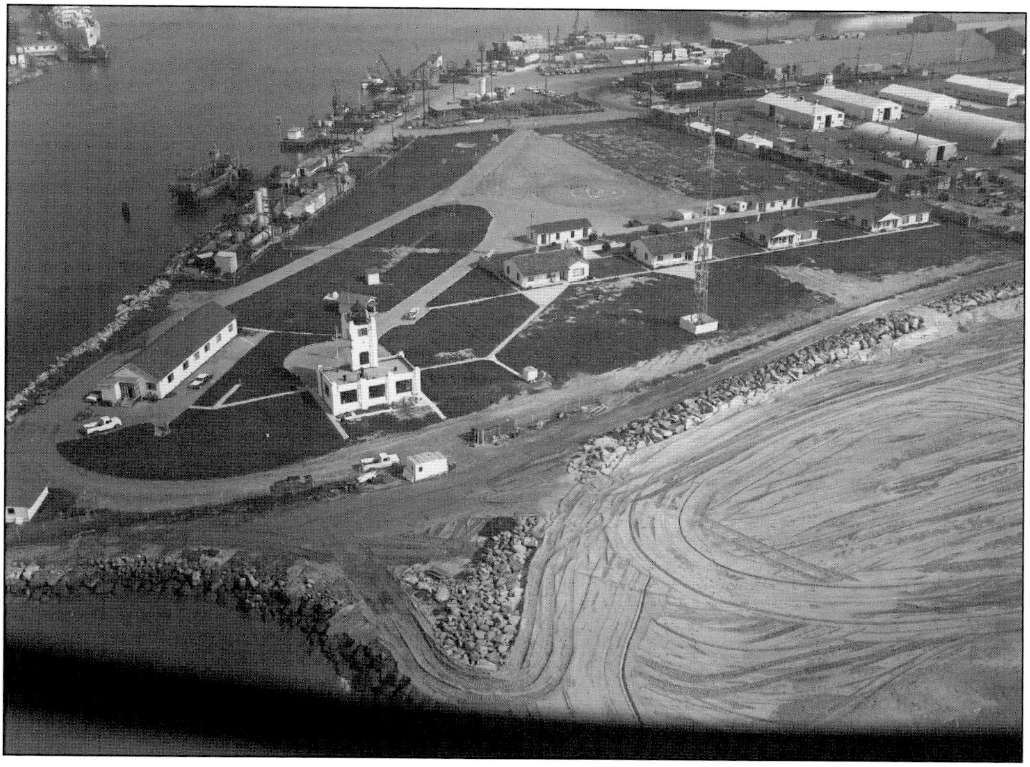

These two photographs were taken in the same session as those on the previous page. The image above shows the lighthouse looking north, including a portion of the sandy beach to the southeast. Below is the view a vessel would have as it approached the port channel entrance. (Both courtesy U.S. Coast Guard.)

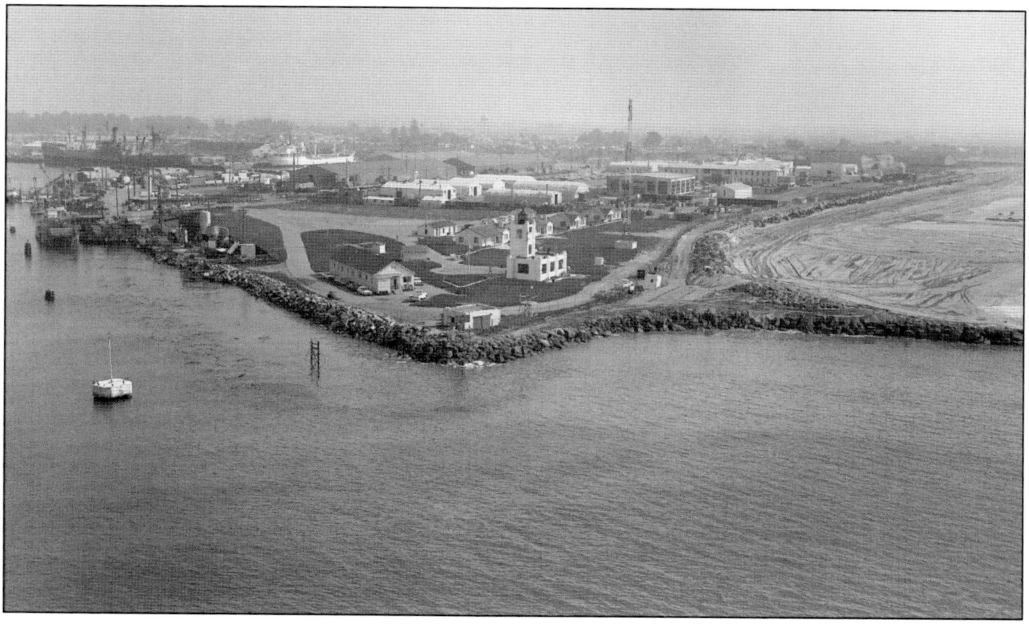

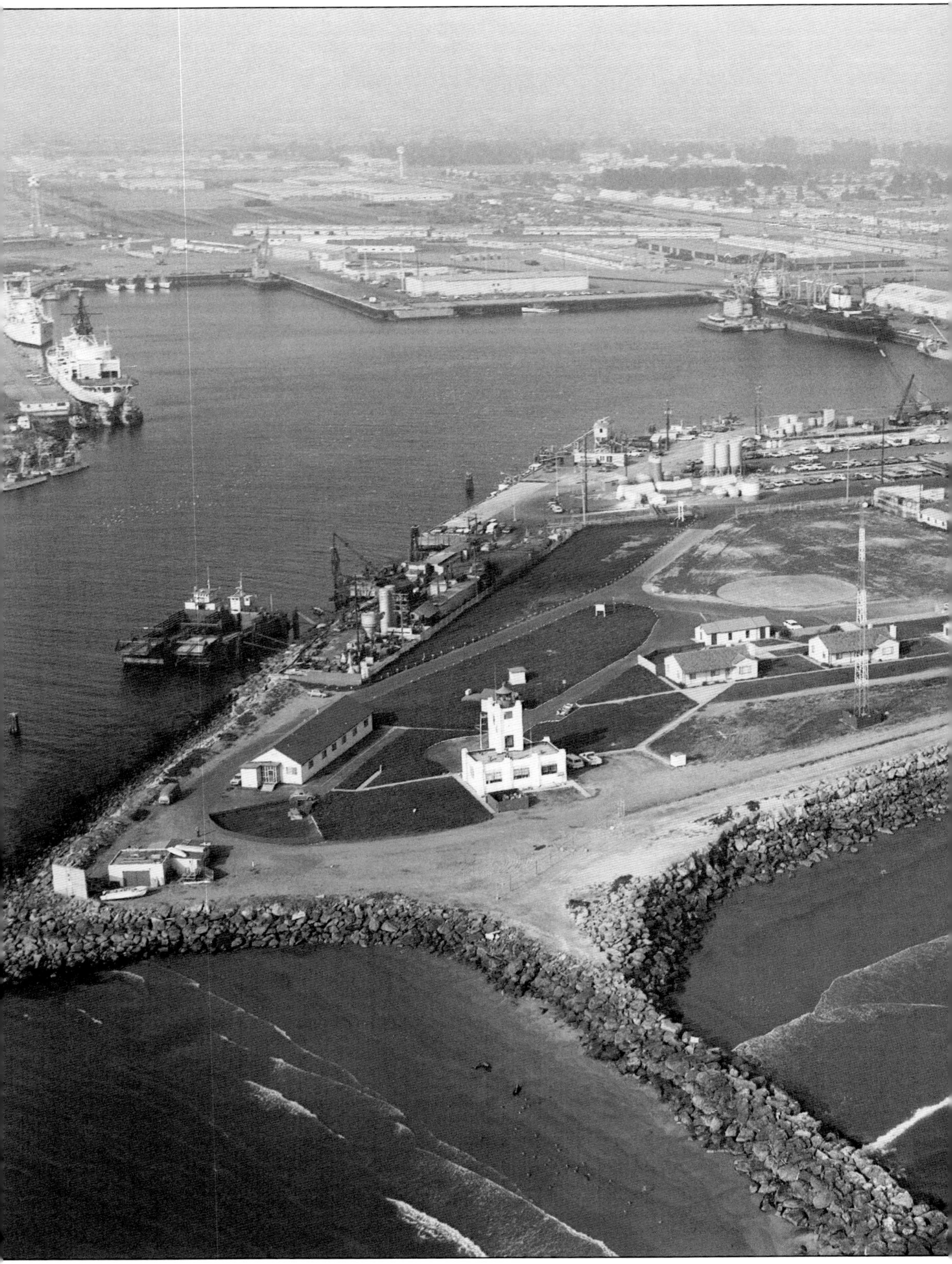

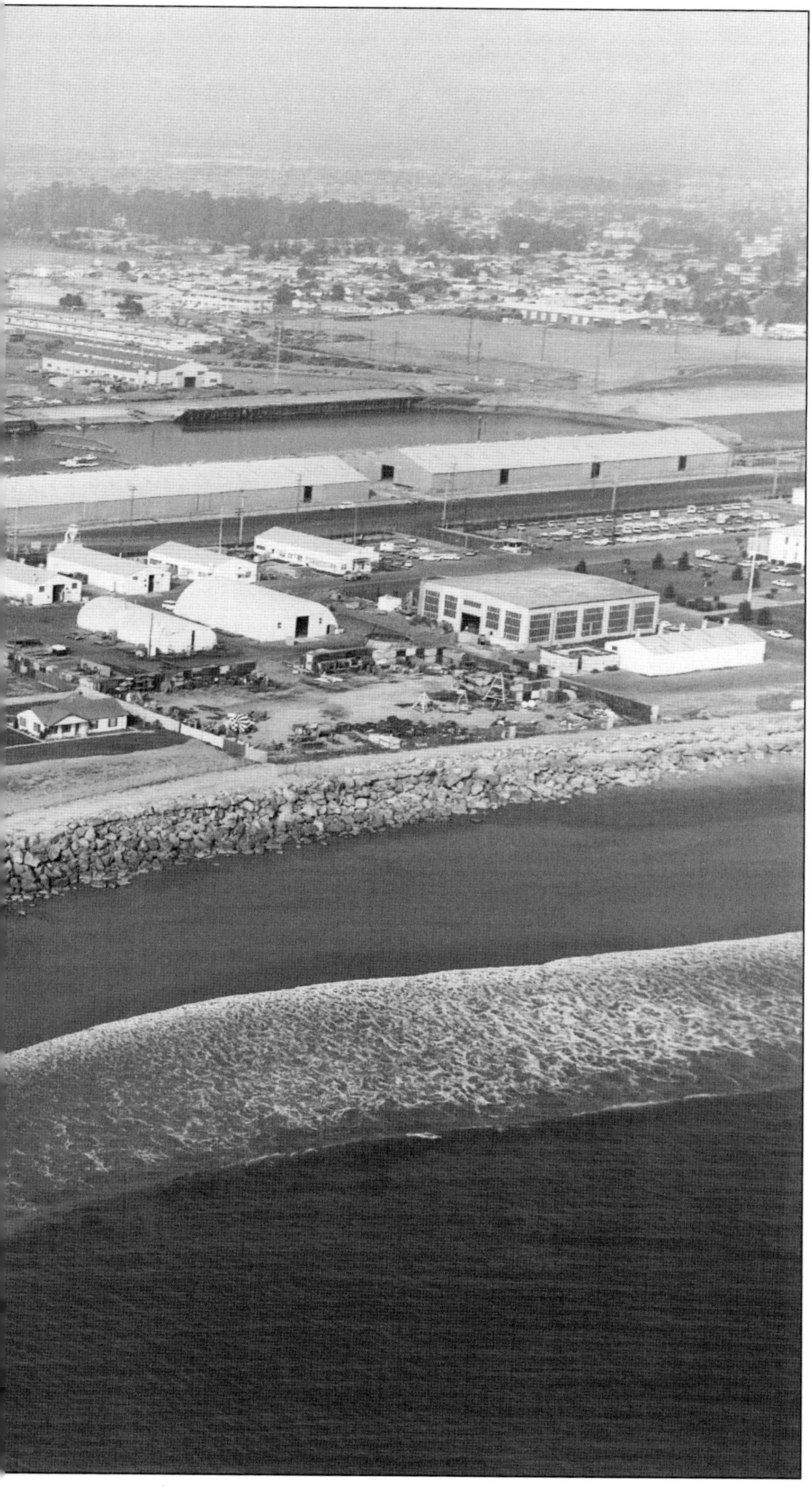

The Point Hueneme Light Station, pictured in this 1950s aerial view of the entire lighthouse grounds, includes areas of the port. The picture shows four similar structures for the keeper's quarters, as two additional buildings were added on to accommodate Coast Guard personnel. A helicopter pad was established on the grounds and is shown as a circle behind the quarters (two smaller structures behind the quarters were for storage). (Courtesy U.S. Coast Guard.)

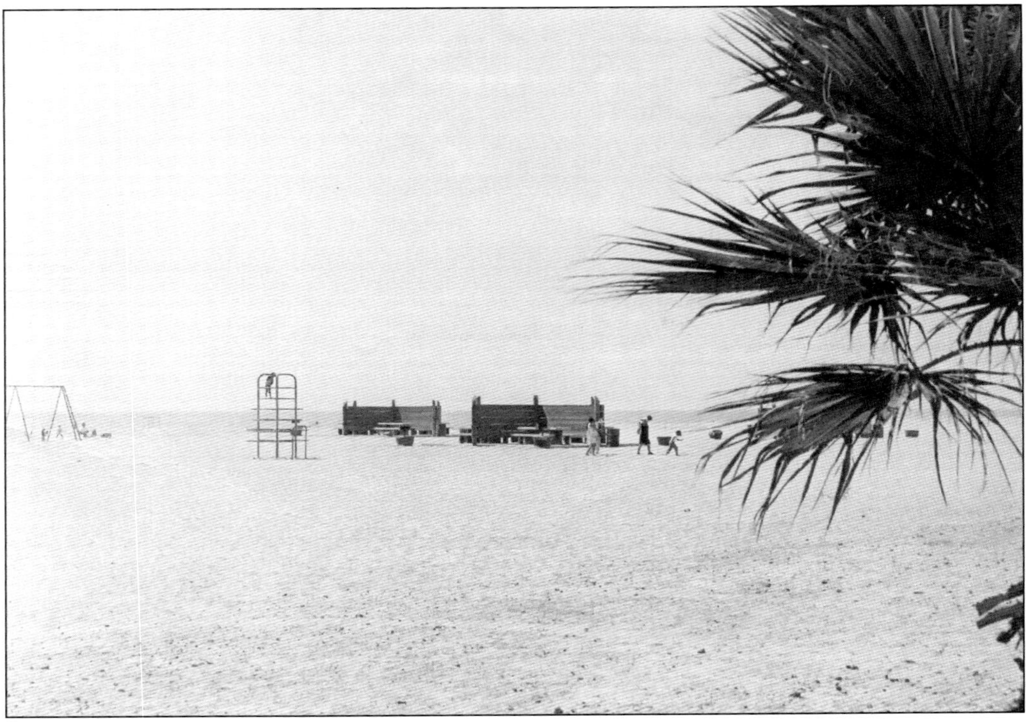

The Port Hueneme Beach Park, pictured here in the 1970s, and Hueneme by the Sea train station became a hot spot for locals and tourists. Famous for its surfing and year-round Mediterranean climate, it also includes an expansive amount of space to lay out, play beach sports, or enjoy an afternoon swim. Even today, Ventura's beaches continue to be a big draw. The beach stretches eastward about a mile from the harbor and naval base and extends to the pier. There are plenty of playground and picnic facilities. (Both courtesy Port Hueneme Historical Society.)

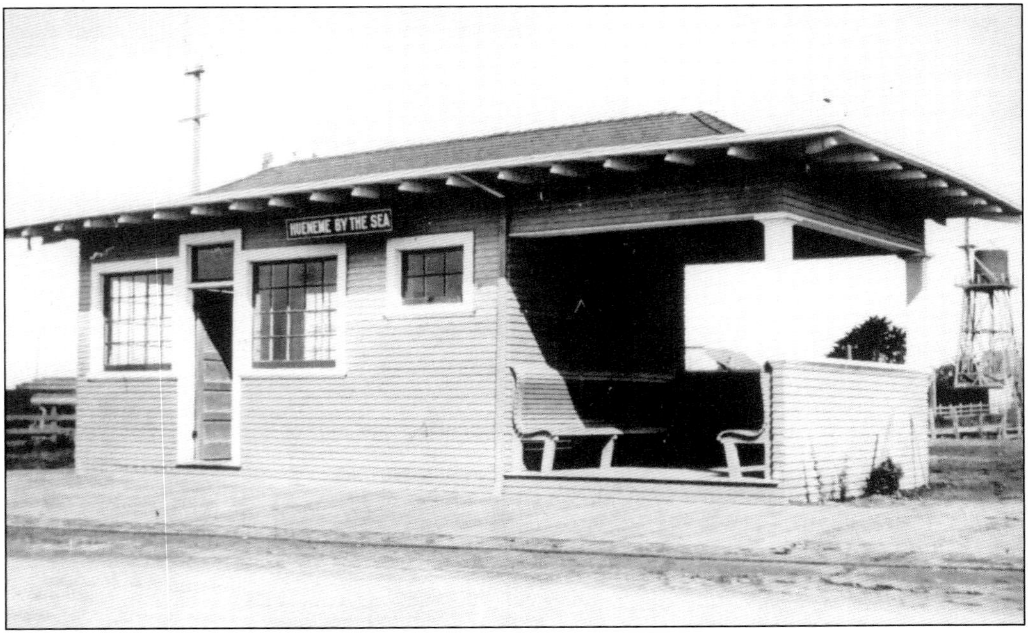

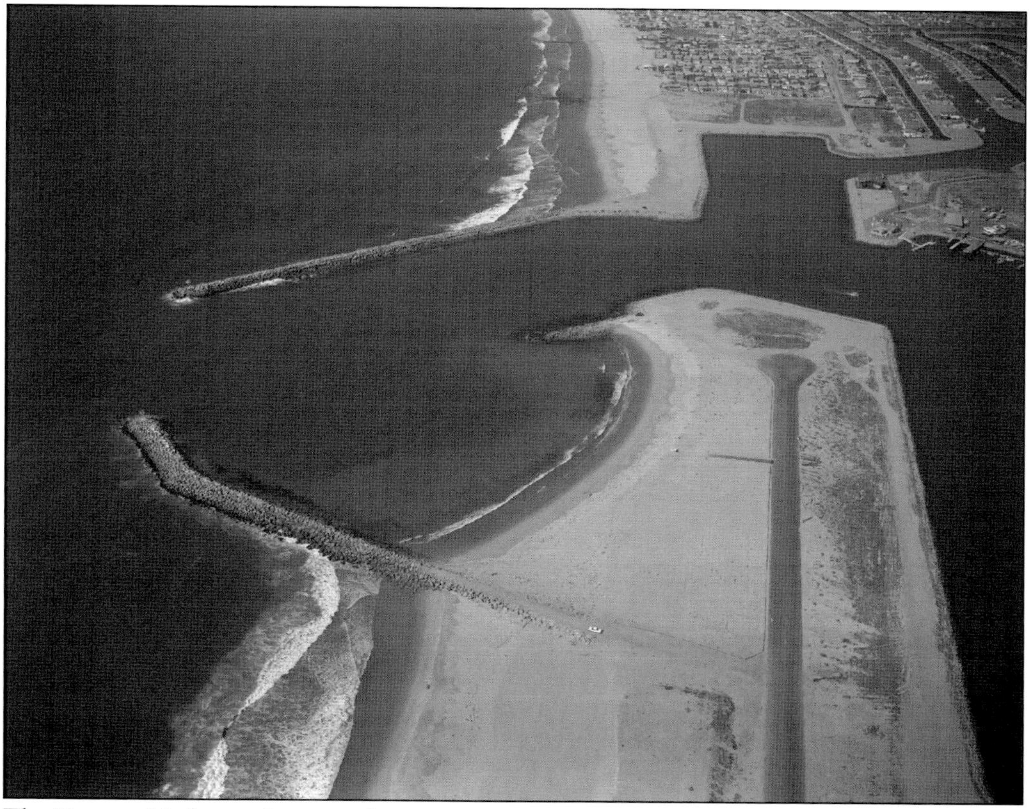

The Ventura Harbor and surrounding area are shown in these aerial views taken in the 1960s. The harbor was constructed in June 1963 at a cost of $4.75 million. The Ventura Port District is the owner/operator of the harbor, which is a 274-acre multiple-use recreational and commercial fishing small craft facility comprised of approximately 152 acres of land and 122 acres of water (except for a 2.74-acre site owned by the National Park Service). It is the official gateway to the Channel Islands National Park and Park Center. (Courtesy U.S. Coast Guard.)

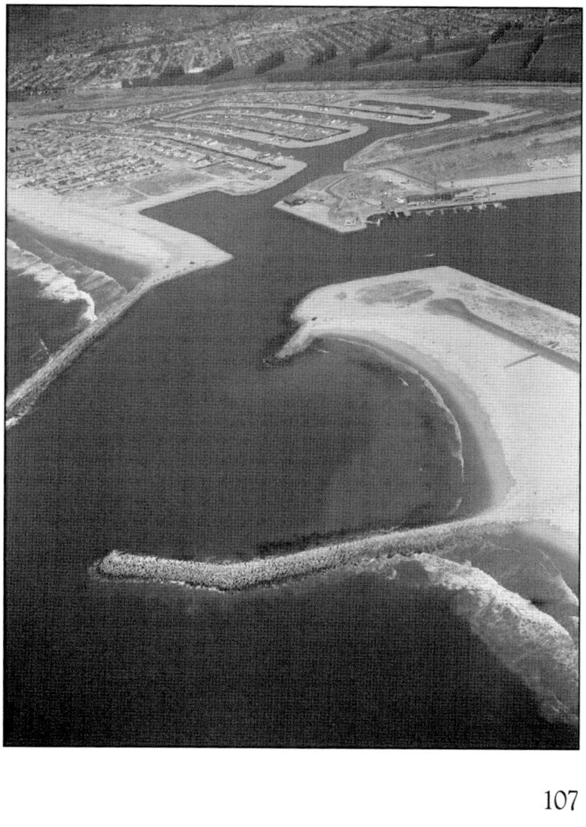

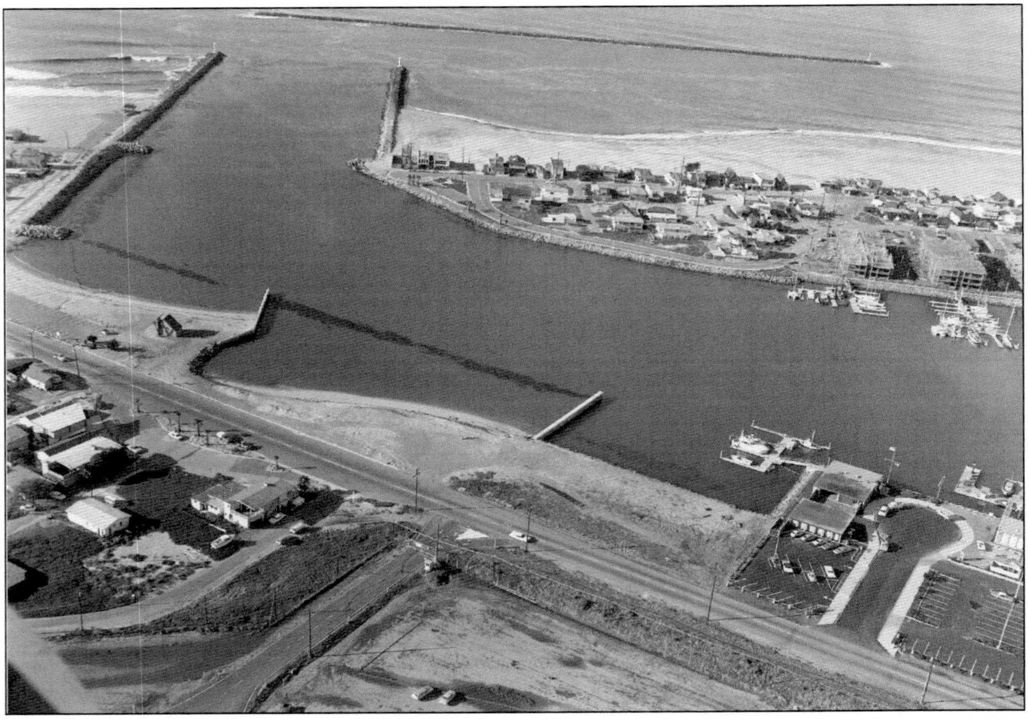

The Channel Islands Harbor is located in western Ventura County in the city of Oxnard. The aerial views here show part of the 310 acres of land and water, houses, and 2,150 wet slips. It was developed throughout the 1960s and 1970s as a small craft recreational harbor. It is designated by the State of California as a "Shallow Small Craft Harbor." (Courtesy U.S. Coast Guard.)

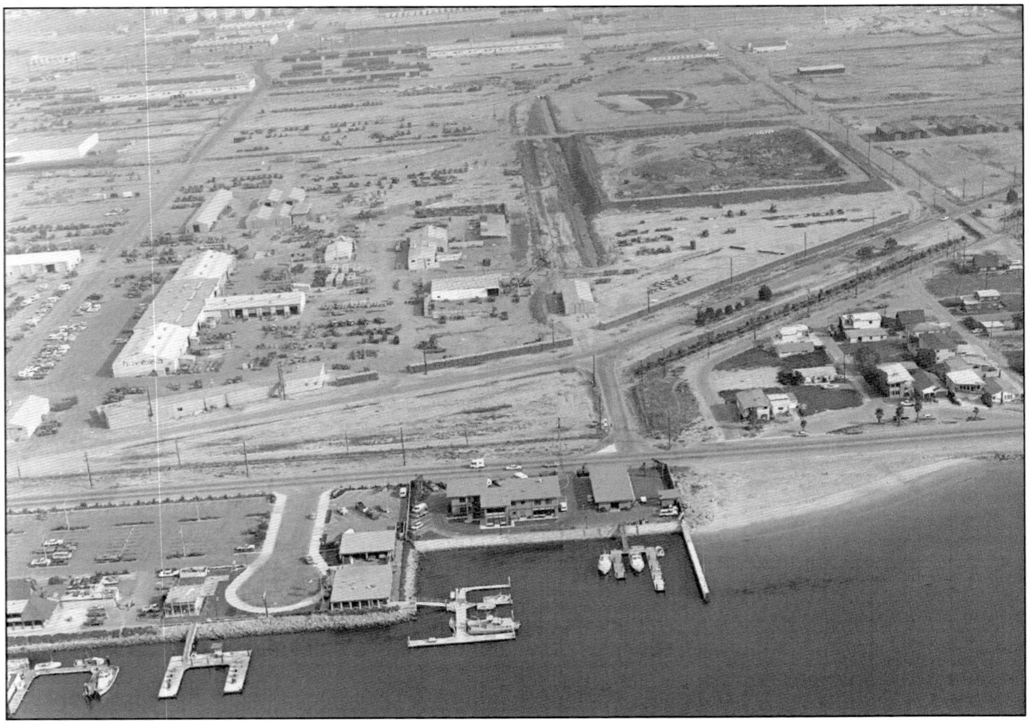

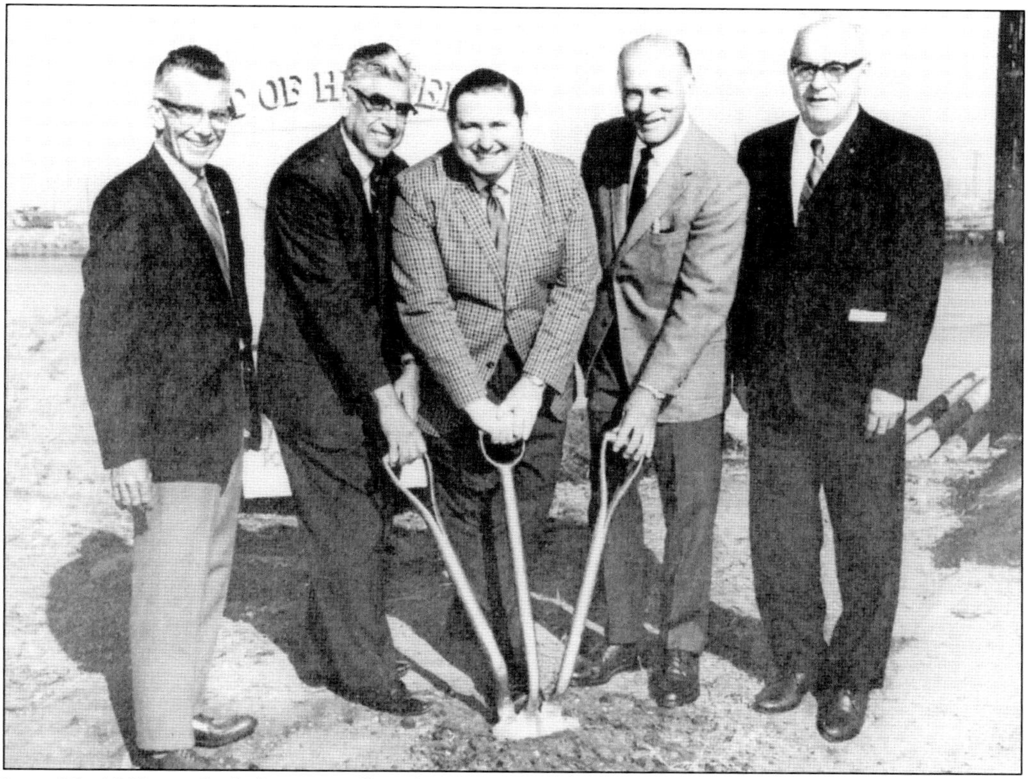

June 30, 1969, marked the groundbreaking ceremonies for the Entrance Channel Wharf. From left to right are Ventura County commissioners Catlin, Ramirez, Jennings, Bennett, and Peterson. (Courtesy Port Hueneme Historical Society.)

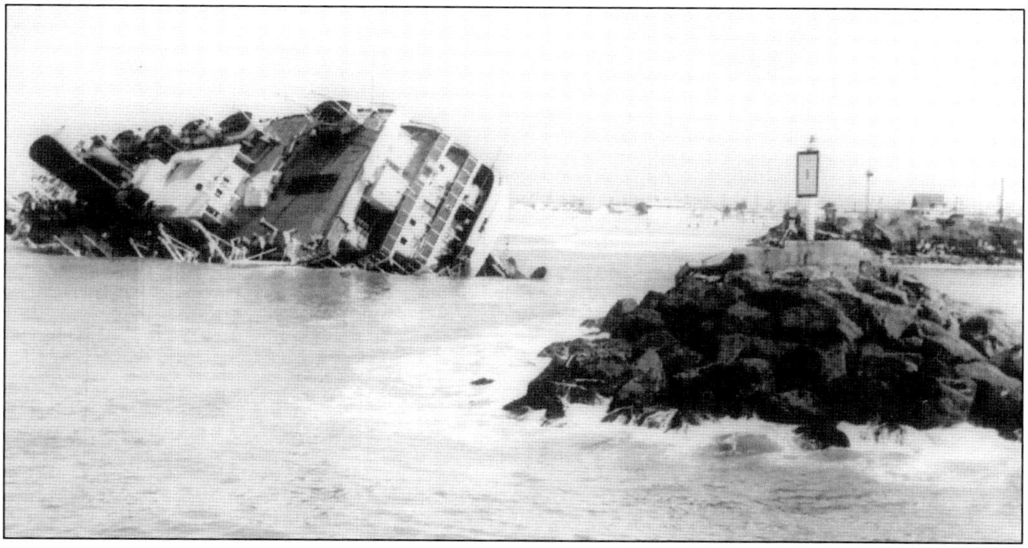

On April 13, 1970, the SS *La Janelle*, a 12,000-ton pleasure ship, ran aground and permanently beached on Port Hueneme Beach after experiencing gale force winds and rough seas. All attempts to salvage the ship failed. The wreck was converted into a fishing jetty by the U.S. Navy Seabees by using a part of the ship to extend the jetty and placing large boulders around the hull. (Courtesy NAVFAC Historian/Naval CEC/Seabee Archive.)

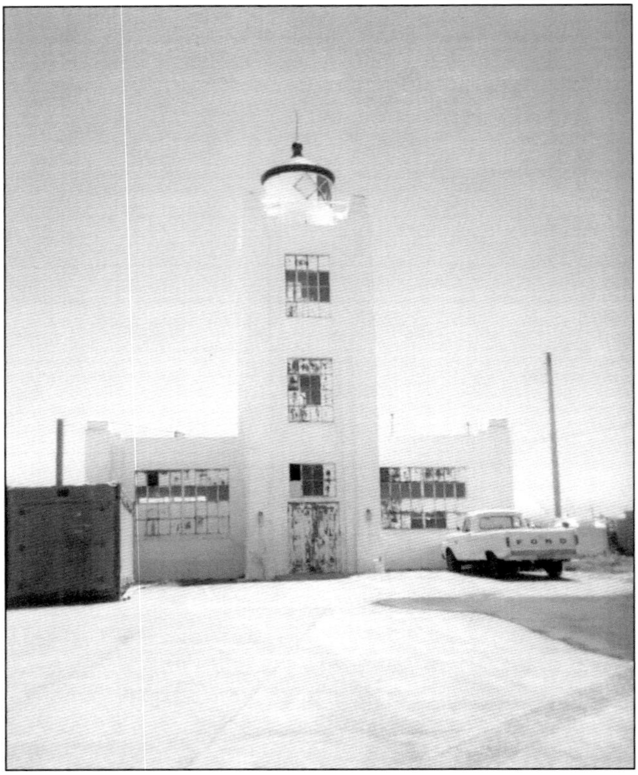

All lighthouses suffer harsh effects from the saltwater spray that causes rapid rust and erosion, and the Point Hueneme Lighthouse is no exception. As illustrated in these photographs, by 1998, the windows on the lighthouse had severely rusted out. (Both courtesy U.S. Coast Guard.)

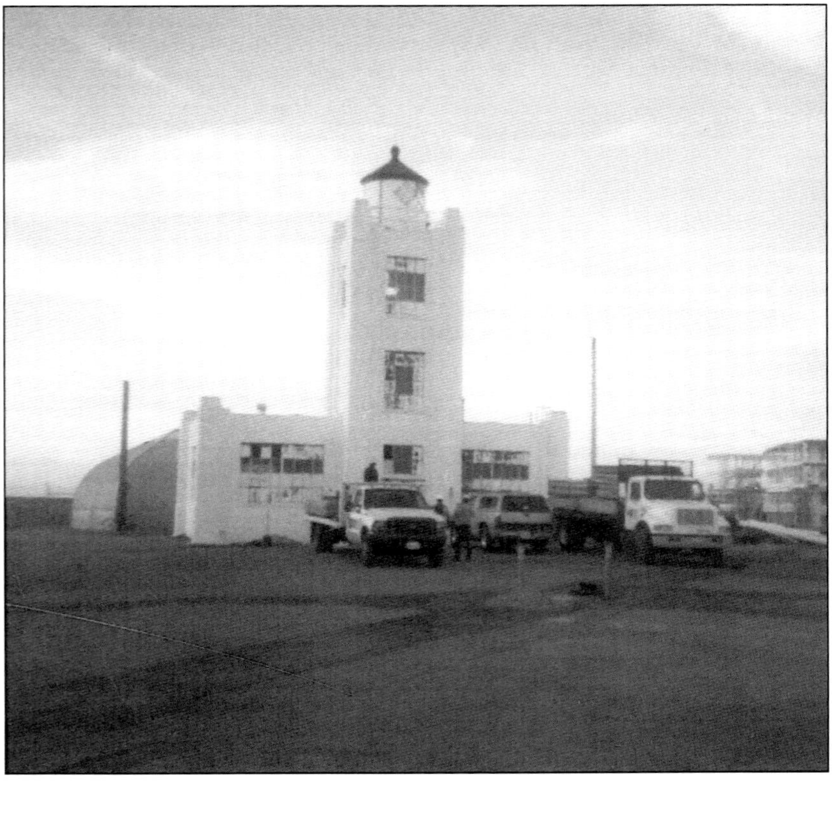

From 1999 to 2000, the U.S. Coast Guard spent $250,000 to renovate the current Point Hueneme Lighthouse, changing the color from black to red. It was a greatly needed facelift. The construction is well underway in the photograph at right. (Point Hueneme Lighthouse collection.)

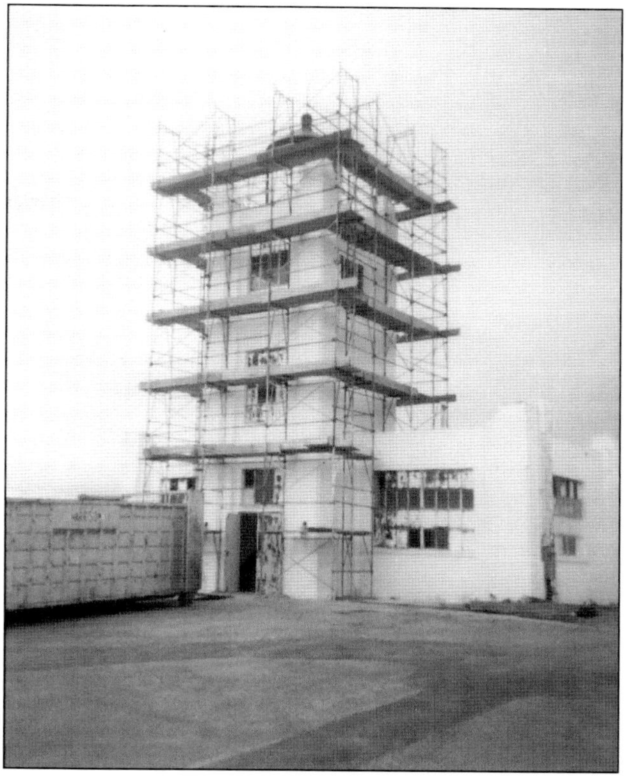

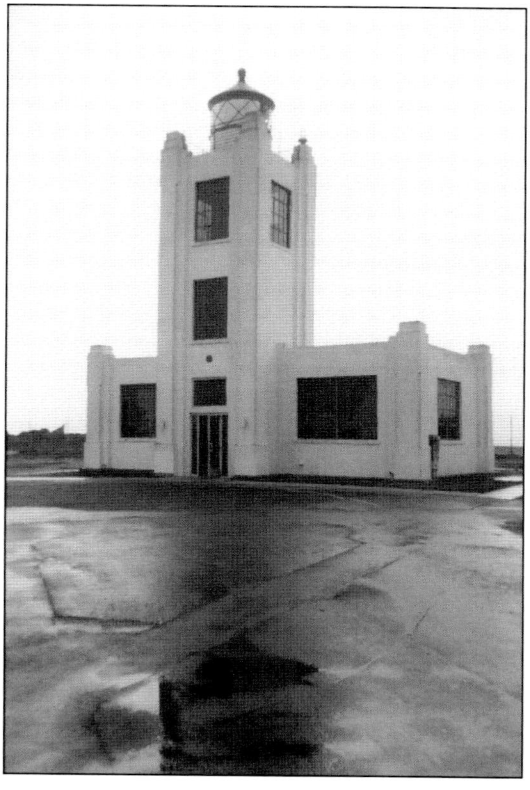

The Point Hueneme Lighthouse is pictured in 2002 after the remodel. The lighthouse was restored back to its original luster, and the new red color gave it a fresh look. (Author's collection.)

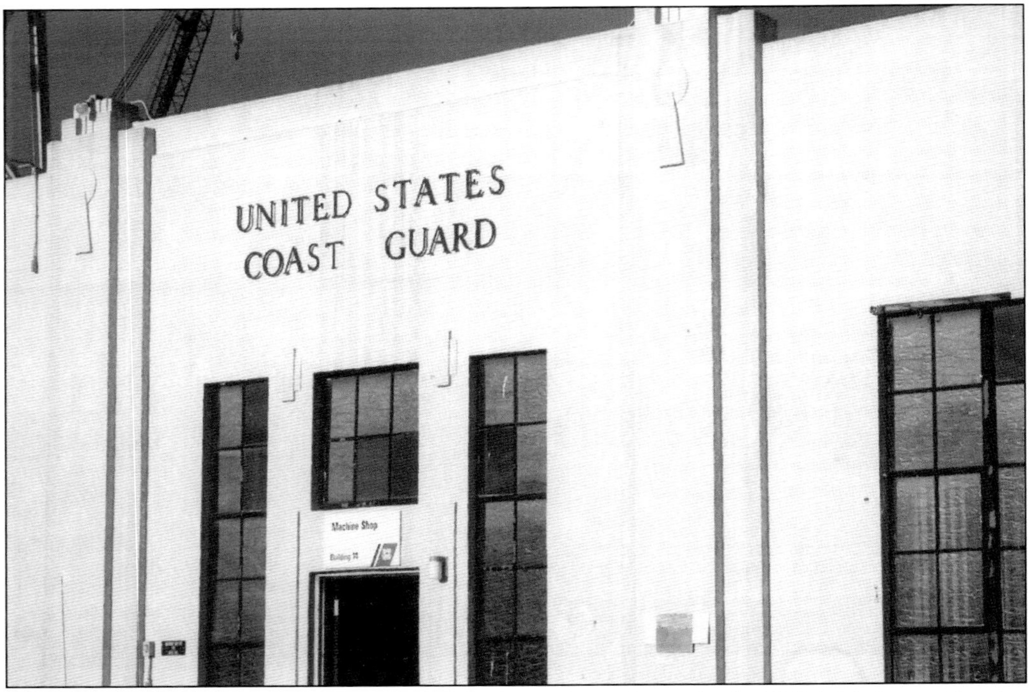

The current U.S. Coast Guard machine shop (above) was formerly the U.S. Lighthouse Service building. It is located at Terminal Island in San Pedro, home to the U.S. Coast Guard Aids to Navigation Team Los Angeles/Long Beach. The emblem (below) includes an ant, which is an acronym for Aids to Navigation Team. They are responsible for servicing Point Hueneme Lighthouse and Anacapa, as well as lighthouses from Dana Point to Morro Bay: Long Beach, Los Angeles Light (Angeles Gate), Point Vicente, Santa Barbara, Point Arguello, Point Conception, and San Luis Obispo Lighthouses. They also perform service on numerous minor aids to navigation. (Both courtesy Point Hueneme Lighthouse collection.)

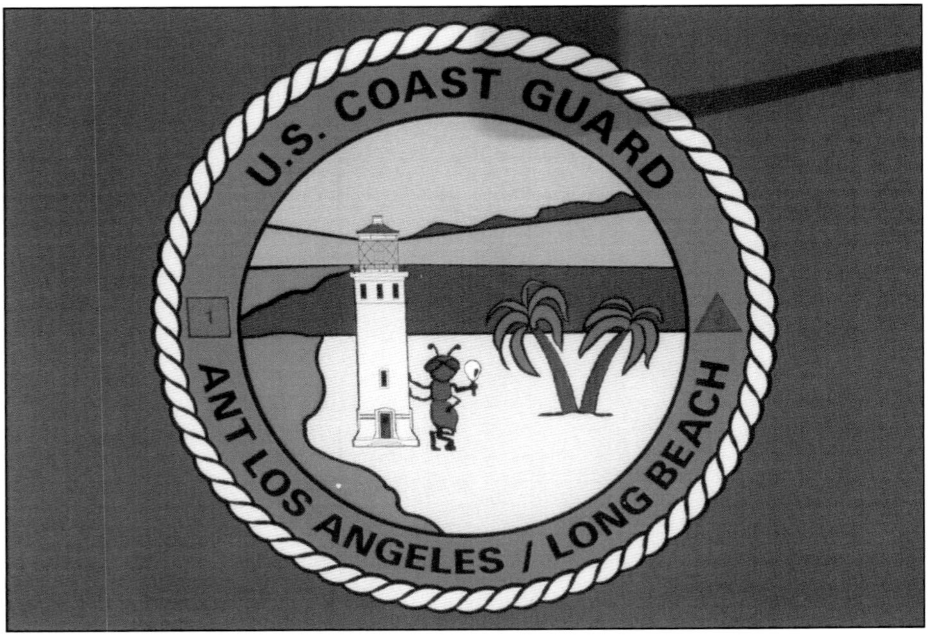

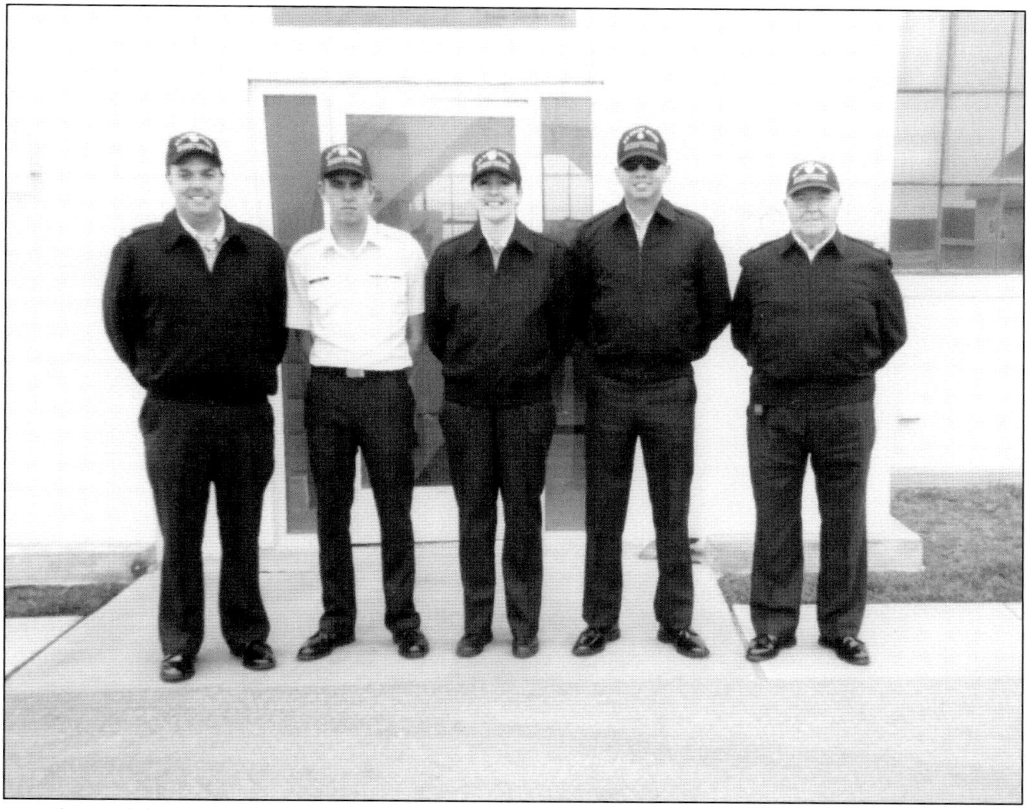

Members of the U.S. Coast Guard Aids to Navigation Team include, from left to right, auxiliarist Kim Castro-Bran, Seaman Travis Hall, auxiliarist Rose Castro-Bran, Petty Officer Matt Jessip, and auxiliarist Eric Castro-Bran. They are standing outside the lighthouse doors and preparing for a group tour. (Point Hueneme Lighthouse collection.)

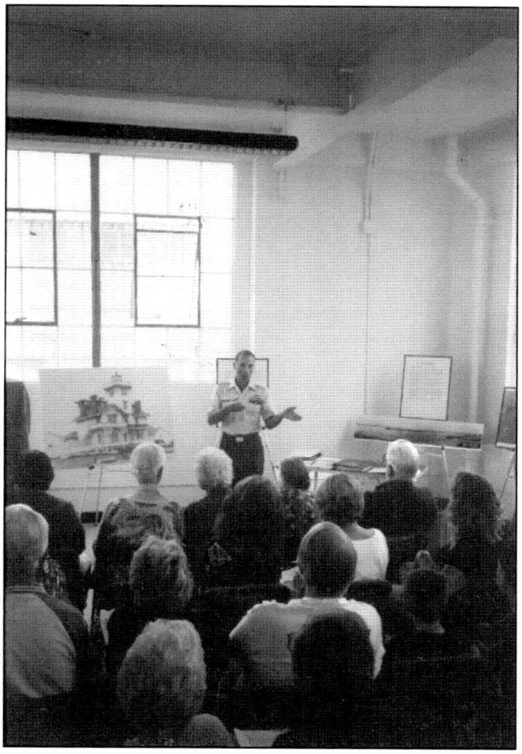

U.S. Coast Guard Chief Sterks, pictured here in 2002, gives a tour and speaks about the history of the lighthouse to a very attentive group. Both Master Chief Petty Officer John Hurst and Chief Petty Officer John Stercks were instrumental in opening up the lighthouse to tours. (Courtesy Eric Castro-Bran.)

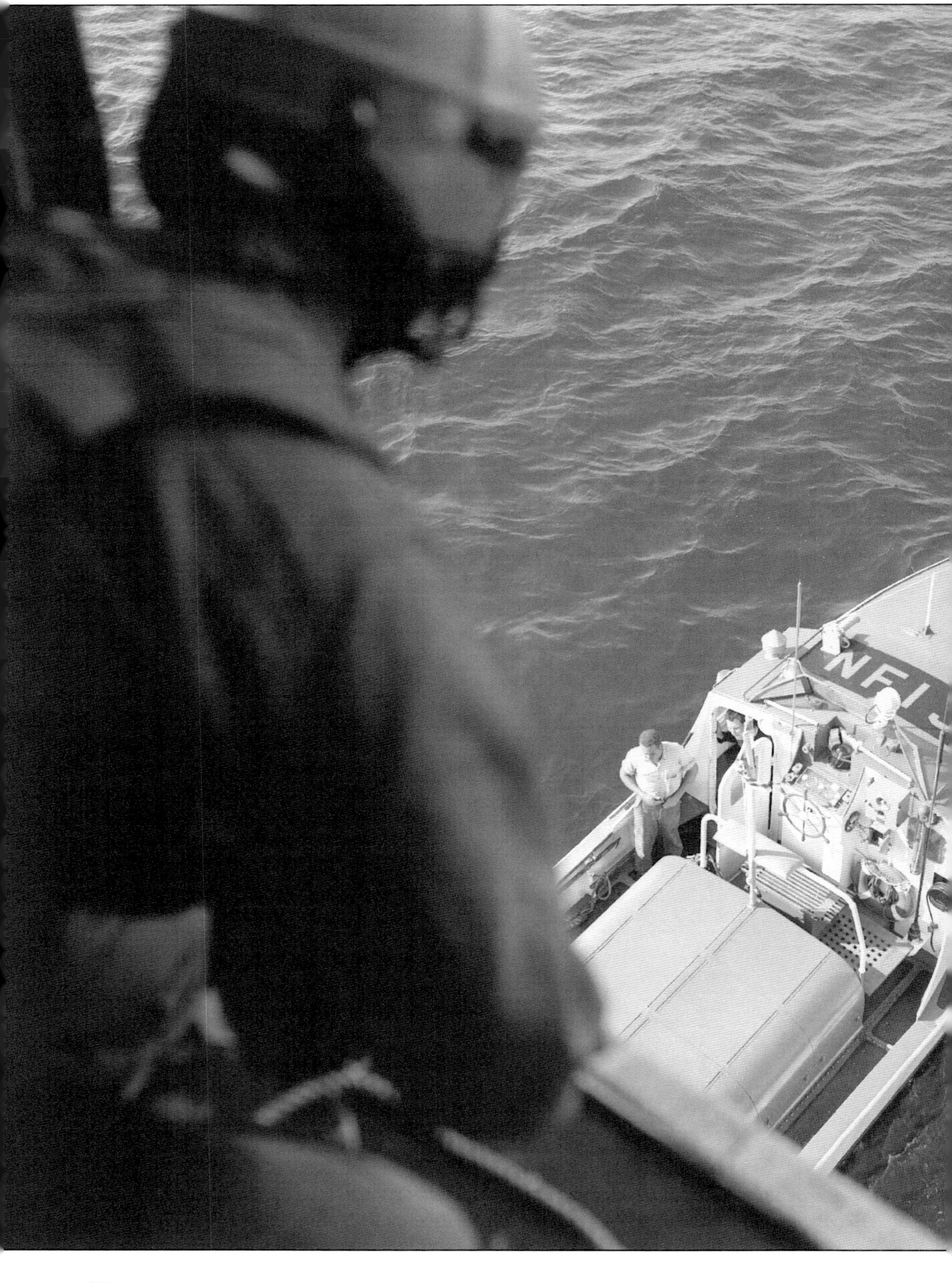
NFI

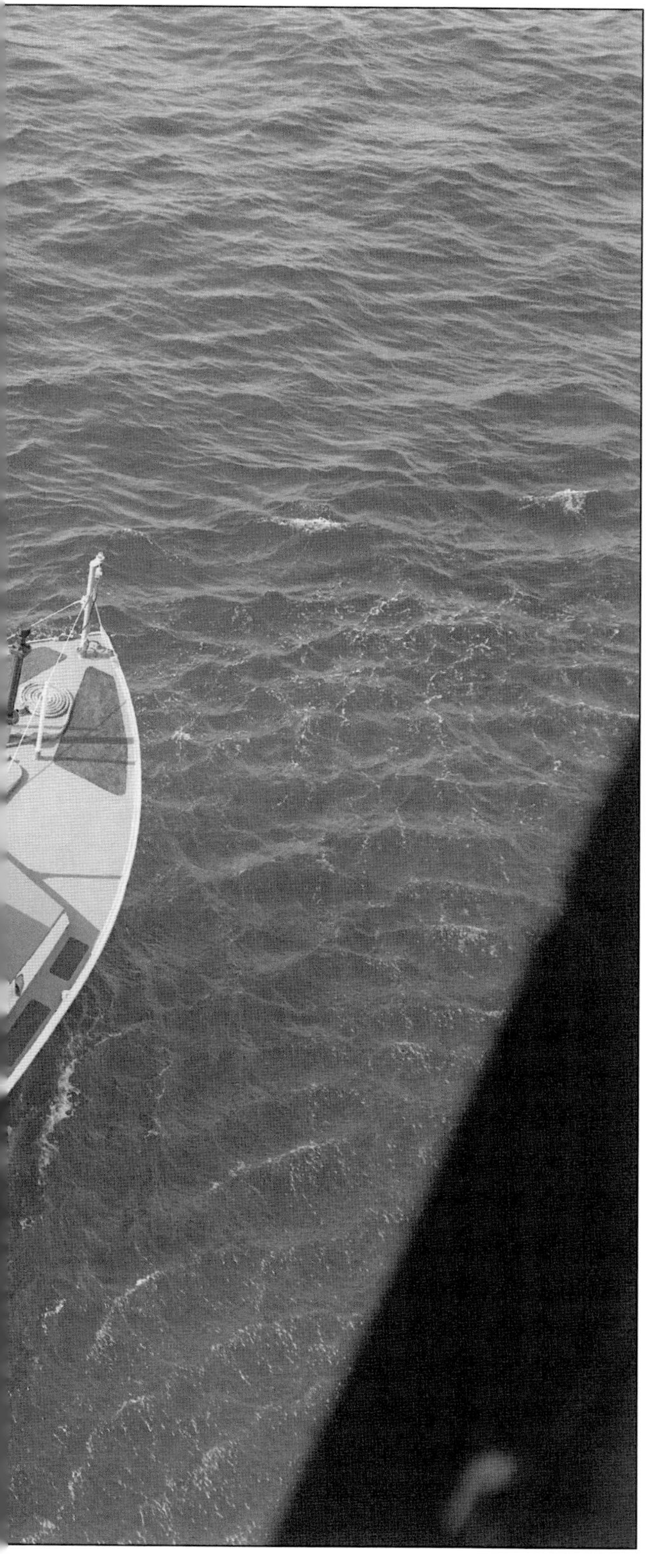

From a Coast Guard helicopter, a Coast Guardsman is responding to a distressed boater. Protecting the waters starts with Search and Rescue (SAR), one of the Coast Guard's oldest missions. Their goal is to minimize the loss of life, injury, or property damage by rendering aid to persons in distress, as well as saving property in the maritime environment. (Courtesy U.S. Coast Guard.)

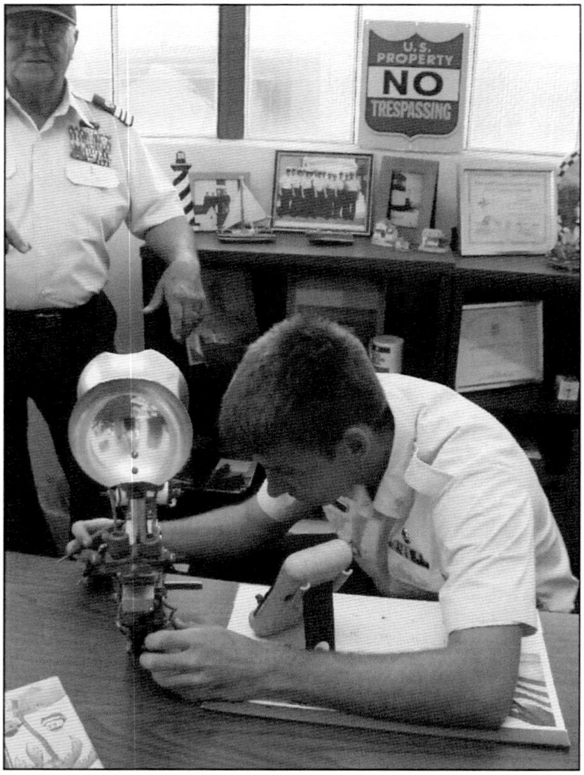

Coast Guard Petty Officer Bart Gaska (foreground) works on the apparatus that contains the 1,000-watt lamp inside the Fresnel lens. Coast Guard Auxiliarist Eric Castro-Bran (background) assists. There are two lamps placed inside the apparatus. When one lamp burns out, it will automatically switch positions so that the second lamp will turn on. When both lamps have burned out, there is an auxiliary light (plastic model) placed outside on the catwalk that will then automatically turn on. (Point Hueneme Lighthouse Collection.)

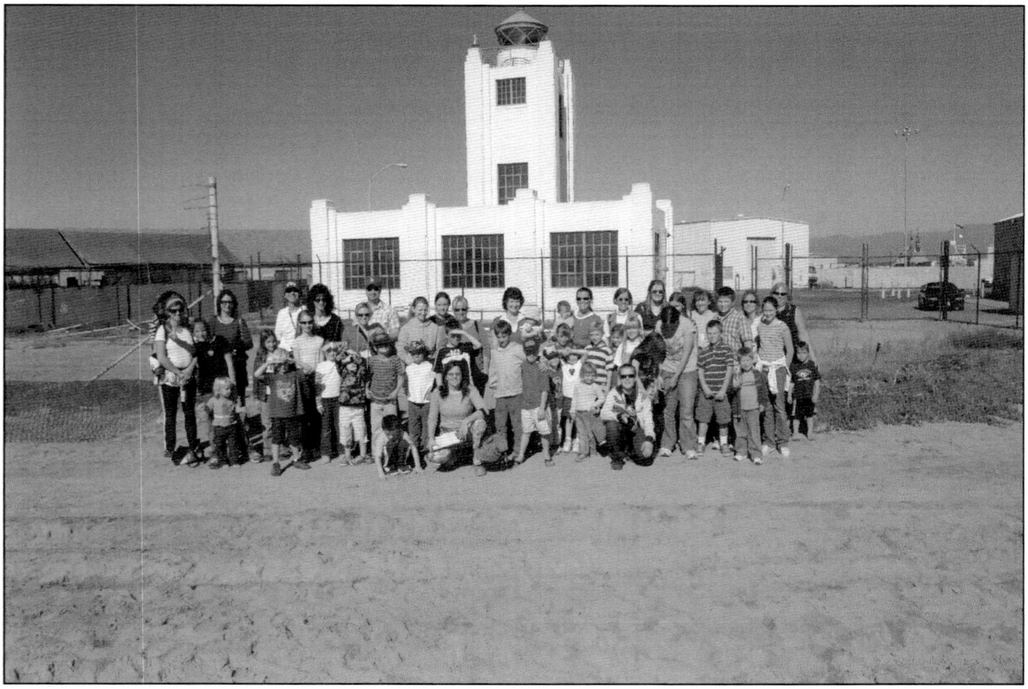

A school group gathers outside the gates of the Point Hueneme Lighthouse following a tour of the lighthouse. The dirt road in front of the children has been completely redone, giving visitors a direct paved path to the lighthouse. (Author's collection.)

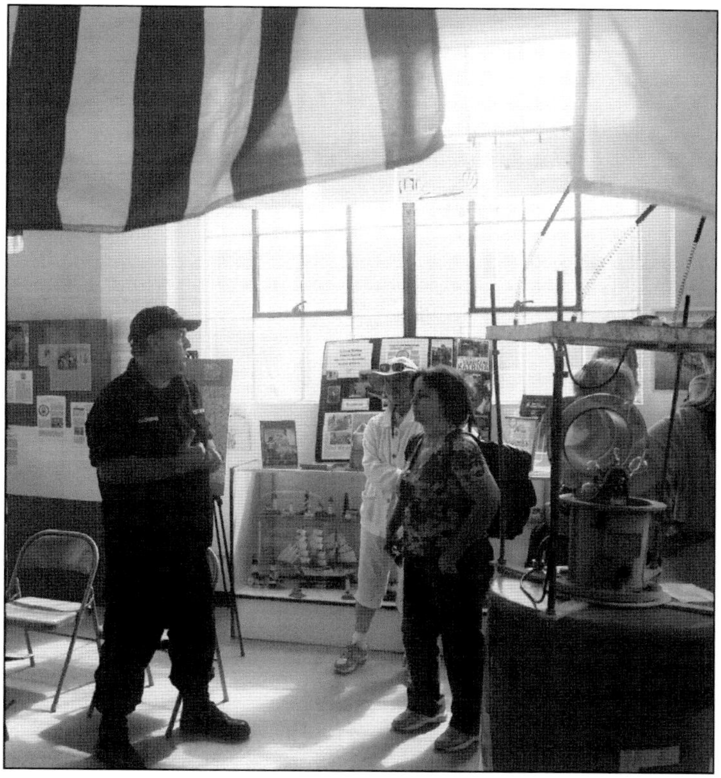

U.S. Coast Guard Auxiliarist Kim Castro-Bran gives a tour of the lighthouse, discussing the history of both the original and the current structure, the construction of the port, and the Fresnel lens. (Author's collection.)

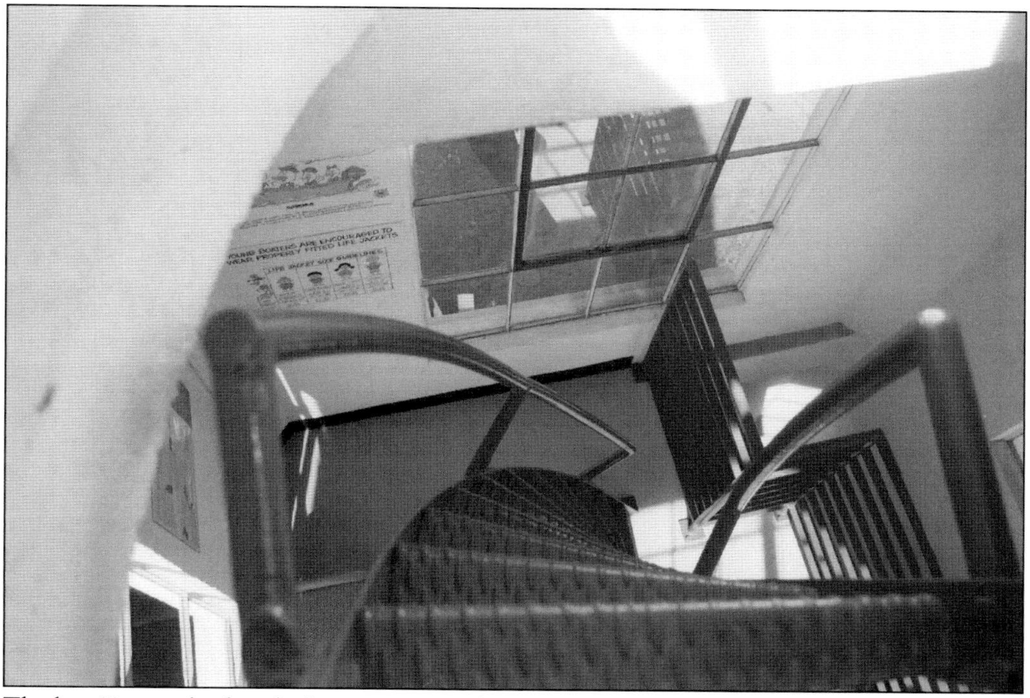

The last 11 stairs lead to the lantern room. The stairs have a slight swirl and are ladderlike. They open to a hole in the ceiling, which is the only entrance to the lantern room and the Fresnel lens. (Author's collection.)

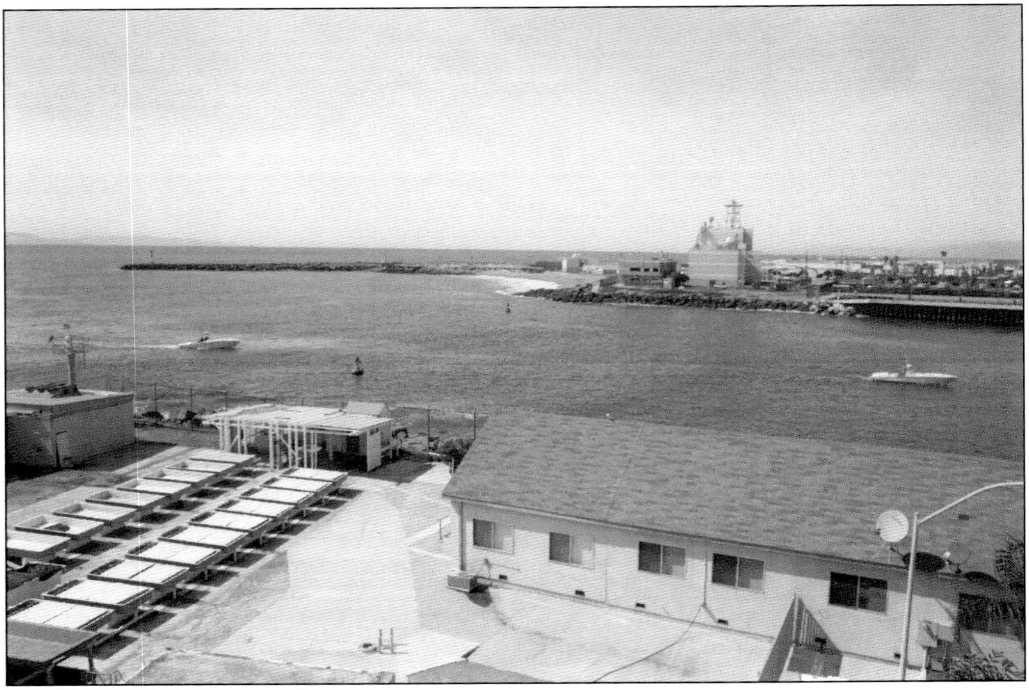

The catwalk of the lighthouses provides an amazing 360-degree view of the port. The view is breathtaking, allowing one to view the Channel Islands and large cargo ships entering the harbor on a clear day. (Both courtesy Point Hueneme Lighthouse collection.)

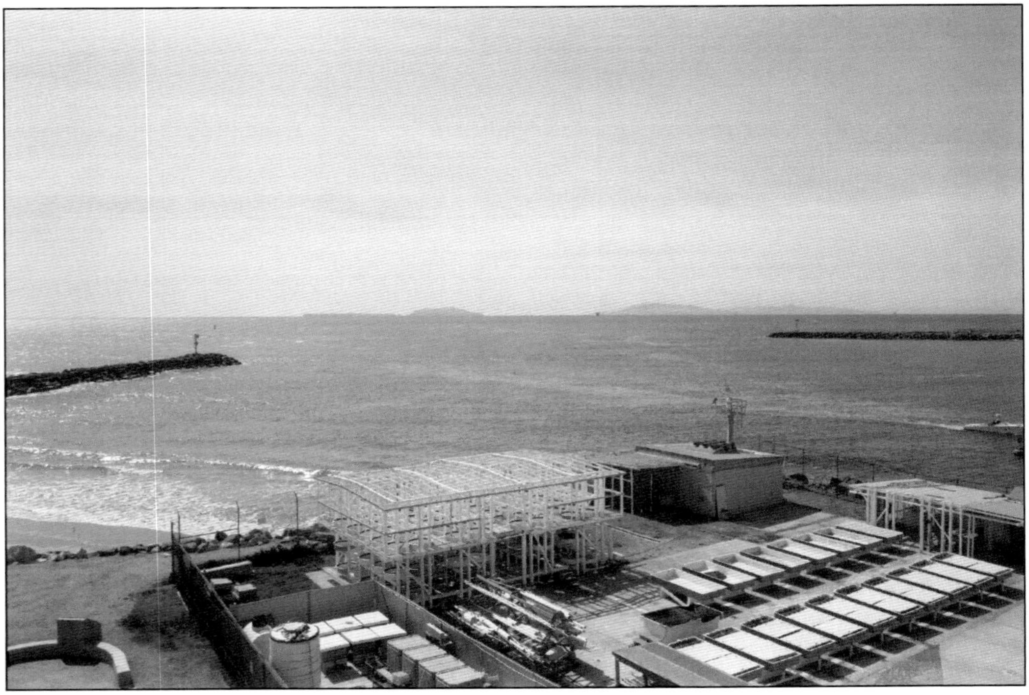

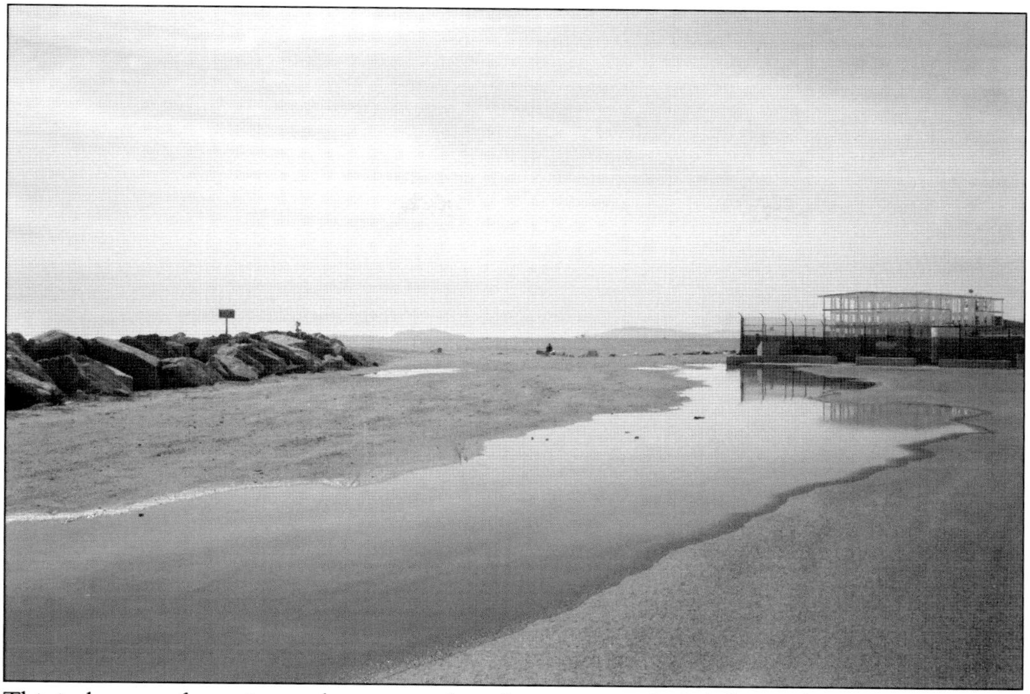

This is the oceanfront view as the promenade makes its way to the lighthouse. (Author's collection.)

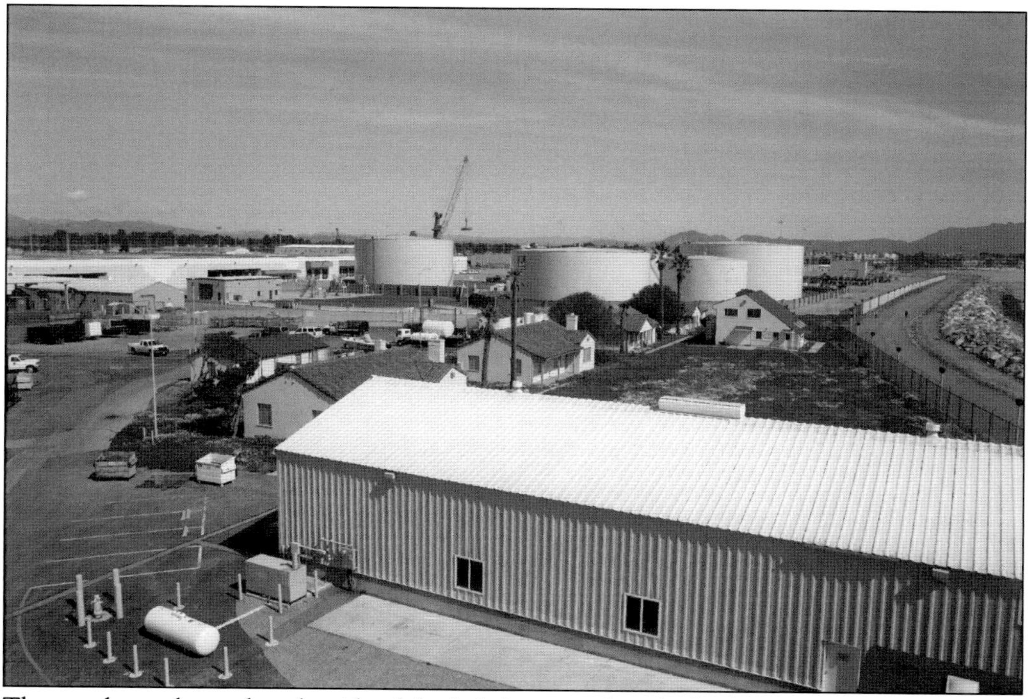

The warehouse located to the side of the lighthouse and in the background is the keeper's and assistant keeper's quarters, which still stand today. (Point Hueneme Lighthouse collection.)

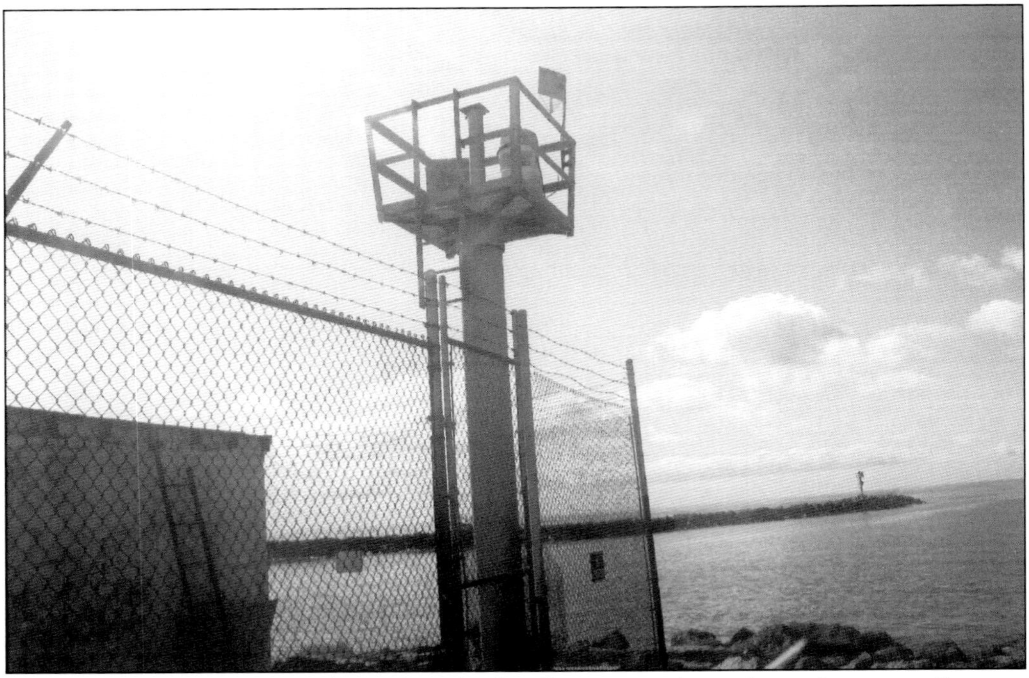

The foghorn, which once was housed on the first floor, is now located outside in a small corner of the port entrance. The foghorn is self-contained and can be turned on and off by the Coast Guard using a cellular phone. (Point Hueneme Lighthouse collection.)

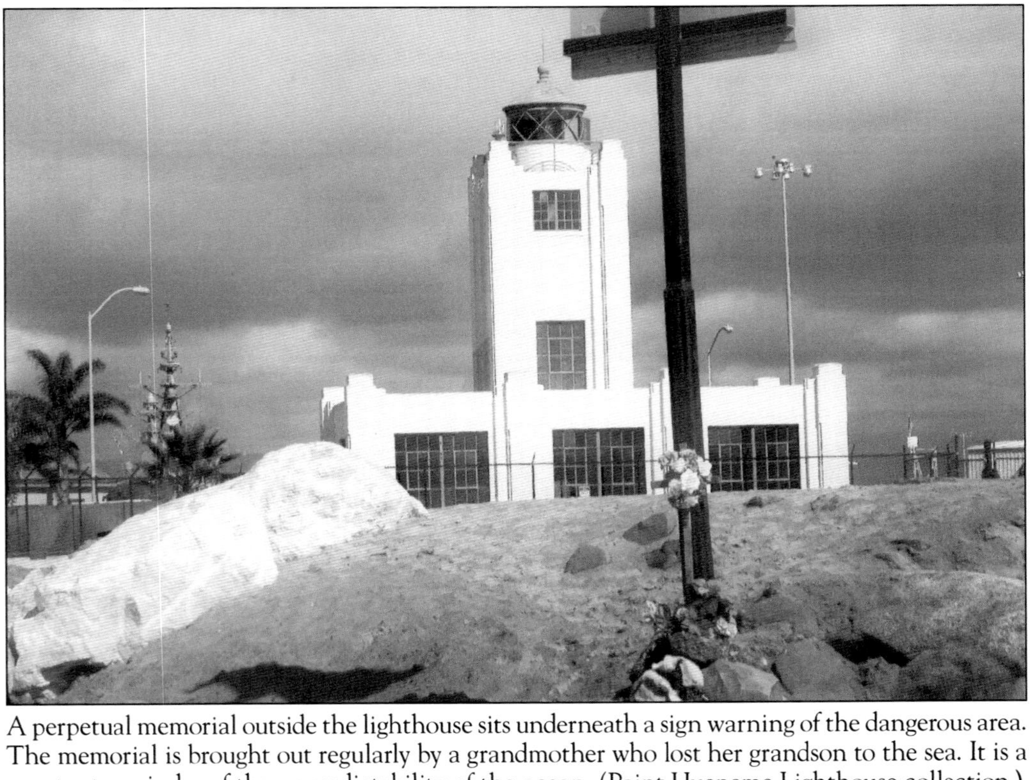

A perpetual memorial outside the lighthouse sits underneath a sign warning of the dangerous area. The memorial is brought out regularly by a grandmother who lost her grandson to the sea. It is a constant reminder of the unpredictability of the ocean. (Point Hueneme Lighthouse collection.)

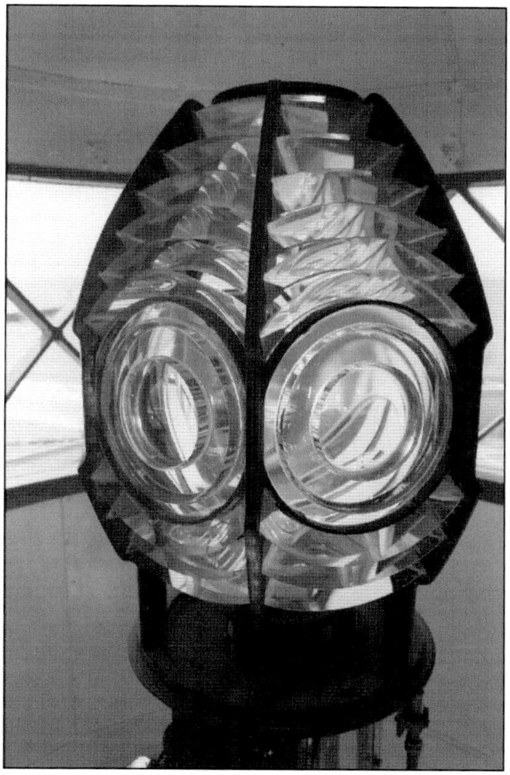

The Fresnel lens manufactured in 1897 in Paris, France, by Barbier and Benard and installed in 1899, is still in operation today. It is still a vital aid to navigation, lighting up the harbor and warning mariners of the nearby rock. The light makes two complete revolutions per minute, with each light throwing out a powerful beam every 5 seconds (with one eclipse flash from a damaged bull's-eye). (Both courtesy author's collection.)

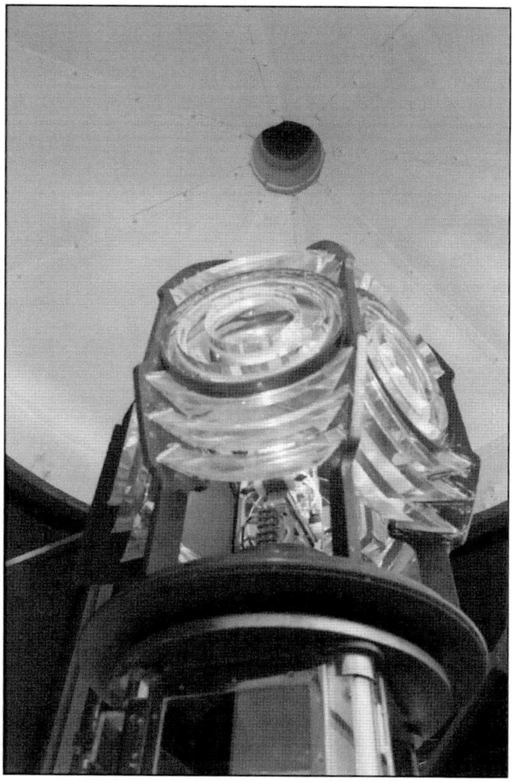

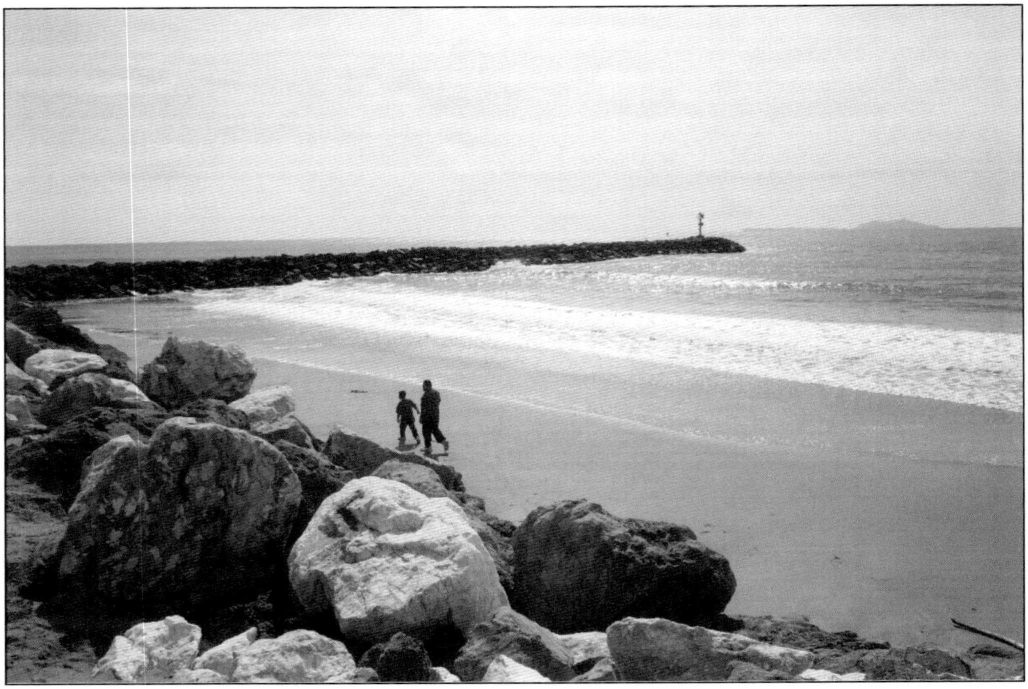

A father and son (above) are enjoying a stroll on the beach, and a bicyclist (below) stops to take in the views. (Both courtesy author's collection.)

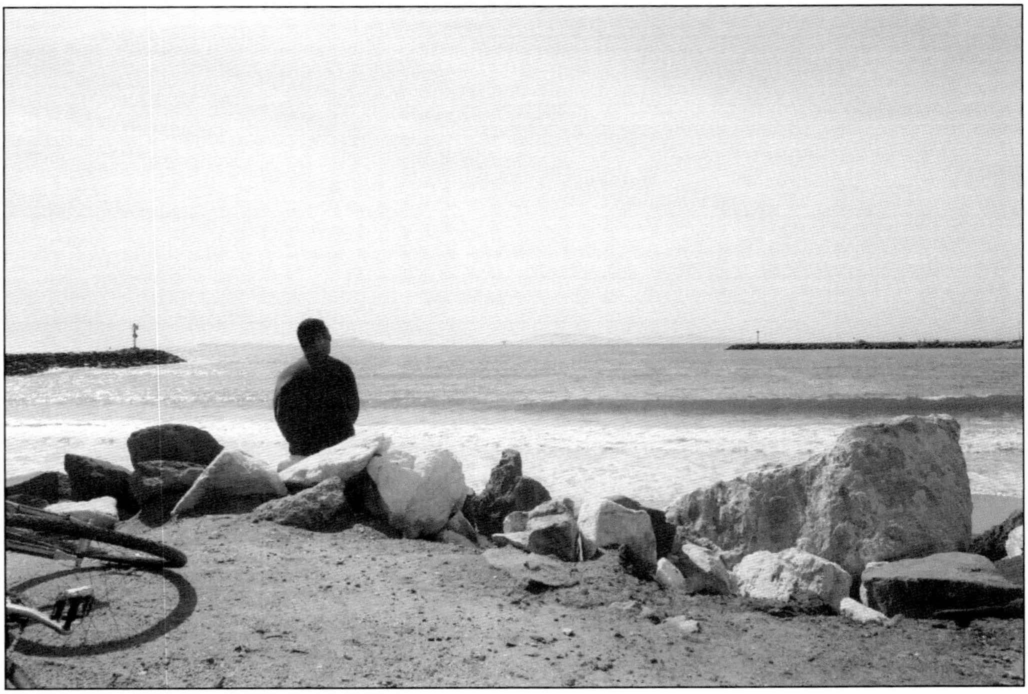

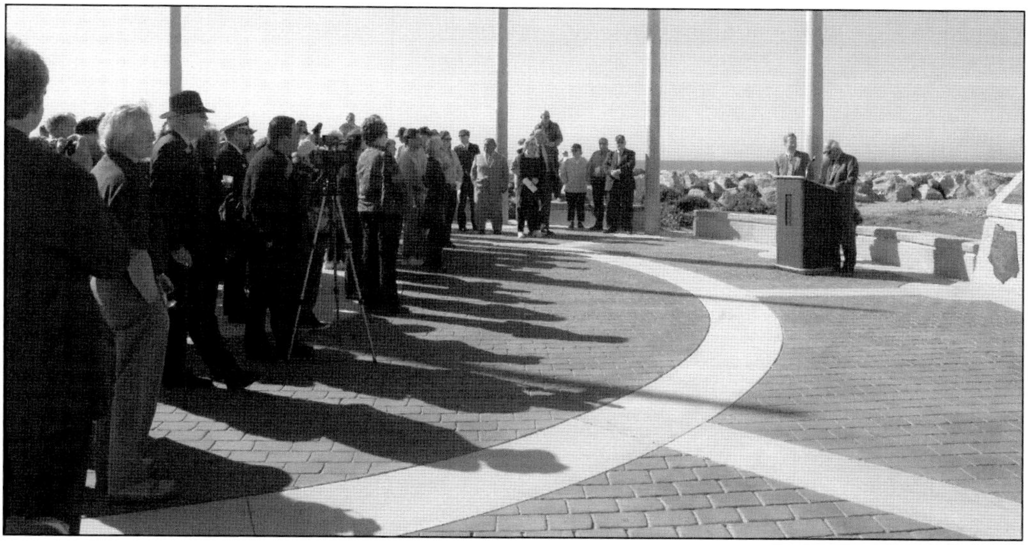

On March 21, 2008, commissioners from the Oxnard Harbor District (port operators), Port Hueneme city officials, U.S. Coast Guard, Coast Guard Auxiliarists, students and faculty from Port Hueneme Elementary, and the public were on hand to witness the inaugural celebration of the opening of the $4.4 million Lighthouse Promenade and Shoreline Protection Project. The Harbor District oversaw the project and funded 82 percent of the cost, while the city of Port Hueneme funded the remaining 18 percent. (Author's collection.)

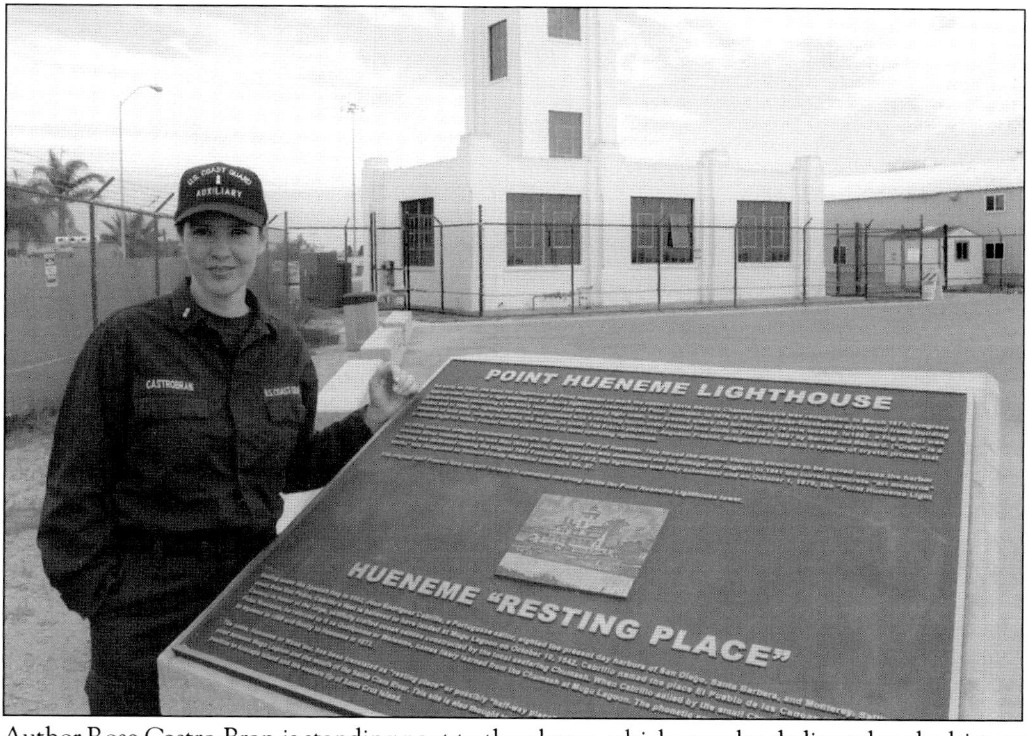

Author Rose Castro-Bran is standing next to the plaque, which was also dedicated to the history of the lighthouse. The beautifully paved promenade is also lined with light poles and leads visitors directly to the beach and the lighthouse. Today the lighthouse is one of the most visited Hueneme destinations, by locals and visitors alike. (Author's collection.)

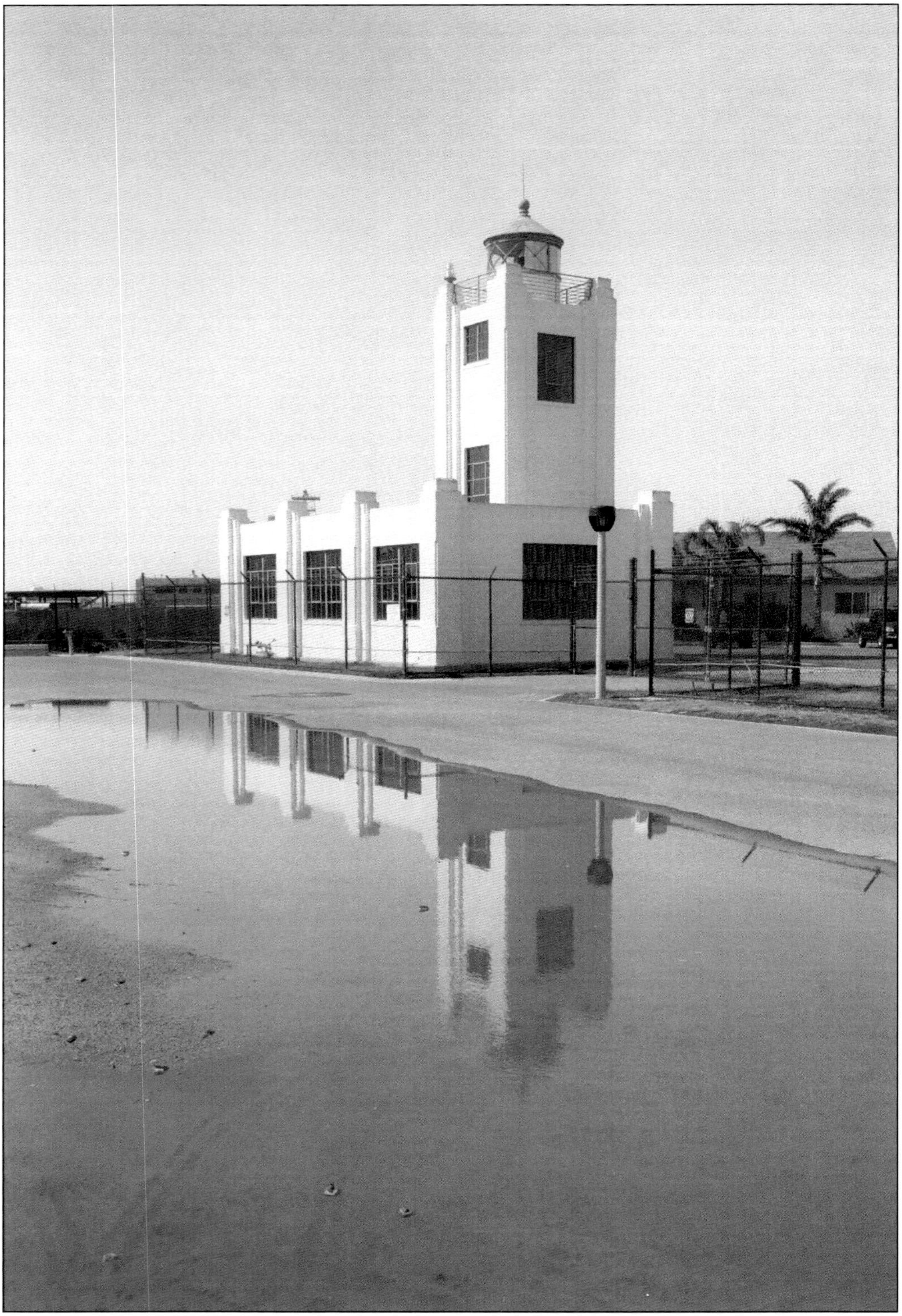
The Point Hueneme Lighthouse continues to aid mariners in safe passage to this day. (Courtesy Kim Castro-Bran.)

THE COMMANDANT OF THE UNITED STATES COAST GUARD
WASHINGTON 20593

07 January 2006

From: Commandant
To: Rose Castrobran, USCG Auxiliary

Subj: AUXILIARY LETTER OF COMMENDATION

1. I note with pride and am pleased to commend you for your performance of duty during the period July 2002 to December 2005 while serving as Lighthouse Keeper. Demonstrating exceptional leadership and managerial ability, Ms. CASTROBRAN maintained the Point Hueneme Lighthouse, turned four bare walls into an information center full of fascinating Coast Guard exhibits, and gave tours to more than 3,500 men, women, and children. Ms. CASTROBRAN created exhibits and displays depicting lighthouse history and lighthouse keepers, the U.S. Lighthouse Service, the Coast Guard and Coast Guard Auxiliary, Fresnel Lenses, Aids to Navigation Team Los Angeles - Long Beach, CGC GEORGE COBB, and the Coast Guard heroes of September 11, 2001. These displays increased the visibility of the Coast Guard to 41 monthly open houses, 14 special tours to senior groups, lighthouse enthusiasts, Boy Scout Troops, and school groups. Equally important to Ms. Castrobran's work on the Point Hueneme information center and outreach mission, was her work with ANT LA-LB to repair outages and conduct routine maintenance to other aids to navigation and lighthouses in the area, such as the Los Angeles and Point Vicente lighthouses.

2. You are commended for your outstanding performance of duty. By your meritorious service you have upheld the highest traditions of the United States Coast Guard and Coast Guard Auxiliary.

For the Commandant,

PETER V. NEFFENGER
Captain, U. S. COAST GUARD
Commander
Sector Los Angeles – Long Beach

J. KIPLING LOUTTIT
Captain, U. S. COAST GUARD
Commanding Officer
Integrated Support Command San Pedro

This letter of commendation was conferred on the author from the commandant of the U.S. Coast Guard in Washington, D.C. (Author's collection.)

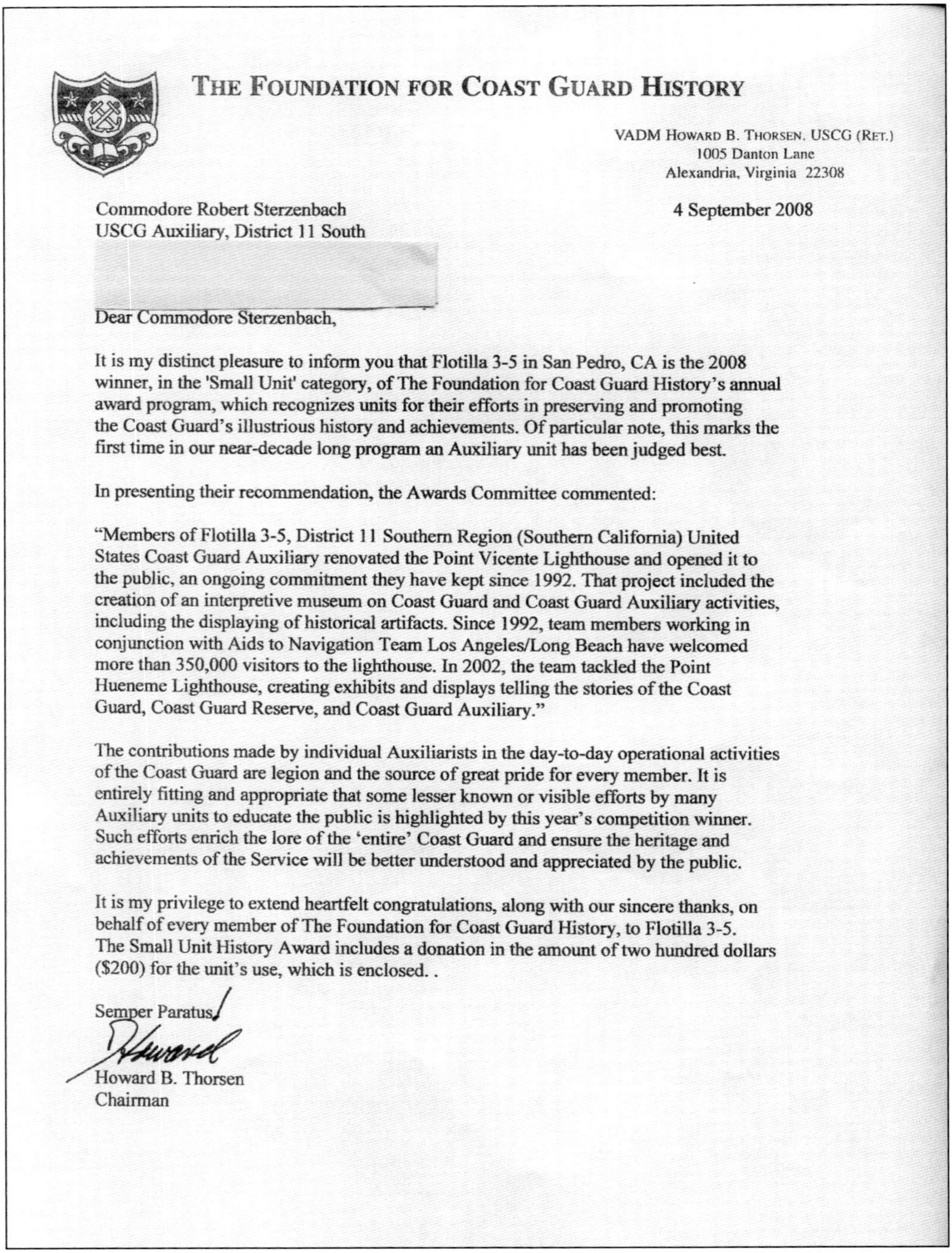

THE FOUNDATION FOR COAST GUARD HISTORY

VADM HOWARD B. THORSEN, USCG (RET.)
1005 Danton Lane
Alexandria, Virginia 22308

Commodore Robert Sterzenbach
USCG Auxiliary, District 11 South

4 September 2008

Dear Commodore Sterzenbach,

It is my distinct pleasure to inform you that Flotilla 3-5 in San Pedro, CA is the 2008 winner, in the 'Small Unit' category, of The Foundation for Coast Guard History's annual award program, which recognizes units for their efforts in preserving and promoting the Coast Guard's illustrious history and achievements. Of particular note, this marks the first time in our near-decade long program an Auxiliary unit has been judged best.

In presenting their recommendation, the Awards Committee commented:

"Members of Flotilla 3-5, District 11 Southern Region (Southern California) United States Coast Guard Auxiliary renovated the Point Vicente Lighthouse and opened it to the public, an ongoing commitment they have kept since 1992. That project included the creation of an interpretive museum on Coast Guard and Coast Guard Auxiliary activities, including the displaying of historical artifacts. Since 1992, team members working in conjunction with Aids to Navigation Team Los Angeles/Long Beach have welcomed more than 350,000 visitors to the lighthouse. In 2002, the team tackled the Point Hueneme Lighthouse, creating exhibits and displays telling the stories of the Coast Guard, Coast Guard Reserve, and Coast Guard Auxiliary."

The contributions made by individual Auxiliarists in the day-to-day operational activities of the Coast Guard are legion and the source of great pride for every member. It is entirely fitting and appropriate that some lesser known or visible efforts by many Auxiliary units to educate the public is highlighted by this year's competition winner. Such efforts enrich the lore of the 'entire' Coast Guard and ensure the heritage and achievements of the Service will be better understood and appreciated by the public.

It is my privilege to extend heartfelt congratulations, along with our sincere thanks, on behalf of every member of The Foundation for Coast Guard History, to Flotilla 3-5. The Small Unit History Award includes a donation in the amount of two hundred dollars ($200) for the unit's use, which is enclosed. .

Semper Paratus,

Howard

Howard B. Thorsen
Chairman

This letter of commendation was conferred on Flotilla 3-5 of the U.S. Coast Guard Auxiliary in San Pedro. Flotilla 3-5 was renamed Flotilla 5-9. (Author's collection.)

Bibliography

Gerold, Charles, and Jack C. Miller. *Official Souvenir Program*. First annual souvenir program, Ventura, CA, November 11–12, 1939.
Greenland, Powell M. *A Troubled Dream*. Los Olivos, CA: Olive Press Publications, 2006.
Holland Jr., Ross H. *America's Lighthouses*. New York: Dover Publications, 1927.
Maulhardt, Jeffrey W. *Port Hueneme*. Charleston, SC: Arcadia Publishing, 2005.
Sonneborn, Liz. *The Chumash*. Minneapolis, MN: Lerner Publications Company, 2007.
Ward, Thomas C. *The Keeper's Log*. Point Hueneme Lighthouse article, San Francisco, CA, U.S. Lighthouse Society, 1992.
Weymouth, Kent, Powell March Greenland, and Cara Converse. *The Journal of Ventura County History*. Ventura, CA: Ventura County Historical Society, Museum of Ventura County, 2010.
Wheeler, Wayne. *The Keeper's Log*. Anacapa Island Light Station article, San Francisco, CA, U.S. Lighthouse Society, 2002.
——— *California Lighthouse Life*. Charleston, SC: Arcadia Publishing, 2000.

Discover Thousands of Local History Books Featuring Millions of Vintage Images

Arcadia Publishing, the leading local history publisher in the United States, is committed to making history accessible and meaningful through publishing books that celebrate and preserve the heritage of America's people and places.

Find more books like this at
www.arcadiapublishing.com

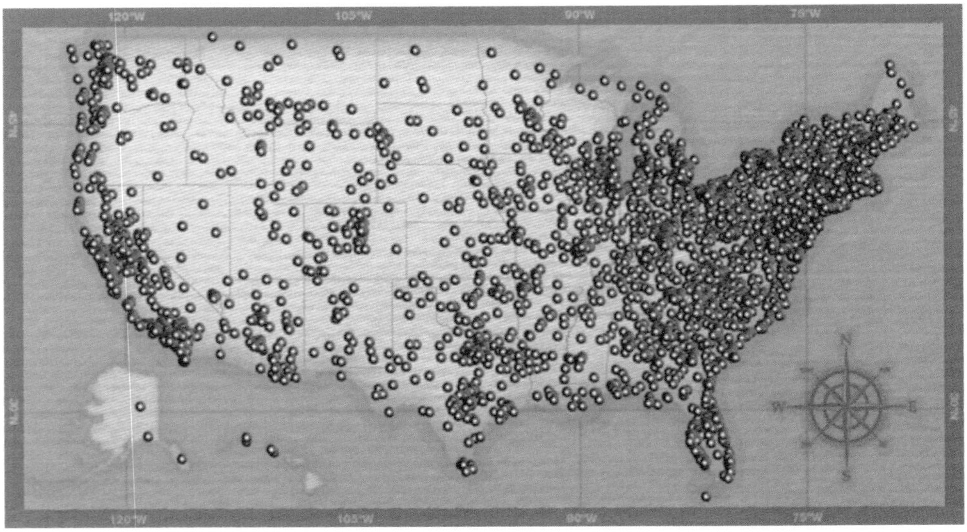

Search for your hometown history, your old stomping grounds, and even your favorite sports team.

Consistent with our mission to preserve history on a local level, this book was printed in South Carolina on American-made paper and manufactured entirely in the United States. Products carrying the accredited Forest Stewardship Council (FSC) label are printed on 100 percent FSC-certified paper.

MADE IN THE USA